Praise for the Conflict of the Ages Series

" ... Great to teach about creation and that theory ... religious approach more than the scientific but I want my children to know both and make up their minds."

" ... Exceptionally well researched and superbly informative ... "

" ... Should be required reading for every college bound teenager ... "

"I can't wait to dive into volume two."

The Conflict of the Ages Part Four, Teacher Edition Ice Age Civilizations

by

Michael J. and Mary C. Findley

Findley Family Video Publications

The Conflict of the Ages Part Four, Teacher Edition: Ice Age Civilizations

Findley Family Video Publications

"Speaking the truth in love."

Table of Contents

a. Written documents v oral traditions

b. geology, geography and artifacts

3. Accuracy

C. It Escapes Their Notice

D. The *Conflict of the Ages* Series

1. Antidisestablishmentarianism

a. What Is an Establishment of Religion?

b. What Is Secular Humanism?

c. What Is Science?

d. What Are the Results of the Establishment of Secular Humanism?

2. Conflict of the Ages Part One: The Scientific History of Origins

3. Conflict of the Ages Part Two: The Origin of Evil in the World that Was

4. Conflict of the Ages Part Three: They Deliberately Forgot: The Flood and the Ice Age

5. Guidelines for all books in the series

a. Partial Fulfillment of Academic Requirements

b. Standard writing style, average reading ease 50%, maximum reading level 10th grade

c. Amount and type of main text limited to the above standards

d. Hyperlinks to articles and books outside of the Main Text

e. The Scriptures are the absolute authority

f. Essential defense against Secular Humanism

II. Foundational Assumptions

A. Assumptions of the religion of Secular Humanism

1. Assume existing birth/death rates for the past

2. Assume a population of 27 million for 2000 BC

3. Assume continued harsh living conditions

B. We assume the Bible to be historically accurate

1. Historical-Grammatical Interpretation

2 The Bible Should be Read Like Other Literature

3. Religion Has a Unity With All Other Academic fields

4. The Bible Was Written to be Understood

C. Secular Humanism is founded on "Deep Time"

1. The earth is millions or billions of years old

2. Special or direct creation by God is not possible

III. Historic Overview

A. Creation

B. The Flood

C. The Ice Age

1. Warm oceans: worldwide temperate zone at sea level

2. Abundant water; probably overabundant

3. Abundant food without intense cultivation

4. Constantly changing conditions favored the nomad

a. Falling temperate zone as the sea levels fell.

b. Rapid retreat and advance of Ice Sheets

c. Pasture lands alternating between marshlands (too wet) and too dry

d. Volcanically active zones would make certain places uninhabitable

IV. Carbon 14 Dating

A. A brief overview of how carbon dating works.

B. Problems with using Carbon 14 dating

1. 5,730 year half-life

2. Assumption of a constant rate of ^{14}C formation.

3. Degree of accuracy diminishes with time

C. Benefits of using Carbon 14 dating

1. Known starting condition

2. Short half-life allows for calibration with written documents

3. ^{14}C can give us useful relative ages.

4. Verifying ^{14}C dates

a. The MSS of the Dead Sea Scrolls

b. The founding of Carthage

c. By 1500 BC, Radiocarbon dates are one or two centuries younger than archaeological timelines

d. The oldest post flood artifacts

e. Materials formed during the flood have ^{14}C dates around 50,000 years

f. Corrected ^{14}C timeline

V. Chronology

A. Calendars

B. Events

1. The Creation 4000 BC

2. The Flood 2350 BC

3. The Crucifixion AD 30

The Conflict of the Ages Part Four
Ice Age Civilizations

I. Overview

II. The Post Flood World: the Ice Age

A. Noah and his family leave the ark

B. God's covenant with Noah

1. *be fruitful, multiple and fill the earth*

2. *Every moving thing that is alive shall be food for you*

3. *Only you shall not eat flesh with its life, that is, its blood*

4. *Whoever sheds man's blood, By man his blood shall be shed*

III. Repopulation of the earth

A. The table of nations

1. Noah's grandchildren became shipbuilders
2. Nimrod
3. Canaan
4. Peleg

B. Babel (confusion)

1. Nimrod is not mentioned
2. Location is not certain
3. Worked on many years
4. Built during Peleg's lifetime
5. No record that the city was ever completed

C. Lifespans of the Lineage of the Messiah after the Flood

IV. The Ice Age records

A. ^{14}C Dating

1. Limits
2. Corrections
3. Benefits

B. Africa

C. Americas

D. Australia/Southeast Asia/Oceania

E. China

F. Europe

G. Egypt

1. Egyptian chronology does not match other chronologies
2. Hebrew History must be rejected to accept Egyptian chronology
3. Egyptian records are inconsistent with each other
4. Carbon-14 dates are younger than Egyptian written records
5. Reconciliation of Hebrew History and Egyptian Chronology

H. Indus Valley

I. Mesopotamia

J. The Foundation of Culture

1. The family
2. Warfare
3. Society
4. Religion
5. Housing

V. Ice Age Literature

VI. Summary

Review and Study Section

I. Review Questions

II. Vocabulary

III. References, Footnotes, Expanded Study and Appendix Materials

Note to the Reader

Note to the Reader

COA4 contains repeated material from COA 1, the first of the previous modules, mostly in the teacher edition, for the benefit of those who may begin the study with this module. For more details of material included in the introduction and back matter please refer to COA 1. Links to the appendix section containing simple endnote source citations or references will be notated alphabetically in the introductory materials and numerically in the main text. (for example: Stephen Hawking[a] or Hammurabi[1]) Because some material is for teachers only, some outline points are omitted from the student edition. The student edition is still continuous, though it does not include as much material.

Endnotes are accessed by hyperlinks.

If there is no letter or number, the link connects to a different appendix section, such as excerpts from *Antidisestablishmentarianism* or our *Elk Jerky for the Soul* blog. In any case, readers can link back from the reference/appendix sections to the place in the text where they left off. Sometimes when the text refers to the same section multiple times (example: "Ch. 14: What Is the Scientific Evidence?" is referenced multiple times throughout the text) there will not be a hyperlink, just a written direction to see that appendix section for more information.

When clicking on a hyperlink, touch or place the mouse on or in a character, not in a space between letters or words, to ensure the hyperlink works correctly.

This work includes three types of material:

1. Our own statements

(This is the majority of the book.)

2. The Scriptures

These will appear in *italic* font. If no version is listed it is the King James Version.

3. Other sources.

Fragment of Jubilees from Qumran Public Domain image

Quotes from other sources vary wildly in accuracy and reliability. One example of highly reliable material outside of the Bible is the *Book of Jubilees*. Source for Jubilees Authority[a] The Coptic Church regards the *Book of Jubilees* as inspired Scripture. Among the Dead Sea Scrolls are twenty-one copies of the *Book of Jubilees*. Our position is that the *Book of Jubilees* is not inspired. It contains errors. Note the testimony from Epiphaneus, a bishop of Salamis (A.D. 310-403?), referenced below.

> "Epiphaneus does not introduce the material from Jubilees as scripture, and Jubilees is not among the biblical books he names in his treatise Measures and Weights; but the

> information in the Book of Jubilees was reliable enough for him to use in refuting a sect that attributed a different origin and nature to Seth."
>
> "He also reproduces Jubilees' connection between the twenty-two works of creation until the Sabbath and the twenty-two generations until Jacob."

With Byzantine historians, "Josephus and Jubilees were regularly cited together, since, in the scope and the material treated, the two works were parallel."

An example at the other extreme is the *Epic of Gilgamesh.* We refer to it because at the time of this writing it is considered to be the world's oldest written document. Its only true purpose was to deify man and support the local tyrant. It is mostly erroneous, sometimes dangerous, and is difficult to read and understand. Still, the *Epic of Gilgamesh* contains some useful information. The multiple extant versions of the *Epic of Gilgamesh* contain considerable variations. While there are fragments of the *Epic of Gilgamesh* dating back to the beginning of the second millennia, maybe even the third millennia, BC, the most complete extant copy is a Babylonian version found in the 7th century BC library of the Assyrian king Ashurbanipal. This is the version we use. It is also the most common version, since it is the oldest complete version.

When Noah's family left the Ark they passed on the true history of mankind to their descendants. Every culture, therefore, was originally founded on accurate information. The various historical accounts included in this work still contain some accurate information. We begin each point with the information taught by the appropriate Scripture passages. That is followed by additional evidence to support the Scriptural teachings. This additional evidence includes various records as well as archeological and geological evidence.

Teacher manual only

cover of book of Jasher from Biblefacts

The *Book of Jasher* needs special explanation. One reviewer stated that the "*Book of Jasher* is not authentic. What is being cited is an 18th century forgery" This reviewer's error concerning the *Book of Jasher* is, sadly, widespread and accepted by many otherwise very well-educated believers. If you are concerned about this error, then please examine the article in the References, Footnotes, Expanded Study and Appendix Materials (near the end of the book) on the *Book of Jasher*.[b]

Many ancient Jewish sources are quoted, including Philo, Josephus, the *Sedar Olam,* the *Book of Jubilees, the Book of the Bee*, the *Cave of Treasures,* the first *Book of Enoch*, various Talmuds and Midrashes, and the *Book of Jasher*. Many non-Jewish sources are also quoted. The Jewish books are from the Second Century AD or older. None of them are inspired by God and all contain errors. Sources quoted in these modules support positions in the Word of God. There is little value in extensive study of any of these works, but they are documented in case you wish to examine them. They are all based on older works and accurately record older Jewish traditions.

I. Introduction

A. The History of Civilization

1. What is the History of Civilization?

The History of Civilization is the record of man either yielding to God's will for His glory or struggling to rebel against God. Beginning with the introductory book *Antidisestablishmentarianism,* this is the thesis of the entire Conflict of the Ages series.

"Nonreligious" history does not exist. All history is religious. We either choose to follow the revealed religion of Jesus Christ or we rebel against the Creator. The forms of this rebellion vary greatly. At this time, the majority of Western culture chooses to rebel against God with the religion of Secular Humanism.

Here is the secular assertion.

> If the time span of our planet-now estimated at some five billion years-were telescoped into a single year, the first eight months would be devoid of any life. The next two months would be taken up with plant and very primitive animal forms, and not until well into December

> would any mammals appear. In this "year" members of *Homo erectus,* the best known species of "near men" would mount the global stage only between 10 and 11 P.M. on December 31.

The university-level history textbook *Civilization Past and Present*[c] opens with this gratuitous assertion. It assumes and asserts that uniformitarianism is a fact. It then uses that assumption to define history.

> History is the record of the past actions of mankind, based upon surviving evidence. The historian uses this evidence to reach conclusions which he believes are valid.

This second assumption is only valid if you understand that the most reliable evidence is the Word of God. Otherwise the only standard for determining what is "valid evidence" is the author. The author then determines what is significant out of the available "valid evidence." History then becomes either the personal opinion of the individual author or the collective opinion of those editing the work.

2. The boundaries or limits to the *Conflict of the Ages* series.

a. It is written as a textbook series to fulfill academic requirements.

Writing style and vocabulary are designed for an average 10th grade student. It is based on the principles and perspective of the Bible. It includes many cultures and literature which are neither Hebrew nor Christian. These works only include what gives the greatest glory to God or demonstrates significant rebellion against the principles of God as revealed in His Word.

b. The amount of material is suitable for students..

Parents and teachers may reduce any section or any material at their discretion. A lack of information would be very difficult for parents and teachers to research to fill in the gaps during the course of a school year. It is the intent of this series to be thorough and complete. Therefore, the text has more material than the average 10th grade student can use in a year.

c. History, vocabulary and literature are combined

The oldest known literature was written hundreds of years after the Flood. This includes Egyptian works composed in hieroglyphics and documents in Mesopotamian cuneiform. Both of these alphabets were in use for more than a thousand years, so the exact time period can be difficult to determine. The Indus script of the Harappan culture (Indus Valley) is from the same time period, but it is still undeciphered.

d. This work is filtered by what we believe

The previous seven works, including the four parts of *Antidisestablishmentarianism,* and the first three modules of the *Conflict of the Ages* series are filtered by what we believe.

All books are filtered by the beliefs of the authors. Unlike the average history textbook, the *Conflict of the Ages* series puts our foundational beliefs in writing. These are spelled out in the prologue to this entire series, the book *Antidisestablishmentarianism.*

3. Antidisestablishmentarianism

Cover of Antidisestablishmentarianism

Clicking on the title of this subpoint takes you to the appendix “Excerpts from *Antidisestablishmentarianism*”. Following are a few brief quotes.

> The Magna Carta opens with the words, “In the first place we grant to God and confirm by this our present charter for ourselves and our heirs in perpetuity that the English Church is to be free and to have all its rights fully and its liberties entirely”. The concept that the English Church is to be free became the basis for the first amendment of US Constitution “Congress shall make no law respecting an establishment of religion, or prohibiting the free exercise thereof...”
>
> “The United States Supreme Court has held that secular humanism is a religion. Belief in evolution is a central tenet of that religion.” (Supreme Court Justice Antonin Scalia in *Edwards v Aguillard, US Supreme Court 1987*).

Secular Humanism is America’s established religion. Those who oppose this establishment of religion such as ourselves are disestablishmentarians. Those in positions of political power, especially in academic positions of power, are fighting to keep their power and privilege. These are antidisestablishmentarians; hence the title of our book.

Antidisestablishmentarianism is the introduction to the *Conflict of the Ages* series.

B. The Tools of the Historian

1. Education

... Scientific history ... is that the method that we use ... something akin to the scientific method. It is based on at least three characteristics ....
The first is to establish that the evidence is reliable.
The second is making certain that the analysis being made is logical.
And third, the analysis must lead to a generalization
that is based on rational argument.
Romila Tharpar

Scientific history ... is that the method that we use ... something akin to the scientific method. It is based on at least three characteristics ... The first is to establish that the evidence is reliable. The second is making certain that the analysis being made is logical. And third, the analysis must lead to a generalization that is based on rational argument.
Romila Tharpar

Education means that you do not have to personally experience something for it to be true. You can rely on the observation and experiences of others to learn things. You cannot personally experience everything that has ever taken place or been done. You do not need to personally experience poison, a fall from a cliff, or an explosion to understand that each of these can be deadly. This understanding of education is widely accepted and seldom questioned.

The foundation of Scientific History is education. George Washington's inauguration took place on April 30, 1789. No one alive today was there, but no truly educated person questions that this event took place. It is documented and verified. We learned about George Washington's inauguration through education.

Yet for some inexplicable reason, when we change from the word "education" to the phrase "an eyewitness account," this same concept of "education" is completely ignored by the true believers in the new religion of "science". By changing the word "education," which they put their faith and trust in, to "eyewitness," they vehemently deny the exact same process. That is reading, an eyewitness account to George Washington's inauguration is an education. But the same people deny that reading an eyewitness account to a crime is an equally valid education. They distort the very definition of terms.

Because the denials are so vehement, widespread and confusing, we need a brief explanation. Every year professionals and academics write millions of papers. We have to trust that these papers are honest, follow scientific methods, and prove what they intend to prove. We are not present at the experiments. The written records of these peer-reviewed papers provide us with an education. We were not present and did not contribute to these observations and experiments. So this is the proper use of the word education. There is very little or no disagreement with this simple definition of the word education.

But when anyone points out that these same people writing these papers, doing research, and performing experiments are scientific eyewitnesses, then an avalanche of complaints descend upon us. Like the proper use of the word education, this is also the proper use of the word eyewitness. These professional eyewitnesses are providing us with an education.

Two justifications exist for such serious complaints against eyewitness accounts.

a. The first is a premeditated and deliberate misuse of the word "eyewitness." Police cadets are taught not to accept eyewitness accounts because they are unreliable. But every single person testifying in a trial is an eyewitness. Crime Scene Investigators, in whom we all place so much faith and trust, are eyewitnesses. The doctors providing expert testimony are eyewitnesses.

The important part of understanding the word eyewitness is the quality of the eyewitness testimony. A witness in shock at a crime scene during the commission of a crime is an unreliable eyewitness. But this is not the only type of eyewitness. A CSI is a very reliable eyewitness. Professionals giving expert testimony are limited to the evidence they examined and their area of expertise. But within those confines they are the best eyewitnesses. So the historian must evaluate the quality of the eyewitness testimony, not reject it before evaluating it.

b. The second is the important reason for the deliberate misuse of the word. Eyewitness accounts of history do not match up with what secular humanists (uniformitarians) want you to believe about history.

Shang Dynasty inscribed scapula by BabelStone – own work. Licensed under Creative Commons Attribution – Share Alike 3.0 via Wikimedia Commons.

Chinese oracle bones, the Mayan *Popol Vuh*, Cuneiform clay tablets of the Sumerian/Akkadian period, Egyptian hieroglyphics, and Sanskrit documents such as the *Laws of Manu* all support a general culture and chronology similar to what is recorded in the Bible.

2. Types of Material used as Sources

a. Written documents vs. oral traditions

It is critically important that scientific history knows the quality of the sources relied on. Oral sources have been respected as reliable eyewitnesses. In US courts, oral testimony is actually preferred over written testimony. Written documents are often "read in" at the time of the trial.

The Exodus of the children of Israel from Egypt is told in the Bible as a straightforward, factual, historical event. Charlton Heston, in his narration of the picturesque Bible video series, presents the Bible as part of the "oral tradition in storytelling" as if teachings passed on orally were understood to be less accurate or reliable and therefore merely legends and myths. Socrates, in Plato's Dialogue "Phaedrus,"[e] actually believes that the combined memory of a society's oral traditions are more accurate and reliable than documents written by individuals.

> "Theuth [Thoth] ... was the inventor of many arts, ... but his great discovery was the use of letters. ... Thammus [the god Ammon] was the king of ... Egypt; ...To him came Theuth ... desiring that the other Egyptians might be allowed to have the benefit of [his inventions]; ... when they came to letters, This, said Theuth, will make the Egyptians wiser and give them better memories; ... Thamus replied: ... you ... attribute to them a quality which they cannot have; for this ... will create forgetfulness in the learners' souls, ... they will trust to the external written characters ... This is an aid not to memory, but to reminiscence, ... not truth, but only the semblance of truth; they will be hearers of many things and will have learned nothing; they will appear to be omniscient and will generally know nothing; they will be tiresome company, having the show of wisdom without the reality." (These quotes are repeated in abbreviated form in the image below.)

"[Writing] will make the Egyptians wiser and give them better memories." said [Thoth].

[Amun] replied:
"You attribute to them a quality they cannot have; this will create forgetfulness in the learners' souls, they will trust to the written characters.

An aid only [to] the semblance of truth; they will be hearers and will have learned nothing; they will appear omniscient and will know nothing; the show of wisdom without reality."

Image by Mary C. Findley of the gods Thammus/Amun and Theuth/Thoth from Illustrated Antidisestablishmentarinism with abbreviated quotes in the text above.

Plutarch,[f] in his discourse on the life of Lycurgus and his rule over Sparta (the Lacedaemonians) in ancient Greece, expresses the belief that only oral tradition can fix the law more firmly in the mind.

> None of his laws were put into writing by Lycurgus, indeed, one of the so-called "rhetras" forbids it. For he thought that if the most important and binding principles which conduce to the prosperity and virtue of a city were implanted in the habits and training of its citizens, they would remain unchanged and secure, having a stronger bond than compulsion in the fixed purposes imparted to the young by education, which performs the office of a law-giver for every one of them.

There is considerable disagreement about whether the Scriptures were in some part orally communicated before being written down. Even if they were, it does not make them less authoritative or reliable. Socrates may not be entirely justified in discounting the value of written records but he reinforces the point that oral communication of history does not make it unreliable or inaccurate. Memorizing and passing on history demands great discipline and does not result in a form of the child's game "gossip."

b. Geology, geography, and artifacts

The geology immediately after the Flood was drastically different from the geology today.

The *Conflict of the Ages Part Three The Flood and The Ice Age* includes details. Geology is often used by uniformitarians as evidence for their mythical timeline. However, after the Ice Age, geology has little bearing on the history of civilization.

Geography is an important aspect of culture and helps explain much of history. However, ancient history had considerably different geography from what we have today. For example, the Sahara desert was at one time a vast savanna. Northern Siberia was inhabited by millions of mammals. Rivers have changed course. The sea level fell then rose again. Deserts have expanded. All of these are important factors in the rise and fall of civilizations.

Secular uniformitarians use artifacts to rewrite history. They place more value on artifacts than oral traditions and written documents combined. While artifacts can be very important, they must be handled with great care. Artifacts by themselves are not history.

3. Accuracy

The key issue is the accuracy, truth, honesty, and importance or *significance* of the information. *If the information is correct, the method of transmission is not important.* So how can we know if the information is both accurate and significant? The mantra of many historians is "chronology is the backbone of history."

The well-known stele of Hammurabi'sg Law Code (pictured above) teaches us dating is not as certain as Secularists would have us believe. It was originally dated to be from the 12th century BC. Within a year that changed to the 25th century BC. Now it now assumed that it was made around 1700 BC.

In A.D. 1901-1902 a French team excavating in Susa, one of the ancient capitals of Elam, then Persia, now modern

Iran, discovered pieces of a basalt stele. It was completely reconstructed and now sits in the Louvre in Paris, France. The head of the French team, M. de Morgan, used the surroundings where it was found to date the stele, the now famous Law Code of Hammurabi, to around 1100-1200 BC.

Excavating in Nippur at the same time was an American/German team headed by the German-born American Hermann Hilprecht. Nippur is in ancient Mesopotamia, an area ruled over by the Assyrians, Babylonians, Persians, Greeks, and Ottoman Turks, and is now modern Iraq. They found a kings list with the name Hammurabi on it. This list made Hammurabi a ruler in the 24th century BC. Hermann Hilprecht immediately (January 1903) proclaimed in a lecture at the University of Pennsylvania that the Hammurabi stele was the oldest law code ever found.

A book entitled *The Oldest Code of Laws in the World by Hammurabi, King of Babylon*, was immediately published in early 1903 and is available as an ebook through Project Gutenberg. It proclaims that Hammurabi ruled from 2285-2242 B.C. The forward is by C.H.W. Johns, M.A., of Cambridge. The book was printed in Edinburgh.

Since 1903, several other Sumerian kings lists were discovered. A rather brief but thorough article in the Roman Catholic online encyclopedia *New Advent*[g] describes the major positions mainstream archaeologists take on the time Hammurabi actually ruled. Most 21st-century archaeologists hold to some type of a "middle" position, that Hammurabi ruled around 1700 B.C.

Uncertain, or even worse, fabricated chronology, is not the standard of accuracy on which to base all of human history. The One Who created the Universe was the only flawless observer. He has communicated accurately to us. This is the true scientific approach. God has left us with physical evidence to examine. That evidence[h] will lead us to honestly conclude that the earth is much less than one million years old.

Our touchstone of truth is the Word of God. The *Conflict of the Ages* series includes worldwide literature, geology, physics, biology, archaeology, and art, which give the greatest possible glory to God or point out the most significant rebellion against Him.

One well-known source which needs special mention is *Wikipedia.*[i] We cite one example of the kinds of problems with *Wikipedia* in *COA3,* Point VI. Material Results of the Flood, D. Radiohalos, 3. The Uniformitarian Answer? This is a *Wikipedia* article which calls Creation Science a pseudoscience. We document how their false charge cannot stand.

It is also true that all scholarly sources are "always in a state of flux." The *Wikipedia* article we use as an example in the above link accurately quotes an incorrect peer-reviewed article. In the example we cite, *Wikipedia* chose to accurately quote an incorrect article because it stated what that author wanted to believe.

You are responsible to understand what is and what is not true. When you are educated well enough to understand the methods used to determine what is and what is not accurate, then *Wikipedia* will be a very valuable resource. It is filled with very simple, basic information and definitions which are accurate enough for most general use. Even though *Wikipedia* contains errors and changes, so do all sources. All major respected sources contain errors.

Wikipedia is a very good starting point with its citations. Even when you realize that the information and conclusions in the main article are inaccurate, you can read the source articles and begin a search using those sources. If you do not learn what you need to know from those sources, they should cite their sources and you can continue your search through their citations.

Whether, then, you eat or drink
or whatever you do, do all to the Glory of God.
(1 Corinthians 10:31).

"Whether, then, you eat or drink or whatever you do, do all to the Glory of God. (I Corinthians 10:31)

C. It Escapes Their Notice

> *Know this first of all, that in the last days mockers will come with their mocking, following after their own lusts, and saying, "Where is the promise of His coming? For since the fathers fell asleep, all continues just as it was from the beginning of creation. For when they maintain this, it escapes their notice that by the word of God the heavens existed long ago and the earth was formed out of water and by water, through which the world at that time was destroyed, being flooded with water.* (2 Peter 3:3-6, NASB)

The Conflict of the Ages Series is designed for believers who must live in a world controlled by mockers. These demonically-influenced people are experts at forcing their religion on others. Their religion appeals to human pride. They proudly classify anyone who refuses to accept their religion as ignorant. Point out that their beliefs are a religion and they usually become enraged.

Our culture indoctrinates into this religion from preschool. This established religion is founded on vast periods of time, often called "deep time." People are indoctrinated to accept this as science. Secular Humanism is a religious belief. Though complete and detailed information can expose this religious belief system, we must understand that *the god of this world has blinded the minds of the unbelieving* (2 Corinthians 4:4 NASB). Evidence and information will not persuade these people. They are blinded so that they might not see the light of the gospel of the glory of Christ (2 Corinthians 4:4 NASB). Only God the Spirit can remove this blindness.

Mockers require acceptance of their religious mockery to obtain a PhD, to be offered a job, to hold any position of authority, and in many cases, to even earn enough money to make a living. Like the First Century Jew facing the Pharisees of his day, people today fear to challenge this establishment of religion because they love the praise of men more than pleasing God.

Still, many among the rulers did believe on Him [Jesus Christ]. But because of the Pharisees they did not confess, lest they should be put out of the synagogue; they loved the glory of men more than the glory of God. (John 12:42,43 NASB)

We are engaged in a spiritual warfare; a war we didn't choose. Mockers dishonestly proclaim that refusal to believe in their religion is opposition to science. But the Flood and the Ice Age are not issues of science. The scientific evidence supports the Word of God. To give an oversimplified explanation, science is how things work, while religion is why things work. Modern Science has completely rejected this basic definition of science and elevated "Science" to an all-encompassing religion. Classical science is based on the orderly collection and observation of knowledge. Einstein's quote "God does not play dice with the universe" defends the foundations of Classical Science, Intelligent Design, and an orderly universe. Stephen Hawking attacked this with the religious "Not only does God[j] definitely play dice, but He sometimes confuses us by throwing them where they can't be seen."

The order of Classical Science is based on the order found in the Word of God. Isaac Newton's laws of physics (Note that Newton wrote more defending his beliefs in Christianity than he did about physics) and Kepler's Laws of Planetary Motion are examples of people professing faith in God who also laid the foundation for entire branches of science (physics and genetics).

Yes, "God created the earth for His glory" is a religious statement. Just as religious is the statement that "the earth came into existence millions of years ago by random chance." It is a religious belief with no verifiable material evidence for support.

What we see in the world around us today is the material evidence for the Flood. This "general revelation," can be compared to the historical record. When compared to any other ancient religious document, the Word of God is the only historical document having a record in chronological order beginning with the creation of the universe. Other ancient documents, such as the Qur'an, describe the Creation and Flood in pieces interspersed throughout these writings. It is also likely that many of the events in these other documents happened near the end of the Ice Age, hundreds of years after the worldwide Flood. We are simply not capable of distinguishing the difference between a global flood and massive local floods in many writings outside the Bible.

All that remains of these floods are rocks. These rocks are often presented as evidence that the Earth is a certain age. However, rocks do not come with labels saying they formed gradually over millions of years. Neither do they have labels saying they were formed cataclysmically less than five thousand years ago.

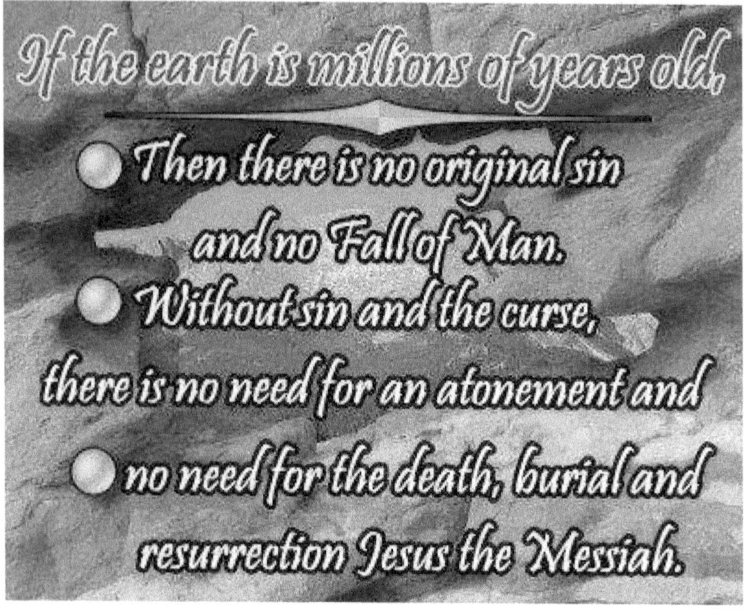

If the earth is millions of years old, then there is no original sin and no Fall of Man. Without sin and the curse, there is no need for an atonement and no need for the death, burial and resurrection of Jesus the Messiah.

As Abraham told the rich man in Hades, *"If they hear not Moses and the prophets, neither will they be persuaded, though one rose from the dead"* (Luke 16:31). Jesus meant that rejection of the Old Testament Scriptures as historically and scientifically accurate and true leads to rejection of Him. *For had ye believed Moses, ye would have believed me: for he wrote of me. But if ye believe not his writings, how shall ye believe my words?* (John 5:46,47) If you don't accept the literal accounts of Creation, the Fall, and the Flood, how can you accept the literal account of the death, burial, resurrection, and atonement of Jesus Christ?

But this is not just an “interpretation” of the Bible in opposition to material evidence. In the appendix at the end of this book you will find “What Does the Scientific Evidence Prove?” which includes some evidences for a young Earth. This is Chapter Fourteen from *Antidisestablishmentarianism*. Secular Humanists usually just ignore this evidence. They will say something like, “those are the usual young Earth arguments. They’ve already been proven false.” Secularists are correct that most of these are “the usual young Earth arguments”. We are not perfect and can make errors in our own presentation of material. However, our works include many of the usual young Earth arguments because they are in fact correct. Getting a Secular Humanist to carefully examine even one of these points is, sadly, very difficult.

They almost always justify their positions with highly complex circular reasoning. Often they wish to rely on authority (Citing education such as a PhD and years experience in this field as authoritative). But they condemn Christians for relying on the authority of a two-thousand-plus-year-old book. Dr. Larry Vardiman,[k] PhD in Atmospheric Sciences, spoke of meeting Carl Sagan. “He immediately began asking me a series of leading questions about how a well trained scientist such as myself could have confidence in a book written by a bunch of ignorant sheep herders thousands of years before any real science had been discovered.” Please notice the hypocrisy.

D. The *Conflict of the Ages* Series

1. The book *Antidisestablishmentarianism* is the introduction to this series

The main body of the work is divided into four sections:

a. *What Is an Establishment of Religion?*

b. *What Is Secular Humanism?*

c. *What Is Science?*

d. *What Are the Results of the Establishment of Secular Humanism?*

(The fourth section includes suggestions on what we should do about Secular Humanism.)

The four sections of *Antidisestablishmentarianism* are each available as a separate book. The section titles from the main book are the titles of the serial versions. It is the introduction to the *Conflict of the Ages* (COA) series. Each student edition is available in individual, numbered units. Teacher manuals each cover three student manuals.

2. COA Part 1 covers origins (*Conflict of the Ages Part One: The Scientific History of Origins*)

3. COA Part 2 covers the origin of evil and the antediluvian world (*Conflict of the Ages Part Two: The Origin of Evil in the World that Was*)

4. COA Part 3 covers the Flood and the Ice Age (*Conflict of the Ages Part Three: They Deliberately Forgot: The Flood and the Ice Age*)

5. Guidelines for all of the books in the *Conflict of the Ages* series

a. Included sources necessary for a complete study of World History are compared with the Scriptures. These should be used to build discernment about what to accept and what to reject.

Mythology (like the *Epic of Gilgamesh*) gives insights into cultures and lifestyles of the people of that time and even what the physical world was like.

False religions helped rulers, as the representative or descendant of a god, unify authority. It was the earliest church-state union. In some cases grains of the original truth of the Scriptures (such as the Flood Epic) remained a part of the religion but in corrupted form.

Historical accounts (like Herodotus) seek to preserve a people's history and culture in the face of internal divisions or external corruptions or attacks. They may contain errors but sometimes include ancient sources no longer in existence. They can add to the knowledge of the ancient world when compared with other sources. Other ancient documents, especially those of Jewish origin, combine religious teaching with history and other knowledge.

b. The writing style is what Microsoft Word calls "standard". The Flesch reading ease target is approximately 50%. The Flesch-Kincaid reading level is no more than 10th grade for the overall average of any individual module. The similarity in writing style should produce similar values. For *COA1*, the Flesch reading ease is 54.6%, and the reading level is 9.7. For *COA2*, the Flesch reading ease is 56.2%, and the reading level is 9.8. For *COA3*, the Flesch reading ease is 48.4%, and the reading level is 10.8. For COA4, the Flesch reading ease is 0%, and the reading level is 0. For COA5, the Flesch reading ease is 0%, and the reading level is 0. For COA6, the Flesch reading ease is 0%, and the reading level is 0.

c. The amount of material has to be suitable for students to absorb. While we do not pretend that the material is easy, it is written on a level which can be grasped by the average high school student.

d. Hyperlinks connect to more difficult books and articles outside of the main text.

There is a main text with hyperlinks to articles and books found in the References, Footnotes, Expanded Study and

Appendix Materials and to reference works outside the main text. There is no attempt keep these expansion articles to the Flesch-Kincaid standards of the main text.

e. The Scriptures are the absolute authority. These other sources can contain valuable knowledge and studying them makes for a well-rounded education as well as fulfilling academic requirements. The key is not to allow secularist beliefs to confuse students into thinking that there are different kinds of truth. Segregating subjects encourages compartmentalizing information that should be taken and evaluated by one standard, God's Word.

f. This is essential information for defending yourself against those who attempt to indoctrinate you into the religion of Secular Humanism. This indoctrination process in Western Societies is done through the educational system, the workplace, entertainment, and through the legal system. This indoctrination process has become so pervasive that it is likely found in the entire western culture as well as many cultures outside of the West.

Our goal is not to answer every possible problem in detail, but to reveal to you, the student, the correct questions and how to think the problem through to the correct conclusion.

Foundational Assumptions

II. Foundational Assumptions

Why do you get up in the morning? Do you go to work? Do you go to school? Do you fix your our own food? Do you eat, bathe, study, work out, talk to friends, pray, sing? Whatever decisions you make, you make because of assumptions. You stay in bed because you assume that it does not make any difference. You go to work or school because you assume that sometime in the future you will need money. Or perhaps you simply believe that you are doing what is right. These assumptions are really what we believe. They are "why" we do what we do.

A. Assumptions of thc Rcligion of Secular Humanism

The real issues are the religious assumptions the formulas are based on. Do not be misled by the use of mathematical formulas, archeological evidence, or physics to prove a point. The mathematics, physics or archeology might be important and necessary points. But they also might be nothing more than a ploy that deludes some people into thinking that they are intellectually superior. When this is the case, it clouds the real issue. The issue is not the language of mathematics, the use of formulas, or the kind of physical evidence. The correct use of a formula does not justify an incorrect underlying assumption. Always carefully examine their *assumptions*. These *assumptions* are *why* they believe what they believe.

Here is just one example of an almost infinite number of possible examples. Noah lived for three hundred and fifty years after the Flood. His son Shem lived six hundred more years. Though men likely died from accidents or murders during this time period, the natural death rate from old age for three hundred forty years after the Flood was, statistically, zero. The first post-Flood death the Bible records was Peleg, 340 years after the Flood. So when anyone claims repopulation after the Flood is a problem, they are using population formulas based on current population growth rates. They are using incorrect assumptions. The following is a list of incorrect assumptions for the assumed "repopulation problem".

1. They assume that existing known birth and death rates should be applied to the past

The historical written record shows a statistically zero death rate combined with a much higher birth rate. Examples are the number of children born to Abraham by Keturah and number of Jacob's children, for example. Noah died 58 years after Abraham was born. Shem died 50 years after Jacob was born. Jacob's first child was born when he was 84 and Jacob died at 147 years old with a household of 70.

2. They assume a population of 27 million for the year 2000 BC

They claim "archeological evidence" for this number, but even a simple examination of the evidence shows an assumption of continuous growth over an assumed period of time. One assumption (evolutionary time scale) is used with a second assumption (that population growth rate in the third century BC was the same as it is now) as "proof" for a third assumption (world's population in 2000 BC).

3. They assume the harsh living conditions immediately after the Flood continued for hundreds of years

They assume harsh living conditions anywhere, any time outside of civilization. They believe that these harsh conditions resulted in very low childbirth rates and high mortality rates. This assumption has no supporting evidence, is impossible to verify even if it were true, which it is not, and contradicts every written record of the time period. The written record of Scripture tells us that Noah did not open the door of the ark and release the occupants until he had evidence of growing vegetation: the olive leaf the dove brought back. Noah also planted a vineyard after the Flood. The scientific evidence shows abundant vegetation at the end of the Ice Age. This evidence is preserved in much of the permafrost of Siberia and the Yukon. How long it took to develop the abundant vegetation is a completely unknown assumption. But secularists desperately need this third assumption to artificially suppress the population numbers in order create an artificial problem where no problem exists.

The slowly falling sea level with high humidity, warm temperatures, abundant rainfall and lack of creatures to eat the vegetation (at first) are optimal conditions for plant growth. A far more reasonable assumption is that within a very few decades the available land would be covered in thick vegetation and animal populations would be exploding. The hunter/gatherer culture, popularly depicted as a primitive, bare subsistence struggle for life, would more likely be a lifestyle based on extreme abundance and laziness. People could wake up each morning and go get whatever they wanted.

The Conflict of the Ages aligns with the scientific testimonies of the eyewitnesses to the historical records contained in the Word of God.

B. The Bible Is Historically Accurate

Everyone builds his life on assumptions. Scientists assume that instruments are accurate. In this COA series, the word *assumption* is a synonym for belief. We assume, that is believe, that the Word of God is True.

If you would like to know more about the scientific basis for the assumption that the Word of God is true, Josh McDowell wrote a book explaining these assumptions: *New Evidence That Demands a Verdict.* Francis Schaeffer's book, *The God Who Is There,* also does a good job of explaining why we believe that the Word of God is true. His series on civilization, *How Should We Then Live? The Rise and Decline of Western Thought and Culture* integrates art, literature, and languages, as we intend to do. We also have numerous short articles explaining our beliefs on our blog, https://findleyfamilyvideopublications.com, where you can also find links to our other works.

The basic assumption that the Word of God is true leads to other assumptions. The Word of God includes accurate history and normal literature.

1. Historical-grammatical interpretation

We take the historical-grammatical interpretation. "When the plain sense of Scripture makes common sense, seek no other sense; therefore, take every word at its primary, ordinary, usual, literal meaning unless the facts of the immediate context, studies in the light of related passages and axiomatic and fundamental truths, indicate clearly otherwise. God in revealing His Word neither intends nor permits the reader to be confused. He wants His children to understand." Dr. David L. Cooper.[l]

2 The Bible should be read like other literature

Examine the evidence honestly. You will conclude that the facts teach that the Bible should be treated like any other literature in its proper historical and grammatical context. It claims to be the Word of God and it cannot be reasonably "interpreted" to be something else. It must be accepted or rejected as a whole.

People who reject the Bible do so because they reject what it says, not because they do not understand what it says.

3. Religion has a unity with all other academic fields

There is a unity of science, history, literature, mathematics, the arts, and the Scriptures. Divorcing the Bible from other subjects allows secularists to put it in a separate category from the "academic" studies. The Bible is scientifically and historically accurate. It also uses literary devices. Other ancient works contain similar poetic devices and figures of speech which can aid in understanding the Scriptures. The order of the universe, the methods God commands men to use for investigation, and the purpose of the universe are all found in the Word of God and are foundational to science. These concepts in the Word of God are the opposite of the concept that the universe is result of random chance and completely without any overriding purpose.

4. The Bible was written to be understood

"Rightly Dividing[m] the Word of Truth": from our blog

Scene from Shakespeare's Romeo and Juliet public domain image

Shakespeare put the words in Mercutio's mouth after he was stabbed in a swordfight, "No, 'tis not so deep as a well, nor so wide as a church-door; but 'tis enough, 'twill serve: ask for me to-morrow, and you shall find me a grave man." (*Romeo and Juliet*, Act 3, Scene 1.) Though Mercutio could still talk, like Adam and Eve, he knew that his wound was fatal. Though Romeo did not grasp the significance of this statement at first, Mercutio knew that he would be in the grave tomorrow.

Anyone who understands Shakespeare has little problem understanding Mercutio. Yet the same people who have no difficulty with Shakespeare suddenly find the Bible incomprehensible. I am told several times a day, by people who have no difficulty comprehending very difficult English literature, "You are not interpreting the Bible correctly." The real issue is not comprehension but a choice, a decision. They do not want to understand. They simply reject the clear meaning of the words of the Bible.

The Bible is a book of literature. It does not need to be interpreted. At least, it should not be interpreted in the sense that it does not mean what it says. They come back with, "So you believe the earth is flat when it says 'the four corners of the earth'?" *After this I saw four angels standing at the four corners of the earth, holding back the four winds of the earth, so that no wind would blow on the earth or on the sea or on any tree.* (Revelation 7:1) The Bible uses literary devices such as the four corners of the earth. As Mercutio used the double meaning of the word grave (serious and death) in Romeo and Juliet, so the Bible is filled with figures of speech.

Just like Shakespeare, or any other literature, the Bible is written to be understood. Since our culture is far removed from Hebrew, Greek, Roman, and even Egyptian, Babylonian, and Persian cultures, some things are difficult for us to understand.

The answers to these, and any other questions we might have about the Bible, are to be found in the Bible itself, not in fanciful personal opinions some glorify by calling them "interpretations." For instance, when the vision of Jesus Christ in Revelation 1 mentions a sword coming out of the mouth of Jesus Christ, we already know that the sword of the Spirit is the Word of God and that God brought all things into existence by the Word.

C. Secular Humanism is founded on "Deep Time"

The foundational assumption needed for this kind of unbelief, rejecting the science and history presented in the Bible, is a belief in deep time. This belief permits not only a rejection of a universe designed, created, and controlled by God, but also is a belief in an entirely materialistic universe.

When we accept the Bible as the Word of God and rightly divide the Word of Truth, other assumptions follow. The Word of God describes in some detail how the world came into existence. Belief that God created the world in six days is an assumption used throughout the COA series. The evidence for a young earth is the greatest material evidence that the Word of God is true and science falsely-so-called is a Satanic lie. Since evolution is impossible in 6,000 years, the evidence for a young Earth and a catastrophic, worldwide flood must be lied about, disguised, and deliberately distorted. It is a religious bias, not a scientific disagreement. The Bible calls this attitude unbelief.

Evolution is impossible without vast amounts of time, which they call deep time. Without deep time, the only possible explanation for life is some form of God who created it. Also known as Intelligent Design, this can take the form of Deism, which seems to be the belief Albert Einstein took to the grave.

Deep time is founded on two basic assumptions or beliefs.

1. The earth is millions or billions of years old

2. Special or direct creation by God is not possible

Unbelievers present many assumptions as evidence for the age of the earth and the universe. Astronomy, the geologic column, radiometric dating, dendrochronology, and the ice age (or multiple ice ages) are probably used more than anything else. They attempt to use two separate arguments; proving deep time and disproving Creation and the Flood.

Astronomy is not proof of "Deep Time." The Geologic Column is not proof of Deep Time." Radiometric Dating is not proof of Deep Time. Dendrochronology is not proof of Deep Time, An Ice Age is not proof of Deep Time.

These five points are detailed the earlier modules.

III. Historic Overview

A. Creation

In the beginning God created. Genesis 1:1

We are not given information about the origin of God Himself.

The earth was formed by God's word out of water and with water. 2 Peter 3:5 ISV

Each day of creation was one rotation of the earth.

And the erev and the boker were Yom Shishi (Day Six, the Sixth Day). Orthodox Jewish Bible[n] [*twilight and dawn* ISV]

The genealogical records are accurate, though the years probably had a different number of days than our Gregorian calendar. The Flood occurred 1656 years after Adam was thrown out of the garden.

As the source of all water on earth, the Garden of Eden had to be one of the highest places on earth. Since one river watered the entire earth, (Genesis 2:10 *And a river went out of Eden to water the garden; and from thence it was parted, and became into four heads.*) there could only be one continent, though there might have been islands. The temperate climate at this altitude made nudity comfortable before the fall.

The Jewish calendar uses creation as the year zero, so the Flood took place in 1656 AM *(Anno Mundi* Latin for "in the year of the world," from the Hebrew "from the creation of the wor**B. The Flood**

ld") according to the Masoretic text.

The globally catastrophic Flood as recorded in all ancient documents, not just the Bible, destroyed all land-dwelling, air-breathing life on earth. Most of the layers of sediment we observe today were deposited during the Flood.

When Noah, his wife, his three sons and their wives, and all the organisms left the ark at the end of a year, vegetation had returned, though the sea level was very high.

C. The Ice Age

The climate had permanently changed. Though the population exploded, changes in topography and climate favored the adaptation of different organisms compared to the antediluvian world. As the volcanically-warmed oceans dropped and the mountains rose (*Mountains rise up and valleys sink to the place you have ordained for them.* Psalm 104:8, ISV), massive snowstorms covered the mountaintops with snow which did not melt during the summers. Mountains continued to rise and sea levels continued to fall until at their lowest point the sea levels were 400 feet lower than today. This caused a moving temperate zone, falling in elevation.

Seal discovered during excavation of the Mohenjodaro "Pashupati" (Lord of Animals) Public Domain in the US due to copyright expiration Wikimedia Commons

Many artifacts support the evidence of abundant wildlife as post-flood civilizations emerged.

When the oceans stabilized approximately four hundred feet lower than the current sea level, the entire earth was connected by land. This is visible as the continental shelf when viewing a satellite map of earth. With the continents connected, men and animals could walk to most places on earth. Noah could pass his shipbuilding skills on to his children, grandchildren, and as many generations as would listen. If they chose to do so, they could travel to any place on earth by ship. Game and wild grains were abundant below the ice-covered elevations. Horses, oxen, and other draft animals survived on the ark and did not need to be "discovered." Men could, and did, travel everywhere on earth, on foot, by ship, riding on animals or using animals to pull carts and wagons.

Ice formation and breakup was very rapid. According to Michael Oard, ice formation is a result of increased snowfall combined with cooler summers which keep the snow from melting. Increased snowfall is primarily the result of volcanic ash. The Ice Age(s?) was probably only a few decades, at most a few centuries. Michael Oard[o] theorizes "This was a unique, fast-acting Ice Age of about 700 years in duration."

From Noah and his family leaving the Ark until the Children of Israel leaving Egypt, the climate was constantly changing. The descendants Noah adapted to these new conditions.

1. The warm oceans caused a worldwide temperate zone near sea level. An abundance of large mammals lived as far north as Siberia. This was the time of woolly mammoths, saber-tooth tigers, and mastodons. History's largest land mammals were alive during the Ice Age. There is also tropical vegetation under the Antarctic ice sheet. The condition of the vegetation seems to be post-Flood.

2. There was abundant, probably too much, water.

3. Game, grains, vegetables, and fruit grew in abundance with little or no cultivation.

Note: The following public domain image depicts reconstructions of hypothetical terrain, plant life, and creatures that may have existed during the Ice Age. Time frames provided by uniformitarians for the so-called Miocene era and the actual appearance of Ice Age creatures, is subject to interpretation. This image is useful for showing the abundance of fauna, the watery conditions, and the lush plant life that was part of the explosive growth of this time period.

Restoration of Miocene fauna of North America, on a mural made for the US government-owned Smithsonian Museum. Includes Moropus, Daphoenodon Paleocastor, Stenomylus, Parahippus, Daeodon, Merychyus, Promerycochoerus. Date 1964 scan from the Time Life book "North America" Author Jay Matternes

4. The constantly-changing conditions favored a nomadic lifestyle.

a. The continually falling sea level would require constant moving, at least at first. This change in temperature would take place over years or perhaps decades.

b. Ice sheets formed, advanced, and retreated rapidly. Melting ice would fill streams and rivers from spring through late fall. This would be neither local nor regional, but worldwide. Controlling floods would be a universal concern with some local exceptions.

c. Pasturelands alternated between being marshlands, usable grasslands, and too dry, requiring a constant movement of animals.

d. Though we have no documents to support this, volcanic activity, including earthquakes, likely continued for centuries.

Carbon 14 Dating

IV. Carbon 14 dating

Carbon 14 dating, abbreviated ^{14}C, is a simple concept with complex problems. ^{14}C is often praised as the absolute authority of dating human artifacts. Others condemn it as a just another inaccurate radiometric dating system. This is not a case of the truth lying somewhere in the middle. It is a case of both sides presenting accurate scientific information to support their positions. However, some, usually believers in deep time, ignore the equally valid scientific information from the other side.

North Ronaldsay sheep. Attribution: Liz Burke 2003 licensed under the Creative Commons Attribution-Share Alike 2.0 Generic license.

Please click here to link to an explanation of the importance of these sheep on the Scottish island of North Ronaldsay to ^{14}C and uniformitarianism.[p]

Like all powerful tools, when the tool is misused it creates massive problems. It is a tool which, when used properly within its limits, completely supports the chronology of the Scriptures. We know that some will find this an astounding statement because they were never told of the limitations of ^{14}C.

A. A Brief Overview of How Carbon Dating Works

The following explanation is simplified and there are exceptions. Cosmic rays, primarily from the sun, constantly bombard the earth, creating a tiny amount of radiation in the atmosphere. This radiation filters down to the soil and eventually into living organisms. Everything living thing on earth absorbs some of this radiation the entire time it is alive. It is fairly evenly distributed and constant. The exceptions should be known and taken into account by the person testing the sample. When an organism dies, it no longer absorbs any of this radioactive ^{14}C. At that time the amount of ^{14}C is equal to the amount of ^{14}C in the general worldwide environment, including the atmosphere. At the point of death the organism begins converting the radioactive isotope ^{14}C into Nitrogen, which will escape into the atmosphere. A tiny sample from the organism can be used to measure the ^{14}C still in the organism. Because radioactive materials decay at a constant rate, the amount measured in the sample can be compared to the number of years required for a known amount of ^{14}C to decay. This number is subtracted from the present date and gives us a date of death for the organism. There are numerous articles which explain this process in detail. This is a very brief overview.[q]

The critical assumption is that organisms have always absorbed ^{14}C at a constant, consistent rate.

B. Problems with Using Carbon 14 Dating

1.)The first problem is well-known and admitted by everyone familiar with ^{14}C dating. ^{14}C has a half-life of 5,730 years. This means that half of the material decays to Nitrogen every 5,730 years. All traces of ^{14}C are gone in less than 120,000 years. This is a theoretical calculated rate. This means that no instrument will ever be able to measure ^{14}C older than 120,000 years old because any sample older than 120,000 will not have any ^{14}C.

But this 120,000 year age limit is more than twice the practical limit. Even those with the greatest faith in ^{14}C recognize that they cannot accurately detect amounts of ^{14}C much older than an assumed 50,000 years, by uniformitarian standards. The amount of remaining ^{14}C after 50-60,000 years is too small to measure accurately.

2. The next problem is just as well-known, though not widely acknowledged. Uniformitarians state with confidence that we know, that is, have established with other methods called calibrations, a 12,000 years BP (Before Present) timeline for correcting ^{14}C dates. This is based primarily on dendrochronology, that is, tree ring dating. The problems with dendrochronology are mentioned in COA3. There is also an article on the problems with dendrochronology in the reference links

from this module.[r] Dendrochronology also relies on the same assumption of a constant past.

Creation and the Flood are assumed to be not true. This assumption is necessary for ^{14}C to accumulate in living organisms at a constant rate throughout history.

Uniformitarians assume a constant rate of ^{14}C formation, which they claim is supported by a constant rate of tree ring formation. For any of these dating methods to be valid, the assumption of a constant rate of formation must be valid. A constant, within strict limits, for the formation of tree rings and ^{14}C is assumed. That assumption is then used to measure samples of tree rings and organic material. Those measurements are then used to proclaim validation of the original assumptions. Assume conditions. Test samples according to those assumptions. Assume that the test results confirm the original assumptions.

3. The degree of accuracy diminishes with time. Again, both uniformitarians and creationists agree with this basic statement. The issue is how much and how fast. Creationists believe that conditions before, during, and soon after the Flood were drastically different from conditions today. Also, the environmental ^{14}C was much lower. Much lower environmental ^{14}C would produce much lower amounts of ^{14}C in the organism. So, using the assumption of a constant rate of ^{14}C formation, any sample from immediately after the Flood would test to be much older than its actual age.

There is no way of knowing when the conditions for ^{14}C formation on earth stabilized. But we can be certain that as we go farther back in time to test older and older ^{14}C samples, the test results will be less and less accurate.

Even today the atmosphere does not appear to be in equilibrium. The earth's magnetic field decay and the

Flood contributed to a lower amount of environmental ^{14}C in the past.[s]

Written documents exist which validate samples of ^{14}C with dates back to the Roman period. Earlier dates become increasingly suspect.

C. Benefits of Using Carbon 14 Dating

1. Unlike other forms of radiometric dating, we know that the clock starts when the organism dies. That is a known starting condition. There is disagreement as to the amount of ^{14}C in the organism at that point, but the original condition is known. When testing for ^{14}C during the written history of mankind, we know the general conditions on earth for any possible organic sample available almost as far back as the Flood. The major assumptions which invalidate all other forms of radiometric dating do not automatically invalidate ^{14}C dating. The centuries immediately after the Flood have actual dates which are considerably younger than the ^{14}C dates.

2. Short half-life allows for calibration with written documents. ^{14}C can date organisms from WWII, the French Revolution, the Black Plague, the building of the Great Wall in China, the Dead Sea Scrolls, and millions of other events which can be checked with written documents. For the historian, it is a useful tool. The historian must understand that ^{14}C is a tool which can be in error, but it is a very useful tool, especially if the results of the tests are less than 2,500 years old.

3. Assuming similar conditions worldwide for ^{14}C formation is reasonable. So, while a sample tested to be 7,000 years old is almost certainly not that age, it is still

older than a sample tested to be 5,000 years old. The actual difference between them could be less than 1,000 years. ^{14}C can therefore reveal relative ages. So even when the tested samples of ^{14}C return dates which are older than the Flood, there is a relative value. It is therefore possible to make relative, not absolute, evaluations of the thousands of carbon-dated samples worldwide. It is very possible that a sample dated 5,000 years old was alive at the same time as another organism which carbon-dated 6,000 years old. For example, if it lived just another fifty years, conditions might have changed enough for the organism to test 1,000 years younger.

Though younger results from the Roman Period to the present are very accurate when properly calibrated with known ^{14}C issues, absolute dates with ^{14}C are impossible. Older dates are still useful as relative dates. Relative dates can be very important. Worldwide thousands of artifacts have been dated by ^{14}C. These tell us the relative ages of all of these artifacts, assuming that regional changes did not alter a specific sample. Relative dating means that we could take fifty samples and arrange them from oldest to youngest. We cannot conclude the actual (absolute) date, even within a range, for test results older than around 2,500 years BP (before present).

But we will understand which sample is the youngest, which sample is the oldest, and arrange each sample in approximately correct chronological order.

4. Verifying ^{14}C dates

Examining a few key dates will give us valuable insight.

a. The Manuscripts of the Dead Sea Scrolls (DSS)

Since their discovery, dozens of ^{14}C tests performed on various DSS manuscripts have given us a range of 408 BC to 318 AD. Each test has its own accuracy range. While there is some question as to the youngest dates (closest to our time period), most of the results are accepted as accurate by Christians, Jews, and secular scholars.

So it is a very reasonable assumption that calibrated ^{14}C test results back to the late (closest to our time) 5th century BC are accurate. As with any test there is the possibility of error, but the basic ^{14}C procedure is sound.

b. The founding of Carthage

Several documents give us information as to the date of the founding of Carthage.[t] Since they compare the founding of Carthage with other known events, all dates are approximates. These dates range from about 850 BC to about 775 BC. Two documents with what is accepted as the most precise information give us dates of 826 BC and 814 BC.

Since both Rome and Islam (AD 698) razed Carthage to the ground, finding material for ^{14}C testing from the foundations is difficult. In spite of the difficulties, some believe that they have found material from the foundation of Carthage.

> "The most recent excavations (by the universities of Hamburg and Gent) date the Greek pottery from the oldest level to the second half of the 8th century. The ^{14}C dates from this level, however, are 50–75 yr older, consistent with the historical foundation of Carthage, which is 814/813 BCE."[u]

So ^{14}C dates back to around 800 BC (the approximate time of Ahab) are still reliable. The complete paper shows considerably more uncertainty than the dates for the DSS. As we progress backwards in time, disagreements become more pronounced.

c. By 1500 BC "radiocarbon dates run one or two centuries earlier than the dates proposed by archaeologists."

> "As in Egypt and the eastern Mediterranean, radiocarbon dates run one or two centuries earlier than the dates proposed by archaeologists. It is not at all clear which group is right, if either. Mechanisms have been proposed for explaining why radiocarbon dates in the region might be skewed."[v]

The Flood altered ^{14}C levels in the environment. As we go back from the founding of Carthage, ^{14}C dating is giving dates which are older than the dates recorded in Hebrew History. So not only are the ^{14}C dates beyond about 800 BC too old as we progress back in time, the existing documents of Egyptian chronology are stretched even more than the ^{14}C dates.

d. The oldest post-Flood artifacts

An article which used Bayesian modeling analyzed 200 artifacts which had already been ^{14}C tested.

> "The researchers used carbon dating to estimate with 68 per cent probability that the first ruler, King Aha, took to the throne between 3111 and 3045 BC, and died between 3073 and 3036 BC. They also concluded that the Predynastic period began in 3800-3700 BC, so it lasted just 600-700 years, several centuries less than previously thought."[w]

As we go back to the Flood, Hebrew history gives us younger dates than these ^{14}C dates. The dates archeologists use are older than the ^{14}C dates. If you are interested, you can examine the older dates proposed by James Breasted. Ussher's dates are used in the COA series without COA claiming that Ussher's dates are entirely accurate. Ussher uses the Masoretic text, not the expanded genealogies of the LXX (Septuagint). He also strictly follows the genealogical records of Genesis without artificially inflating them. Ussher relies on information which is no longer available to us, so some of his sources cannot be verified. The amount of time the Children of Israel were in Egypt and the exact dates of the Hebrew kings are also questionable. Ussher is used as a well-known frame of reference, not an absolute standard. We use Ussher's timeline as an approximation, though a very close approximation. For example, Ussher has 588 BC as the fall of Jerusalem to Nebuchadnezzar. That date is very accurate, though it might off by a few years. Ussher has the date of Solomon dedicating the temple as 1004 BC. This date is likely off by several decades. Ussher has the date of the Exodus from Egypt as 1491 BC. This date is likely off by almost 50 years. So we understand that by using Ussher's date for Noah leaving the ark, 2348 BC, COA is using it only as a close approximate.

^{14}C dates the first Egyptian ruler beginning his rule as early as 3111 BC. It is a very reasonable assumption that this first Egyptian ruler was Noah's grandson Mizraim. It is also a reasonable assumption that he took the throne of Egypt shortly after the tower of Babel, approximately 2100 BC.

The Name Mizraim is a transliteration of the Hebrew characters into the English alphabet. It is usually translated using the word *Egypt* throughout the Old Testament.

So the ^{14}C dates are approximately 1100 years too old in 2100 BC. Making the very reasonable assumption that people moved to Egypt less than 100 years after the Flood, the actual beginning of the predynastic period was about 2250 BC. Since ^{14}C dates for Egypt go back to 3800 BC, we can reasonably assume that ^{14}C dates of 3800 BC are 1550 years too old.

e. Materials formed during the Flood have ^{14}C dates around 50,000 years.

Fossils, coal and diamonds formed during the Flood have ^{14}C dates from 20 to 55,000 years old.[x]

f. Corrected ^{14}C timeline

Using assumptions which might need modifications with the discovery of additional information, we can make certain corrections to a ^{14}C timeline. This is very general and there is always the possibility of specific errors. From the present to the 8th or 9th century BC ^{14}C dates can be accepted as presented by ^{14}C laboratories. From that point back, ^{14}C dates begin to give us results which are slightly older than the actual dates. By 2000 BC actual date, ^{14}C dates are giving results which are more than a thousand years too old.

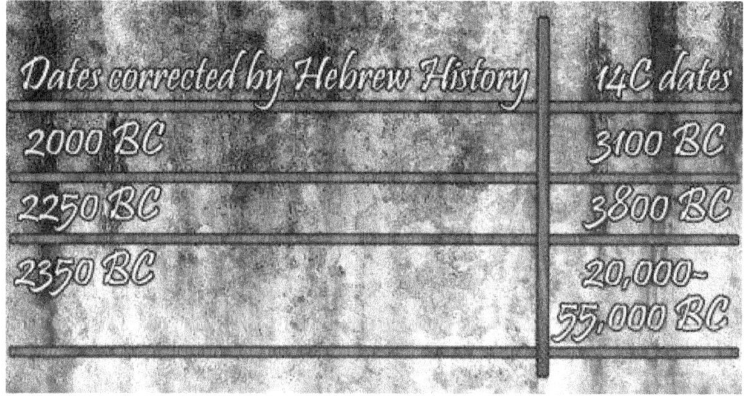

^{14}C dates corrected by Hebrew History 2000 BC – 3100 BC; 2250 BC; 3800 BC; 2350 BC; 20,000-55,000 BC

From approximately 800 BC where ^{14}C dates are somewhat vague though still reliable, to 2000 BC, ^{14}C dates become inaccurate by more than a thousand years. This is due to the amount of ^{14}C in the general environment at that time. It is not due to inaccurate measurements or deliberate dishonesty, except for making the assumption that the environment was constant.

The most important point is the very rough approximation of one hundred years of actual dates of approximately 2250 BC to approximately 2350 BC show a jump in ^{14}C dates from 3800 BC to dates in the tens of thousands of years. So any ^{14}C date of that age is unreliable because the conditions on earth were stabilizing from the Flood. Understand that Secular Humanism with their faith in deep time will not tolerate such error correction.[y]

"If you mistakenly assume that the radiocarbon levels in the atmosphere and biosphere have always been the same as they are today, you would erroneously estimate much older dates for early human artifacts, such as post-Babel wooden statuettes in Egypt. And that is exactly what conventional archaeology has done." Dr. Snelling[z]

V. Chronology

A. Calendars

Julius Caesar reformed the Roman calendar in the 1st century BC for the purpose of collecting taxes. This Julian Calendar has undergone several revisions since then. The Gregorian Calendar, used in much of the West, is a revision of the Julian Calendar. Italy, Poland, Portugal, and Spain converted in October, 1582 AD.

JULIAN 1582	October				Gregorian 1582	
Sun	Mon	Tues	Wed	Thurs	Fri	Sat
	1	2	3	4	15	16
17	18	19	20	21	22	23
24	25	26	27	28	29	30
31						

Visual example of the official date change from the Julian calendar to the Gregorian
Date 15 September 2014 Author Asmdemon

Visual example of the official date change from the Julian Calendar to the Georgian Date

The COA series uses both the Gregorian and the Jewish AM *(Anno Mundi)* calendars. The Gregorian calendar is the most common calendar in the Western world and is used by most of our readers.

The Julian Day calendar began with the year 0 as 4714 BC of the Gregorian calendar. It is a reconciliation of many calendars worldwide and counts days of the year without using months. There are many variations of both the Julian and Julian Day calendars.

The abbreviation BC after a date means Before Christ (His birth). The abbreviation AD before a date means *Anno Domini,* Latin for *In the Year of Our Lord.* AD also counts from Christ's birth. There was no year zero.

The abbreviation AM or A.M. after a date means *Anno Mundi* which is Latin for "in the year of the world." That comes from the Hebrew "from the creation of the world." While there is some slight disagreement, the year Zero AM corresponds to 3,761 BC.

This headstone uses an Anno Mundi date Rotunda yard, Thessaloniki: Jewish tomb remains – 5664 is a Hebrew year that began in the evening of September 22, 1903 and ended September 9, 1904. 16 December 2008 Author Pvasiliadis

Every culture on earth has its own calendar. While the Jews were in captivity in Persia, they used the Persian calendar, the Babylonian calendar, the civil Jewish calendar of the Northern kingdoms, the civil Jewish calendar of Judah, and the Mosaic calendar found in the Torah. In Egypt, each new Pharaoh introduced a new calendar. It seems that the Egyptians also used separate civil and religious calendars.

This is why most conservative books which agree with the COA dating concept still vary in the specific year. Correlating hundreds of events and calendars can be done, but there is still disagreement.

The Gregorian calendar is based, after centuries of corrections, on the regularity of astronomical movements. It is not perfect, but most calendars are based on events important to a particular culture. Usually kings based a calendar on their ascension to the throne. Probably the most famous example is the Sumerian Kings list.

There is more agreement in dating among conservatives than you would expect. The chronologies of Genesis are accepted as accurate and without gaps. The two major periods of disagreement are the exact dates of the Hebrew kings during the monarchy and the length of time the Jews were in slavery in Egypt. During the period of the monarchy, the greatest possible legitimate disagreement is only a matter of decades. During the period of slavery in Egypt, there is potential disagreement of about a century.

COA follows the dates of the Masoretic Hebrew text and not the expanded dates of the Septuagint (LXX).

B. Events

Most dates are approximations.

The easiest way to grasp history is to memorize events. The three most important events in human history are the Creation, the Flood, and the death, burial, and resurrection of Jesus the Christ. Using approximations of Archbishop Ussher's dates, these would be
1. Creation 4000 BC,
2. the Flood 2350 BC, and
3. the crucifixion of Christ AD 30.

Once you have this basic time frame memorized, you can add other important events:
Israel moves his family to Egypt, 1700 BC;
the Exodus from Egypt, 1450 BC;

Solomon begins building the temple, 970 BC;
the fall of Jerusalem to Nebuchadnezzar, 585 BC;
the Battle of Thermopylae, 480 BC.
From this point, dating is more certain:
the fall of Rome, AD 476,;
Muslim defeat in Europe at the battle of Tours, AD 732;
death of Genghis Khan, founder of the Mongolian Empire, the largest empire in the world, AD 1227;
Columbus discovers America, AD 1492;
Martin Luther nails the 95 thesis to the church door in Wittenberg, AD 1517.

It is easy to add more dates. However, except for the last two dates, they are spaced out in intervals designed to provide an overview of human history.

The Conflict of the Ages Part Four Ice Age Civilizations

I. Overview

Secularism teaches a very long, slow progress for humans. They believe that the discovery of fire, the wheel, and how to domesticate animals took millennia. With much trial and error, one culture very slowly evolved into another. The evidence, however, shows a very rapid, sudden, even explosive growth of population, civilization, and advanced technology from the very beginning.

Although the following image of a Mesopotamian Cylinder Seal impression does not date from the Ice Age Era, it does appear to show some type of flying machine. Many ancient artifacts and manuscripts refer to flying devices. These indicate that technology was developed by man very early.

1st Millennium Mesopotamian seal
19 February 2005 (original upload date)
Original uploader was IronyWrit
This image is in the public domain.

1st Millennium Mesopotamian seal 19 February 2005 (original upload date) original uploader was IronyWrit this image is in the Public Domain.

Rapid, even explosive growth fits the records available in Hebrew History. Noah and his family left the ark about 2350 BC (Ussher's date). Arphaxad was born two years later. Arphaxad and his wife gave birth to Salah thirty-five years later, followed by Eber thirty years later. Thirty-four years later, one hundred and one years after leaving the ark, Noah's great-great-great grandson Peleg was born. And Noah lived another 249 years.

During Peleg's lifetime men decided to rebel against God by building a tower. Ussher tells us that they went

> "into the valley of Shinar. Ge 11:2 Here the people impiously conspired as we find in the book of Wisdom /APC Wis 10:5 to hinder this dispersion of them as commanded by God and began by Noah (as may be gathered from Ge 11:4,6,8,9 compared together)."[1]

This took place during Peleg's lifetime, somewhere between 101 and 340 years after the Flood.

Josephus tells us, "Now it was Nimrod who excited them to such an affront and contempt of God. He was the grandson of Ham, the son of Noah…"[2] At this time there was only one language and only one culture. Under Nimrod's leadership, they hunted down people to work on a tower. Some people fled to escape from this manhunt. This explanation fits in with the rapid dispersion of nomad groups such as the Australian Aborigines and the Clovis people of the Americas. It also helps explain why the oldest artifacts show cave dwellers, since these would be first, temporary residences.

The Lord God intervened in the building of the tower. The languages were confounded and various people groups were divided. After the division, the various language groups began fighting among themselves. Unrepentant, they moved off and founded their own civilizations. Nimrod attempted to recapture these people for his own kingdom. These conflicts, plus the need to escape Nimrod, explain why civilizations suddenly appeared in China, Egypt, Europe, and the Indus Valley, as well as throughout Mesopotamia, at nearly the same time. It shows why the Sumerian and Akkadian cultures are slightly older than the rest. It also explains why the oldest aspects of human culture are large buildings and warfare.

The tower of Babel and the confusion of languages took place near the beginning of the Ice Age. Meteorologist Michael Oard believes that the physical evidence shows that "the total length of time for a post-Flood Ice Age is about 700 years."[3]

Using a seven-hundred-year period for the end of the Ice Age, we look for an event to indicate the end of this time period. The seven years of plenty in Egypt began in 1715 BC [Ussher] when Joseph was vizier of Egypt. That was about 635 years after the Flood ended, according to Ussher's dating. While there is nothing which says that the seven years of famine ended the ice age, it was a worldwide famine and the timing fits. *The people of all the earth came to Egypt to buy grain from Joseph, because the famine was severe in all the earth.* (Genesis 41:57 NASB)

It is a reasonable assumption that Egypt, which depends on the flooding of the Nile, would experience greater harvests as the rapidly melting ice caps added more soil and nutrients and increased the areas flooded. It is another reasonable assumption that the areas formerly covered by ice in central Africa, which had supplied the Nile with annual floodwater, would become bare and unable to retain both rainwater and water from the annual snow thaws. These areas which were barren because they were covered by ice needed time to grow vegetation. The vegetation would keep the melted snow from immediately rushing down the Nile and out to sea and so maintain Egypt's annual floods. It is also possible that this is the time Lake Victoria formed. Whatever the reason, at the end of seven years of drought, the Nile River returned to annual flood cycles. These are assumptions, but they are reasonable assumptions based on the facts.

II. The Post-Flood World: the Ice Age

"And the *Chaldaeans* boasted further, that they had observed the stars 473,000 years; and there were others who made the Kingdoms of *Assyria, Media,* and *Damascus*, much older than the truth." (emphasis added) Sir Isaac Newton.[4]

When Noah and his family left the ark, the volcanic activities of the Flood made the oceans warmer than any time in earth's history. It is probable that near the end of the Flood the mountains rose and the valleys descended.

> *You covered it with the deep as with a garment;*
> *The waters were standing above the mountains.*
> *At Your rebuke they fled,*
> *At the sound of Your thunder they hurried away.*
> *The mountains rose; the valleys sank down*
> *To the place which You established for them.*
> *You set a boundary that they may not pass over,*
> *So that they* [the waters] *will not return to cover the earth.* (Psalm 104:6-9 NASB)

As the sea level lowered, ice formed on the rising mountain peaks and the Ice Age began. This began soon after they left the ark; perhaps immediately but within decades at the most.

A. Noah and Family Leave the Ark

The chronology of James Ussher is a useful, accurate approximation. The reader should understand that his dates, though well researched, could be in error. Throughout the COA series alternatives to Ussher's dates will be offered, along with explanations why these alternatives seem to be more accurate dates. These alternative dates are usually close to Ussher's dates.

The Chronology of Ancient Kingdoms Amended by Sir Isaac Newton was published posthumously from collected notes. Though it is incomplete, and does not go back to the Flood, it is better than Ussher's work.

> 40. When Noah was 601 years old, on the 1st day of the 1st month (Friday, October 23rd), the 1st day of the new post-Flood world, the surface of the earth was now all dry."[5]

Eight people left the ark and immediately began producing children. Arphaxad was born two years after the Flood. There were no recorded deaths for 340 years and families were large. A new generation began about every 35 years. The human population exploded.

B. God's Covenant with Noah

This covenant includes all of Noah's descendants. It is not just a covenant with Noah the individual man, or just his immediate family. This is the eternal covenant Isaiah wrote about. *The earth lies defiled beneath its inhabitants; because they have transgressed the laws, violated the statutes, and broken the everlasting covenant.* (Isaiah 24:5 ISV)

> *And God blessed Noah and his sons and said to them, "Be fruitful and multiply, and fill the earth. The fear of you and the terror of you will be on every beast of the earth and on every bird of the sky; with everything that creeps on the ground, and all the fish of the sea, into your hand they are given. Every moving thing that is alive shall be food for you; I give all to you, as I gave the green plant. Only you shall not eat flesh with its life, that is, its blood. Surely I will require your lifeblood; from every beast I will require it. And from every man, from every man's brother I will require the life of man. "Whoever sheds man's blood, By man his blood shall be shed, For in the image of God He made man. "As for you, be fruitful and multiply; Populate the earth abundantly and multiply in it."* (Genesis 9:1-7 NASB)

1. *Be fruitful, multiply and fill the earth.* God began by repeating the command given to Adam. God repeated it a third time by closing the covenant with the same words. The word translated *fruitful* can also be translated *productive*. While *multiply and fill the earth* both refer to producing children, *be productive* or *fruitful* in both Genesis 1:28 and the two places here includes the idea of responsibility and control. It is the idea of proper management using the tool of engineering and technology, not only in marriage but in everything.

2. *Every moving thing that is alive shall be food for you.* Next God gives permission to eat meat. In the Garden God gave Adam plants as food. This does not mean that antediluvian mankind was obedient and never ate meat.

It simply means that now God gave His permission. The animals are aware of this.

> *The fear of you and the terror of you will be on every beast of the earth and on every bird of the sky; with everything that creeps on the ground, and all the fish of the sea, into your hand they are given.*

Damaidi, Beishan Mountain Ningxia Hui Autonomous Region more than 10,000. 3,172 sets of early Chinese petroglyphs 8,453 individual figures public domain image

The harmonious relationship between mankind and animals is destroyed until God makes all things new.

3. *Only you shall not eat flesh with its life, that is, its blood.* Humans are prohibited from eating any animal while it is still alive. Humans are prohibited from eating raw meat with the blood still in it. Humans are prohibited from eating cooked meat where the blood has not been drained before it is cooked. God repeats this command again in Leviticus where the eating of blood is connected with divination. *'You shall not eat anything with the blood, nor practice divination or soothsaying.'*

Leviticus 19:26 The armies of Israel disobeyed this command by slaughtering animals on the ground and eating the animals on the ground so their blood could not drain out. *The army grabbed the spoil, took sheep, oxen, and calves, and slaughtered them on the ground, and then the army ate them with the blood.* I Samuel 14:32 ISV

4. Whoever sheds man's blood, by man his blood shall be shed. God requires capital punishment. The Mosaic Law allows for exceptions such as accidental death or what we might call manslaughter. But what we call first degree murder requires execution of the murderer. God will require the blood of anyone who refuses to execute a convicted murderer.

> *Thus says the Lord, "Because you have let go out of your hand the man whom I had devoted to destruction, therefore your life shall go for his life, and your people for his people."*
> (I Kings 20:42, NASB)

III. Repopulation of the Earth

A. The Table of Nations

Genesis chapters Ten and Eleven document the repopulation of the earth. Chapter Ten is called the Table of Nations. It lists the most significant of Noah's early descendants. Combined with genealogical records in Chapter Eleven, we learn that our forefathers settled the entire earth in a few hundred (not thousand) years. Chapter Eleven is the genealogy of the Messiah through Shem and Abraham. Though Josephus is not entirely trustworthy, he provides interesting information about these men as well as expanding the list.[6]

Assuming very little mortality for the first 350 years, thirty years per generation, and large families, means concluding that the earth's population was in the millions, including women and children, by the time the Tower of Babel was attempted. The widespread introduction of warfare at the division of languages along with the beginning of natural death due to old age ended the period of explosive population growth.

1. Some of Noah's great-grandchildren became shipbuilders and lived on sea coasts.

> *Javan's descendants included Elisha, Tarshish, Kittim, and Dodanim, from whom the coastal peoples spread into their own lands and nations, each with their own language and family groups.* (Genesis 10:4,5 ISV)

> After this they were dispersed abroad, on account of their languages, and went out by colonies every where; and each colony took possession of that land which they light upon, and unto which God led them; so that the whole continent was filled with them, both the inland and the maritime countries. There were some also who passed over the sea in ships, and inhabited the islands. (Josephus)[7]

The pyramids of Giza have some underground storage pits containing disassembled boats. Made from cedars from Lebanon, one boat has been removed and re-assembled. It is in a museum at the base of the great pyramid. Though it is called Khufu's solar boat, there is no direct evidence of a connection with Khufu. The name "solar ship" or "solar boat" is the belief that they were buried to help in the afterlife to travel with Ra (or Re) the sun god.

Solar boat Edifu Temple of Horus stock xchng free image

About twenty-six ships have been found buried in boat pits throughout Egypt. Most of these go back nearly to the founding of Egypt. The existence of these ships makes perfect sense if they were made within a few centuries of the Flood. If the Nile region was, as Herodotus records, a marsh with a high water table, and the region to the west consisted of vast savannahs filled with game, these were likely very common ships throughout the Ice Age.

Gizeh Sonnenbarke BW 2CC by SA 3.0 Berthold Werner own work Wikimedia Commons

The oldest images in tombs also have ships.[8]

2. "...there sprang from Cush *Nimrod*, the founder of the first imperial kingdom..." wrote Keil and Delitszch.

Barque-photo2-sesostris3 by Jaques de morgan – fouilles a Danchour (1895) via Wikimedia Commons

Noah's great-grandson Nimrod was the world's first tyrant. *Now Cush became the father of Nimrod; he became a mighty one on the earth. He was a mighty hunter before the Lord; therefore it is said, "Like Nimrod a mighty hunter before the Lord." The beginning of his kingdom was Babel and Erech and Accad and Calneh, in the land of Shinar. From that land he went forth into Assyria, and built Nineveh and Rehoboth-Ir and Calah, and Resen between Nineveh and Calah; that is the great city. Mizraim became the father of Ludim and Anamim and Lehabim and Naphtuhim and Pathrusim and Casluhim (from which came the Philistines) and Caphtorim.* (Genesis 10:8-14 NASB)

Cush fathered Nimrod, who became the first fearless leader throughout the land. He became a fearless hunter in defiance of the LORD. That is why it is said, "Like Nimrod, a fearless hunter in defiance of the LORD." Genesis 10:8-12 ISV

The Legacy of Nimrod

Rulers Seeking Worldwide Physical and Spiritual Domination

(Note: Not all images are as ancient as the Ice Age but represent the influence of Nimrod on world cultures)

(Mesopotamia, Canaan, Egypt, India)

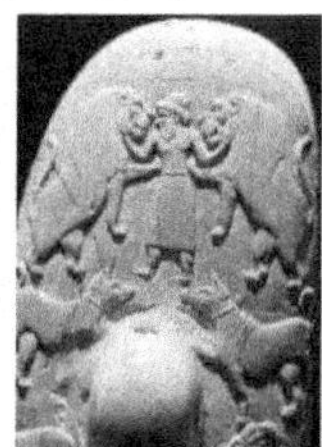

Subduing dangerous or supernatural creatures without weapons

(Indus Valley, Celtic, Babylonian)

Surrounded by tame creatures and small, subordinate humans
Rulers control and are superior to everything

(Egypt, Phonecia, India, Greek, Celtic)

Godlike beings with control over animals appear in similar poses in widely separated cultures Riding fish/dolphins, served by elephants, furniture or stairs with lions, sphinx, etc., flanking

(Note that in the graphic above, these are examples of rulers seeking to subjugate apart from God. They distort and redefine scriptural promises of man being able to rule nature and have great physical and spiritual power with obedience. They sought this power apart from God. Ancient biblical rulers were given power over animals and men, as well as great wealth and land, because of their faith and trust in their Creator, not in themselves.)

"The name itself, *Nimrod* ... 'we will revolt,' points to some violent resistance to God." wrote Keil and Delitszch.[9]

> "Now it was Nimrod who excited them to such an affront and contempt of God. He was the grandson of Ham, the son of Noah, a bold man, and of great strength of hand. He persuaded them not to ascribe it to God, as if it was through his means they were happy, but to believe that it was their own courage which procured that happiness. He also gradually changed the government into tyranny, seeing no other way of turning men from the fear of God, but to bring them into a constant dependence on his power." wrote Josephus.[10]

Indus Priest King Statue found in Mohenjo-daro in 1927 National Museum Karachi Pakistan Photographer Mamoon Mengai Creative Commons Attribution Share alike 1.0 generic license

It is very likely that the Mesopotamian hero *Gilgamesh* was designed to exalt Nimrod. It is also very likely that he was known as *Herakles* in the Indus valley, to the Greeks as *Heracles*, and became *Hercules* to the Romans. In the Indus Valley, the birth of Hinduism transformed *Herakles* into *Shiva*. In Egypt he was transformed into *Osiris*. The differences of these various demigods are overshadowed by their similarities. This does not mean that Nimrod personally possessed these abilities. It means that Nimrod invented the *Epic of Gilgamesh* and had it publicized in various cities to deceive people into believing that he had these abilities. Without the aid of demonic deception, it does not seem possible that so many people in so many different cultures would accept the same lie in the same form.

Knife Canaanite deity ivory and flintstone blade from Gebel el Arak South of Abydos, Louvre Museum Photographer Rama Creative Commons Attribution-Share Alike 2.0 France license

3. Canaan

Canaan became the father of Sidon, his firstborn, and Heth and the Jebusite and the Amorite and the Girgashite and the Hivite and the Arkite and the Sinite and the Arvadite and the Zemarite and the Hamathite; and afterward the families of the Canaanite were spread abroad. The territory of the Canaanite extended from Sidon as you go toward Gerar, as far as Gaza; as you go toward Sodom and Gomorrah and Admah and Zeboiim, as far as Lasha. (Genesis 10:15-19 NASB)

Canaan, Mizraim and Cush were sons of Ham. Canaan was the brother of Cush, the father of Nimrod. Mizraim, [Egypt] *the brother of Cush and Canaan, was the father of Casluhim, (of*

> *whom came the Philistines)* (1 Chronicles 1:12, NASB.)

Canaan's territory began in Sidon and extended to the edge of his brother Mizraim's, that is, Egypt's, territory. Egypt's territory extended from the edge of his brother Canaan's territory to the edge of his brother Cush's territory in Africa. Note this passage from the *Book of Jubilees.*

> "28. And Ham and his sons went into the land which he was to occupy, which he acquired as his portion in the land of the south. 29. And Canaan saw the land of Lebanon to the river of Egypt that it was very good, and he went not into the land of his inheritance to the west (that is to) the sea, and he dwelt in the land of Lebanon, eastward and westward from the border of Jordan and from the border of the sea. 30. And Ham, his father, and Cush and Mizraim, his brothers, said unto him: "Thou hast settled in a land which. is not thine, and which did not fall to us by lot: do not do so; for if thou dost do so, thou and thy sons will fall in the land and (be) accursed through sedition; for by sedition ye have settled, and by sedition will thy children fall, and thou shalt be rooted out for ever. 31. Dwell not in the dwelling of Shem; for to Shem and to his sons did it come by their lot. 32. Cursed art thou, and cursed shalt thou be beyond all the sons of Noah, by the curse by which we bound ourselves by an oath in the presence of the holy judge, and in the presence of Noah our father." 33. But he did not hearken unto them, and dwelt in the land of Lebanon from Hamath to the entering of Egypt, he and his sons until this day. 34. And for this reason that land is named Canaan."[12]

Public domain depiction of Egyptian Osiris as ruler-god

While the *Book of Jubilees* is not inspired, this certainly fits in with God's later command to the Children of Israel to take the land.

4. Peleg: *"unto Eber were born two sons: the name of one was Peleg; for in his days was the earth divided..."* (Genesis 10:25)

This is a clear reference to the division of languages and the forced divisions of mankind when God scattered mankind by dividing people into different languages at the tower of Babel. There is considerable disagreement over when the original single continent was divided. Was it divided into the continents we know today during Peleg's lifetime or were they divided at the end of the Flood?

Several Jewish traditions clearly state that the division of the continents took place during the lifetime of Peleg. The *Book of Jasher* says “to Eber were born two children, the name of one was Peleg, for in his days the sons of men were divided, and in the latter days, the earth was divided.”

This belief is also stated in the *Seder Olam.*

> “You can’t say the division of the continents happened at Peleg’s birth because the children of his younger brother Joktan had 13 families of their own at the division of Languages. Nor can you say this happened when Peleg was middle-aged because Scripture does not come to hide but to reveal. Therefore, this verse must mean that the division of languages happened near the last year of Peleg’s life.”[13]

Mike Beauregard from Munavut, Canada – rebounding beach uploaded by PDTillman (9404384095) CC 2.0

While the oldest Jewish tradition clearly states that the physical earth was divided during the lifetime of Peleg as well as the languages, most creation scientists today do not believe this to be accurate. Dr. Tim Clary explains the reasons[14] why he and most creation scientists believe the evidence teaches the physical division of the continents was a continuation of the Flood. He does not believe that the physical evidence allows for more than three centuries from the end of the Flood to the division of the continents. Instead, Creation Scientists believe that the physical evidence leads to the conclusion that the physical division took place during the flood. They believe that the continents were in their current locations within a few decades of the end of the flood.

Further evidence comes from Dr. John Baumgartner.[15] "It plausibly leads to intense global rain as hot magma erupted in zones of plate divergence, in direct contact with ocean water, creates bubbles of high pressure steam that emerge from the ocean, rise rapidly through the atmosphere, radiate their heat to space, and precipitate their water as rain. That no air-breathing life could survive such a catastrophe and that most marine life also perished is readily believable. "

Using Ussher's chronology, Peleg was born in 2247 BC and died in 2008 BC.

It is best to develop a hypothesis which explains all the data. Modern creation geologists believe the evidence shows that the physical division of the continents took place at the end of the Flood, so let's accept that as a premise. Let us also accept that the sea levels during the Ice Age were 400 feet lower, as NASA evidence indicates. So, during the Ice Age, the lowest point of the sea level would have been at the edge of the continental shelves. That means the continents stopped their rapid movement and settled in approximately their current locations decades after the Flood. Most likely much of the movements were over before Noah left the ark. But the low sea level allowed men during the Ice Age to walk to all of the continents. If all of this is correct, The division of the continents recorded in ancient Jewish traditions does not means that the continents moved when languages were divided at the tower of Babel, but that sea levels rose enough to cut the continents off from one another.

B. Babel (Confusion)

The historical record of Babel (Confusion) is the beginning of what we call civilization. Antediluvian civilization was completely destroyed. Though those antediluvian shipbuilding, metallurgy, agricultural, and engineering skills were passed on through Noah and his family, this was the first post-Flood civilization.

The history of civilization is usually a lengthy praise of man's accomplishments. However, this is not God's perspective.

> *And the whole earth was of one language, and of one speech. And it came to pass, as they journeyed from the east, that they found a plain in the land of Shinar; and they dwelt there. And they said one to another, Go to, let us make brick, and burn them thoroughly. And they had brick for stone, and slime had they for mortar. And they said, Go to, let us build us a city and a tower, whose top {may reach} unto heaven; and let us make us a name, lest we be scattered abroad upon the face of the whole earth. And the Lord came down to see the city and the tower, which the children of men builded. And the Lord said, Behold, the people is one, and they have all one language; and this they begin to do: and now nothing will be restrained from them, which they have*

imagined to do. Go to, let us go down, and there confound their language, that they may not understand one another's speech. So the Lord scattered them abroad from thence upon the face of all the earth: and they left off to build the city. Therefore is the name of it called Babel; because the Lord did there confound the language of all the earth: and from thence did the Lord scatter them abroad upon the face of all the earth. (Genesis 11:1-9)

The Tower of Babel may have been a ziggurat, resembling step-pyramids like this one in Peru. Image from World Photo Cube.

1. The proud leader, Nimrod, is not mentioned here. Moses wrote the phrase *the people*. We will not be able

to blame others for the decisions we make. We know that Nimrod was the leader because of Genesis 10:10; *the beginning of his kingdom was Babel.*

2. The location[16] is not certain. Based on the research of Anne Habermehl, we can be confident the city of Babylon on the Euphrates River, which means *gate(s) of (the) god(s)* is almost certainly not Nimrod's city Babel *(confusion).* The LXX (Septuagint) actually translates the name of the city as Confusion, not using the word Babel in the Greek OT.

3. The tower was under construction for years, though we do not know how many. According to Ussher, it was under construction for thirteen years when the Lord God intervened. According to the *Book of Jubilees* 10:21 it was worked on for forty-three years.

The Rosetta Stone in the British Museum. 21 November 2007 Hans Millewaert Creative Commons Attribution share alike 4.0 International license

God's confounding of the languages is echoed in the inability to understand ancient Egyptian writings until the re-discovery of the Rosetta Stone in 1799.

4. The confounding of the languages and scattering of the people was during Peleg's lifetime, 101 to 340 years after the Flood. Peleg died forty-eight years after the birth of Abraham. Ussher takes the name of Peleg, meaning division, to mean that Noah divided the entire earth between his children in 2247 BC, the year Peleg was born, 101 years after the Flood. Instead of accepting this division, men decided to start building the tower of Babel.

5. There is no record that Babel was ever finished. Josephus writes that the Sibyl said,

> "When all men were of one language, some of them built a high tower, as if they would thereby ascend up to heaven, but the gods sent storms of wind and overthrew the tower, and gave every one his peculiar language..."

This is also mentioned in the *Book of Jubilees*, [82:4]

> "The Lord sent a mighty wind against the tower and overthrew it upon the earth, and behold it was between Asshur and Babylon in the land of Shinar, and they called its name 'Overthrow'."

This passage from the *Book of Jubilees* clearly states that the tower of Babel was north of the city of Babylon, because Asshur is the land of Assyria.

C. Lifespans of the Lineage of the Messiah after the Flood

Noah lived 58 years after the birth of Abraham. His son Shem, who survived the Flood, died fifty years after the birth of Jacob (Israel).

Noah lived 952 years.
Shem lived 600 years.
Arphaxad lived 438 years.
Salah lived 433 years.
Eber lived 468 years.
Peleg lived 239 years.
Reu lived 239 years.
Serug lived 230 years.
Nahor lived 149 years.
Terah lived 205 years.
Abraham lived 175 years.
Isaac lived 180 years.
Jacob lived 147 years.
Joseph lived 110 years.
We do not have the lifespans in Egypt until Moses.
Moses lived 120 years.

If any of Noah's sons, Shem, Ham, and Japheth, married young women, those women could have lived more than eight hundred years after the flood. They could have been alive during the lifetime of Moses. This would make the generation led by Joshua into the land of Canaan the first generation without the opportunity to talk to a person who lived before the flood.

The Ice Age Records 

IV. The Ice Age Records

Meteorologist Michael Oard concludes based on the evidence that the length of the Ice Age was approximately 700 years. The Ice Age then includes civilizations from Noah leaving the Ark until Joseph became vizier of Egypt.

The oldest surviving artifacts are found in protected environments; tombs, buried ruins, and caves. Sometimes these include written documents. The oldest written documents are written in cuneiform, hieroglyphs, and languages which today cannot be deciphered. One of the oldest complete works of literature is the *Epic of Gilgamesh*. Though there are many ancient fragments, the most complete copy is from the library of the 7th century BC Assyrian King Ashurbanipal. This 7th century version is the version which is normally translated into English.

Dating the oldest human artifacts is difficult at best and often impossible. We do have some tools, though their usefulness is far more limited than skeptics would like us to believe. The graphic below shows an archaeological dig in Turkey. This city is considered by some to be one of the oldest in the world.

Gobekli Tepe, Sanliurfa 6 Sept 2011 photographer Teomancimit creative commons attribution share alike license

A. Carbon 14 Dating

Radiocarbon (^{14}C) dating assumes a constant rate of Carbon-14 formation for at least 60,000 years. While the decay rate is accurate, the assumed formation rate is not. ^{14}C dating is covered in more detail in the Teacher Manual Introduction. It is important to understand that ^{14}C, like all dating methods, does not measure time. It measures the amount of ^{14}C decay. Dendrochronology counts tree rings. *All* dating methods count or measure something which exists today. Assumptions are made as to the rate of formation and decay. These assumptions are applied to the existing data for an assumed date.

1. Limitations

The flood is recorded not only in the Bible, but also the *Epic of Gilgamesh*, the *Sumerian King's List,* and hundreds of other sources. The worldwide catastrophe of the Flood as well as a series of catastrophes after the Flood make all ^{14}C dates before the Roman Empire too old. As we go backward in time, the radiocarbon dates become increasingly less accurate.

This is due to lower amounts of environmental ^{14}C as the timeline gets older. It is not because of any change in the decay rate of ^{14}C. Skeptics assume that there were only minor or no environmental changes in the past. They assume that a worldwide catastrophic flood never happened. A worldwide catastrophe like the Flood requires adjusting dates based on ^{14}C. The formation rate of the ^{14}C was less in the past than it is today. As the samples test progressively older, adjustments to ^{14}C dates are required to make them accurate. As the timeline approaches the Flood the actual date will be much younger than the ^{14}C results.

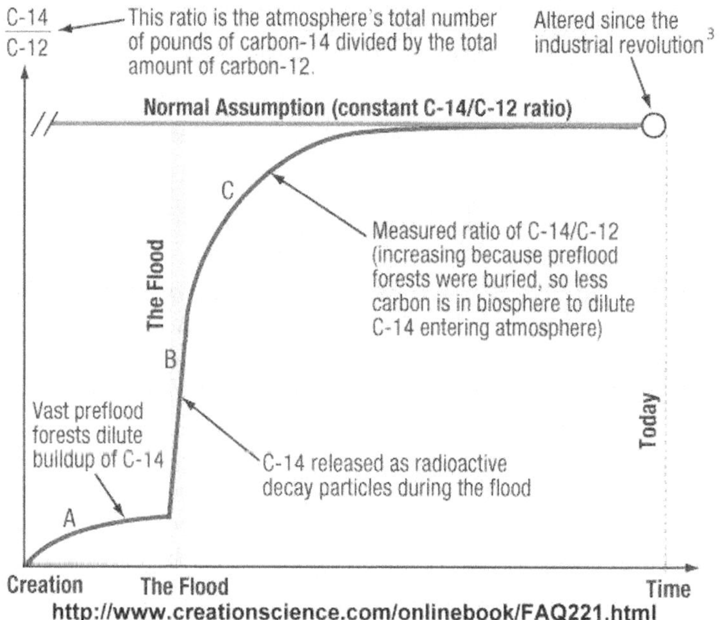

diagram of 14C timeline from creation through the flood to today from Creation Science website

Skeptics also understand that a worldwide catastrophe as described in all ancient literature would make ^{14}C unreliable as the timeline approached the Flood.

Therefore, they reject a worldwide catastrophic event such as the Flood because of their presuppositions – their belief system – not because of evidence. As archaeologist David Down said,

> 'I've used Carbon-14[17] dating', David chuckled. 'Frankly, among archaeologists, carbon dating is a big joke. They send samples to the laboratories to be dated. If it comes back and agrees with the dates they've already decided from the style of pottery, they will say, "Carbon-14 dating of this sample confirms our conclusions." But if it doesn't agree, they just think the laboratory has got it wrong, and that's the end of it. It's only a showcase. Archaeologists never (let me emphasize this) never date their finds by carbon-14. They only quote it if it agrees with their conclusions.'

2. Corrections of ^{14}C dates are necessary.

Hebrew history helps us understand both the benefits and limitations of ^{14}C dating. The Dead Sea Scrolls (DSS) are ^{14}C dated between a very late 5th century BC date and the 4th century AD. While any scientific procedure is capable of error, the ^{14}C dates for the DSS conform to other documents and artifacts and match the known history of the region for that time period. The ^{14}C dates of the Dead Sea Scrolls are accepted by both conservatives and liberals. There is little debate on the ^{14}C dating of the DSS. Many different documents of the Dead Sea Scrolls have been successfully dated using ^{14}C dating. So we can assume that ^{14}C dates for all artifacts tested from the present back to the 5th century BC are reasonably accurate, using known corrections.

Public domain Isaiah Scroll from the dead Sea Scrolls, Qumran

The oldest document[18] from the Dead Sea Scroll collection has not been ^{14}C dated as of this writing. J. T. Milik dated the MUR 17 papyrus fragment as 8th century B.C.

The uncalibrated ^{14}C dates for the city of Jericho[19] are 1550 BC for the layer which best matches the destruction described in the book of Joshua. However, there are many reasons for calibrating this date to 1400 BC, which matches the historical record of Joshua's destruction of Jericho. This layer of the city of Jericho had both a functioning spring and grain stored from a recent harvest (Joshua 3:15). It means that the city was prepared for a protracted siege. Little of the grain was eaten, so the siege was short. It also means that the invaders did not take the valuable grain. The city was set on fire. The fire includes houses and utensils in the homes which were considered valuable. The bricks of the outer fortifications are piled on top of each other (they fell down flat). There is one section of the wall, wide enough for a house, which did not collapse at the same time the rest of the wall collapsed. So this is a ^{14}C correction based on Hebrew History of 150 years to 1400 BC.

Corded ware pottery dated to ca. 2500 BC Museum of Prehistory and Early History Berlin 28 June 2011 Einsamer, Schuetze GNU Free Documentation License

Since ^{14}C dates are primarily calculated from artifacts found in tombs or buried in the destruction of a city, the accuracy of the ^{14}C dates depends on the age of the material (often wood) used in making the artifact. For example, an old tree has both new growth and also parts which are hundreds of years old. The wood used in a tomb might be centuries old before it is placed in the tomb. The sample of wood used for ^{14}C testing could be centuries older than the mummy in the same tomb.

Sample from the Pyramid Texts from an Egyptian tomb. Image from World Photo Cube.

The name of Noah's grandson (Genesis 10:6) Mizraim is elsewhere translated as Egypt. Mizraim is a transliteration; that is, the Hebrew letters are given English equivalents. Throughout the Old Testament the word Mizraim is translated as Egypt. It is probable that Egypt (Mizraim) founded the country of Egypt approximately 2150 BC following the dispersion after the tower of Babel. Not only is there uncertainty about the date and the spelling of the name of the first king of Egypt, there is uncertainty as to who the first king of Egypt was. These are names of at least three different men who might be the first King of Egypt. (see III. G. 1. For more information on the first King of Egypt) Yet ^{14}C dates for the first king of Egypt, known as Menes, Mena, Meni, Min, Narmer, or Aha (Hor-Aha) are ^{14}C dated back to approximately 3100 BC. Knowing exactly when he died and the age of the artifacts placed in his tomb is problematic. It is a reasonable assumption that approximately 2150 BC, worldwide actual dates are at least 1000 years younger than ^{14}C dates.

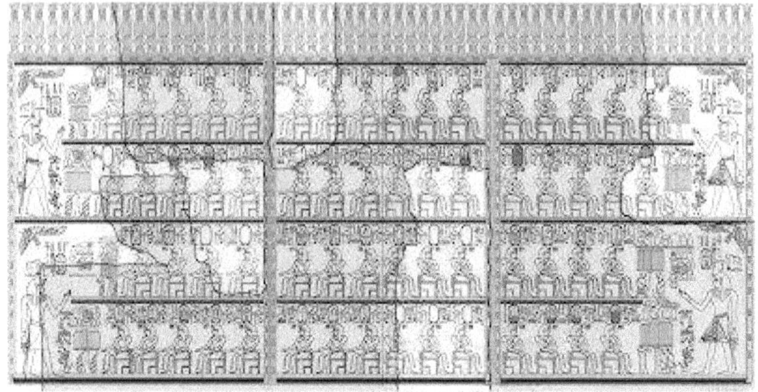

**Drawing of the Karnak King List 2009 Author PLstrom
Creative Commons Attribution-Share Alike 3.0 Unported license.
White areas indicate missing portions**

Drawing of the Karnak King List 2009 author PLstrom CC attribution share alike 3.0 unported license white areas missing portions

Farther back in time,[20] coal, diamonds, and fossils were formed during the Flood approximately 2350 BC. Yet samples of coal, diamonds, and fossils have been ^{14}C tested and returned dates of 20-60,000 years BP (before present). It is a reasonable assumption that all ^{14}C dates older than 3100 BC (^{14}C tested date) are actually dates from 2200 to 2350 BC. The rapidly changing conditions on post-Flood earth account for these increasingly unreliable dates. ^{14}C dates from 3100 BC to 60,000 BC are actual dates spanning from the first Pharaoh of Egypt back to the Flood, only about 200 years. Understand that in addition to the potential problems listed in this section there are many highly technical issues which must be taken into account to make a radiocarbon date accurate.

3. Radiocarbon dating has benefits in spite of its problems. ^{14}C results for a given sample are, with significant exceptions, the same worldwide. This assumes that conditions were roughly same throughout the world at the same time. This foundational

assumption of ^{14}C dating is likely correct. So an artifact which tests to be about 4,000 years old (BP, Before Present) in North America is probably the same age as artifact which ^{14}C tests to be about 4,000 years old BP in Egypt, China, the Indus valley, or most places on earth. It is also only slightly older than an artifact which tests to be 3,700 years old BP and only slightly younger than an artifact testing to be 20,000 years old BP.

Lower amounts of environmental ^{14}C "stretch" or elongate ^{14}C dates. It was somewhere around 500-800 BC before conditions on earth put as much ^{14}C in the environment as we see put into our modern environment. Even today, the environmental ^{14}C is not in complete equilibrium. Changes in the environmental ^{14}C began during the Flood. Environmental ^{14}C was added until we reached the current environmental levels of ^{14}C. The Flood period had significantly lower levels of ^{14}C. Understanding these limits, these relative dates can be used to correlate artifacts worldwide. All of the cultures described in this section were contemporaneous. These are the oldest human artifacts from immediately after Flood. Based on ^{14}C evidence, some nomadic groups traveled throughout the earth within the first few decades after Noah left the Ark. Perhaps they were outcasts. Perhaps they were actually traveling for the cities of Nimrod and were collecting minerals, metals, or other things the cities lacked.

The time period just after the Flood was highly unstable. Decades after Noah and his family left the ark, the environment was very likely changing quickly. So, when ^{14}C dates for human artifacts come up over 4,000 years old BP, it simply means that these artifacts where created very soon after Noah and his family left the ark. Due to the rapid environmental changes, these dates are unreliable. Additional information might change the exact numbers. It is doubtful that the basic concept will change.

obsidian handaxe from Ethiopian acheulean period, found near Lake Langano, Ethiopia – Moika Kunture Museum 2007 GNU free documentation license Wikimedia commons

B. Africa

Like Australia, Oceania, and the Americas, there are abundant fragments of human occupation in Sub-Saharan Africa which date from this period. The fragments are small and there is little agreement about them. These Africans also left tools such as spears behind.

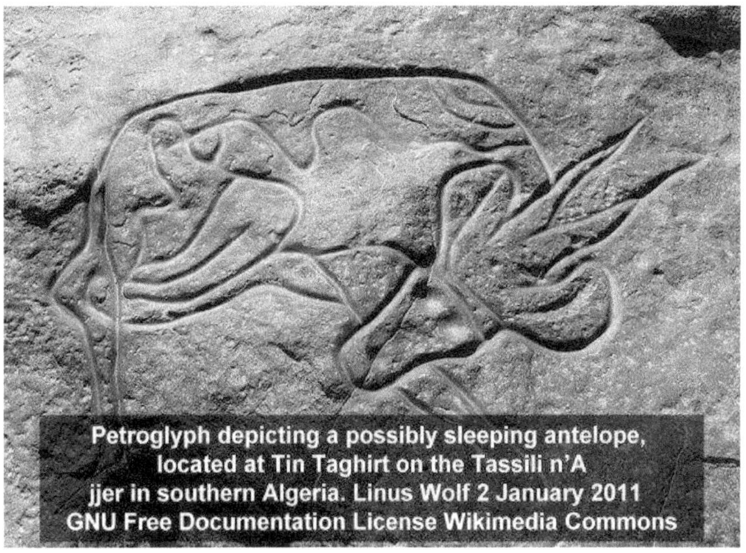

Petroglyph depicting a possibly sleeping antelope located at Tin Taghirt on the Tassili n'A jjer in southern Algeria Linus Wolf 2 January 2011 GNU free documentation license Wikimedia commons

C. Americas

While there are many claims to earlier cultures, the Clovis people are the oldest well-documented people in the Americas. They are named for the area where they were first discovered, Clovis, NM. They were hunters, made drawings on rock, wore jewelry and are identified by the type of flint spears they left behind. Remains of the Clovis people are found from the Yukon to Venezuela. They left a variety of tools behind. There is considerable disagreement whether the distinctive Clovis spearhead represents a unified people or a technology adopted by many different peoples.

Clovis points from the Rummelis-Maske Site, 13CD15, Cedar County, Iowa. State Archaeologist collection Bill Whittaker GNU free documentation license Wikimedia commons

D. Australia/Southeast Asia/Oceania

polished Japanese ax heads this work has been released into the public domain by its author, PHG at the English Wikipedia project.

There are abundant fragments of human occupation which date from this period. The fragments are small and there is little agreement about them. They also left tools and spears behind.

Bradshaw rock paintings in the Kimberley region of Western Australia, taken at a site off Kalumburu Road ne ar the King Edward River. 20 09 Author TimJN1 Creative Commons Attribution-Share Alike 2.0 Generic license.

E. China

Shang Dynasty inscribed scapula by BabelStone – own work. Licensed under Creative Commons Attribution – Share Alike 3.0 via Wikimedia Commons.

Unlike Africa, the Americas, Australia, and Oceania, archaeologists discovered the remains of agricultural implements, animals which were domesticated, buildings, structures, clothing, plumbing with pipe and thousands of other objects. Professional archeologists refer to these remains as the Erlitou culture. Later documents such as the *Records of the Grand Historian* and the *Bamboo Annals* refer to this time period in Chinese history as the Xia dynasty. However, it is sometimes referred to as a predynastic period. The COA series refers to this time period as the Xia dynasty for simplicity. The Xia dynasty is also mentioned in the *Book of Documents,* or *Classic of History,* or *Shangu* (the same document goes by all three titles).

Public Domain image of a bamboo book. More recent Chinese histories refer to ancient works that no longer exist.

The Yellow Emperor might have ruled over the Xia dynasty. It is claimed that the Xia dynasty had fifteen emperors, lasted for hundreds of years and passed on the concept of *the Mandate of Heaven. The Mandate of Heaven* is similar to the European concept of divine right, that is the ruler rules by the authority of heaven. However, unlike the divine right, *The Mandate of Heaven* requires the ruler to rule justly. If he is not a just ruler, then *The Mandate of Heaven* is transferred to someone else who is responsible to be a just ruler. It is the right to rebel against unjust authority. Most of the teachings attributed to the Xia dynasty are moral teachings.

Like the Indus Valley, Mesopotamia, Egypt, and Europe, there were many tribal wars. Later records indicate that flood control was the major issue. Like Europe and the

Indus Valley of this time period, the Xia dynasty left no written documents which have been translated with certainty.

F. European

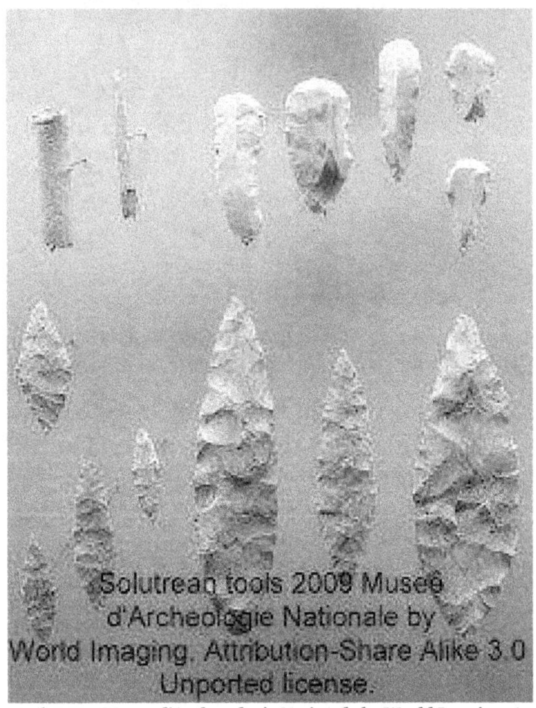
Solutrean tools 2009 Musee d'Archeologie Nationale by World Imaging. Attribution-Share Alike 3.0 Unported license.

Solutrean tools 2009 Musee d'Archaeologie Nationale by World Imaging. Attribution-Share Alike 3.0 unported license

Large monuments, buildings, farm implements, canals, and many other evidences of civilization exist throughout Europe for very early civilizations. There are no known written documents from this early period. For having left so much evidence, very little is known about these people. This evidence includes the famous pile dwellings. They exist throughout Europe, but were first found in Switzerland. First thought to be lake houses, it was discovered that the lakes were lower but flooded periodically. The dwellings were built on piles to keep them from being flooded. All of these structures throughout Europe seem to include various types of fortifications. This shows that the concept of warfare is as old as civilization.

Skara Brae, Scotland. Europe's most complete Neolithic village, House 9 of Skara Brae. 2007 Wknight94 GNU Free Documentation License Wikimedia Commons

The continuous habitation of the coastlines has covered over or destroyed any evidence of the earliest coastal inhabitants. Perhaps the most well-known cultures from this time period are the Minoans on modern Crete, the Philistines, Phoenicians, Trojans, and Hittites (who may or may not be related to the Trojans.)

One of the most interesting mysteries these civilizations left behind is a written language as yet undeciphered known as Linear B. Linear B was an early form of the Greek language spoken by the Mycenaean Greeks. The Mycenaean Greeks followed Minoan culture on Crete.

The Phoenician language became the international trade language because of Phoenician ships and trade. The Phoenicians were Semitic and lived in many coastal cities, but were famous for the city of Tyre.

Linear B tablet from Nestor's Palace Archaeological Museum at Hora near Pylos. copy of the original tablet

Linear B tablet from Nestor's Palace Archaeological Museum at Hora near Pylos. Copy of

original tablet. 2010 Author Fae Creative Commons attribution-share alike 3.0 unported license.

Wikimedia commons Ggnantija Temples Malta copyright @ Daniel Hausner Taken August 2004 released under the GNU free documentation license

G. Egypt

Plato[21] approximately 375 BC wrote;

"One of the [Egyptian] priests, who was of very great age; said, 'O Solon, Solon [7th century BC Athenian statesman], you Hellenes [Greeks] are but children, and there is never an old man who is an Hellene.'

Solon, hearing this, said, 'What do you mean?'

'I mean to say,' he replied, 'that in mind you are all young; there is no old opinion handed down among you by ancient tradition, nor any science which is hoary with age. And I will tell you the reason of this: there have been, and there will be again, many destructions of mankind arising out of many causes.

Karnak. Image from World Photo Cube

'There is a story which even you have preserved, that once upon a time Phaëthon, the son of Helios, having yoked the steeds in his father's chariot, because he was not able to drive them in the path of his father, burnt up all that was upon the earth, and was himself destroyed by a thunderbolt.

'Now, this has the form of a myth, but really signifies a declination of the bodies moving around the earth and in the heavens, and a great Phaethon, conflagration of things upon the earth recurring at long intervals of time:

when this happens, those who live upon the mountains and in dry and lofty places are more liable to destruction than those who dwell by rivers or on the sea-shore; and from this calamity the Nile, who is our never-failing savior, saves and delivers us.

Helios, sun god temple of Athena in Ilion (Troy). Pergamon-Museum in Berlin, Germany. 2007 Author Gryffindor Public Domain Wikimedia Commons

Helios sun god temple of Athena in Ilion (troy). Pergamon Museum in Berlin, Germany. 2007 Author Gryffindor public domain Wikimedia commons

'When, on the other hand, the gods purge the earth with a deluge of water, among you herdsmen and shepherds on the mountains are the survivors, whereas those of you who live in cities are carried by the rivers into the sea; but in this country neither at that time nor at any

> other does the water come from above on the fields, having always a tendency to come up from below, for which reason the things preserved here are said to be the oldest.
>
> 'The fact is, that wherever the extremity of winter frost or of summer sun does not prevent, the human race is always increasing at times, and at other times diminishing in numbers. And whatever happened either in your country or in ours, or in any other region of which we are informed--if any action which is noble or great, or in any other way remarkable has taken place, all that has been written down of old, and is preserved in our temples; whereas you and other nations are just being provided with letters and the other things which States require; and then, at the usual period, the stream from heaven descends like a pestilence, and leaves only those of you who are destitute of letters and education; and thus you have to begin all over again as children, and know nothing of what happened in ancient times, either among us or among yourselves.

Secular historians regard Egyptian records as the oldest and most reliable in the history of the world. Secular historians also understand that these early records have problems. Yet even before Plato, Egyptian records were and still are the standard. James Breasted's massive multi-volume work *The Ancient Records of Egypt* is considered the standard work for establishing the timeline of Egypt, and therefore world history, since all other history is correlated with Egyptian history. Even with modifications, Breasted's timeline is still the standard.

Public Domain image of James Henry Breasted

The works of James Henry Breasted PhD, though filled with errors, contains pictures, drawings, diagrams and information which is no longer available any other form. When the tombs were opened, few of them were properly preserved and many of the paintings and artifacts have deteriorated to the point of being unrecognizable. Therefore, the human race depends on Dr. Breasted's works as the only surviving record of many of these ancient artifacts.

Egyptian bracelet. Public Domain Wikimedia Commons

Egyptian bracelet public domain Wikimedia commons

The Egyptian chronologies are the starting point and standards by which all other records, worldwide are judged. However, those judgments are not accurate for the following reasons:

1. Egyptian chronology does not match the chronologies of other nations. While we do not expect perfect correlation, the ancient Egyptian records do not correlate with *any* other records. For example, the Egyptians rarely recorded defeats. Therefore we would not expect to find a thorough defeat such as the plagues and the exodus. But even their recorded victories, major events and even their recorded observations of celestial sightings do not correlate with the records of other nations.

"Egyptologists[22] began to realize traditional chronology had serious issues when inconsistencies with Assyrian and Hittite discoveries surfaced."

Egyptian chronology [23] also contradicts astronomical records. The theory that Egyptian chronology is based on astronomical events is called the Sothic theory. Modern astronomy has proven that this link is not true.

History is from the Greek word for inquiry. The Greek "father of history" Herodotus[24] explains that the Egyptians

> "told me that the first man who ruled over Egypt was Min, and that in his time all Egypt, except the Thebaic canton, was a marsh, none of the land below Lake Moeris then showing itself above the surface of the water. This is a distance of seven days' sail from the sea up the river.
>
> [The Egyptians] "said that when Moeris was king, the Nile overflowed all Egypt below Memphis, as soon as it rose so little as eight cubits. Now Moeris had not been dead 900 years at the time when I heard this of the priests; yet at the present day, unless the river rise sixteen, or, at the very least, fifteen cubits, it does not overflow the lands."

If this Min[25] mentioned by Herodotus is Noah's grandson Mizraim, as many believe, then Egyptian history begins about 2150 BC. This does not match with Egyptian documents claiming their history began around 5500 BC.

Manetho says the first king was Menes, which can be related to the Hebrew word Mizraim. As mentioned under the corrections to ^{14}C Dating, (III. A. 2.), it is not possible to know for certain who the first king of Egypt was. The most probable names are Menes, Mena, Meni, Min, Narmer, or Aha (Hor-Aha). There is no known linguistic connection between Mizraim and Narmer or Aha (Hor-Aha). This does not rule out that they are the same man, just that there is no direct linguistic connection.

In Genesis 10:6, the word Mizraim is simply a

transliteration of the Hebrew letters. From Keil and Deilitszch (K&D) to modern translations such as the Holman Christian Standard, Amplifed, ISV and the NIV, his name is translated as *Egypt.* It is the same Hebrew word which is translated as Egypt throughout the Old Testament.

Mizraim/Egypt was born in the same generation as Arphaxad. Arphaxad was born 2 years after the Flood and died 440 years after the Flood. Since God did not give us a chronology of Mizraim (Egypt), the lifespan of Arphaxad is used as a rough comparison by generation. Arphaxad outlived Noah, but died before his father Shem, before his son Salah, before his grandson Eber, but outlived his great grandson Peleg, his great-great grandson Reu, his great-great-great grandson Serug, his great-great-great-great grandson Nahor, his great-great-great-great-great grandson Terah, and only died twenty-seven years before his great-great-great-great-great-great grandson Abraham. Born only 2 years after the Flood, Arphaxad died only twenty-seven years before Abraham died in 1881 BC according to Ussher. This means that Abraham could meet and talk to Noah, Shem and Mizriam (KJV, NASB), *Egypt.* Since Abraham journeyed to Egypt, it very likely that he met and talked to Mizriam, *Egypt.* As Josephus writes:

"Abraham Teaching Astrology to the Egyptians 1665" (Should be astronomy, not astrology) Antonio Zanchi ca. 1631-1722, Venice Italy Public Domain

Egyptians were formerly addicted to different customs,[26] and despised one another's sacred and accustomed rites, and were very angry one with another on that account, Abram conferred with each of them, and, confuting the reasonings they made use of, every one for their own practices, demonstrated that such reasonings were vain and void of truth: whereupon he was admired by them in those conferences as a very wise man, and one of great sagacity, when he discoursed on any subject he undertook; and this not only in understanding it, but in persuading other men also to assent to him. He communicated to them arithmetic, and delivered to them the science of astronomy; for before Abram came into Egypt they were unacquainted with those

> parts of learning; for that science came from the Chaldeans into Egypt, and from thence to the Greeks also.

The Flood ended in 2350 BC, according to Ussher's chronology. The first child Arphaxad, was born 2 years after they left the ark. The first recorded death was Peleg 340 years after they left the ark.

"1816d AM, 2526 JP, 2188 BC " Constantinus Manasses states that the Egyptian state lasted 1663 years. Counting backward from the time that Cambyses, king of Persia, conquered Egypt, leads us to this period. About this time Mizraim, the son of Ham, led his colony into Egypt. Hence Egypt was called sometimes the land of Mizraim, sometimes of Ham, Ps 105:23,27 106:21,22 From this it was that the Pharisees later boasted that they were the sons of ancient kings."

Saqqara pyramid of Djoserin Egypt 2007 Author Charlesjsharp creative commons attribution share alike 3.0 unported license

We know that building the pyramids took considerable manpower. If the Egyptian state began in 2188 BC, as

Ussher says, there had to be enough to time raise enough children to adulthood to build them. So the oldest pyramid could not have been built before about 2100 BC, probably later. We can also estimate, assuming that he lived as long as Arphaxad, that Egypt (Mizraim) died approximately 1850 BC. If Josephus was correct that Abraham brought advanced mathematics and astronomy to Egypt from Mesopotamia, then the first of the great pyramids of Giza, which display very advanced engineering skills, could not have been built much before 1975 BC. That would certainly explain why the Egyptians first built mastabas with mud bricks, then step pyramids, which are mastabas of decreasing size stacked on top of one another, next the bent pyramid of Sneferu, and suddenly the massive pyramids of Giza. The Egyptians certainly learned advanced engineering skills very quickly. To understand how massive the pyramids of Giza, here is an account of a 12th century AD attempt to destroy them.

Pyramid of Menkaure date July 2008 photographer Daniel Mayer GNU free documentation license

"When king Al-Aziz Othman,[27] son of [Saladdin] succeeded his father, he let himself be

> persuaded by some people from his Court, who were devoid of good sense, to demolish the pyramids. One started with the red pyramid, which is the third of the great pyramids, and the smallest. So the sultan sent sappers, miners and quarrymen, lead by some of the main officers and the first emirs of his Court and ordered them to destroy it. To carry out the orders they had received, they put up their camp near the pyramid. They brought there a large number of workmen from all around, and supported them at great cost. They stayed there for eight whole months ..., extracting one or two blocks each day, with a lot of difficulties and having exhausted their strength. Some pushed from above with levers while other workers pulled down with ropes and cables. When one of these stones would tumble down, it would make a lot of noise, which was heard from afar and shook the earth and caused the mountains to quake. In falling it would bury itself in the sand. It was then necessary to use great efforts to pull it out. Afterwards, grooves were chiselled into which wedges were driven to divide the blocks into several fragments. Then each piece was loaded on a wagon to pull it to the foot of the nearby mountain where it was thrown down.[...] This happened in the year 593 (i.e. 1196 A.D.)."

The 5th century BC writer Herodotus records how the pyramids were built. He has a section in his book *Histories* where he transcribes what an Egyptian priest told him. (Follow this link to the appendix for our blog post on this topic.)

The pyramids stand as the most expensive monuments in human history, but we do not know why they were built. The three great pyramids of Egypt at Giza have no bodies buried in them, though the bodies could have been robbed in antiquity. Examine the pyramids closely. The pyramids of Giza yield more questions than answers.

2. To accept Egyptian chronology, Hebrew history must be rejected.

Inscription seal using Paleo-Hebrew Alphabet from Lachish public domain

Hebrew History includes not only the Bible, but everything written by and about the Hebrews, such as *the Talmud, the Book of Jubilees, The Book of Enoch, the Apocrypha, the Seder Olam, Josephus, Philo,* and many other Jewish works.

The most important problem with mainstream history basing their chronological timetables on Egyptian kings lists is the required rejection of the chronologies of the Bible. These genealogical records are so far apart, if you accept Manetho's dates, that there is no simple reconciliation. The rejection of Hebrew history is a choice to use the oldest possible dating scheme. Egyptian records provide the oldest possible chronology for human civilization. It is the desire to make civilization older which makes people reject Hebrew history. The evidence does not support this choice.

3. Egyptian records are inconsistent with each other. There are several versions of Egyptian records. From the Persian period to the present, there are few differences. These differences are easily reconciled. But beginning with the Persian period and moving backward in time, these differences are increasingly magnified. The oldest records are so different as to be completely useless for dating.

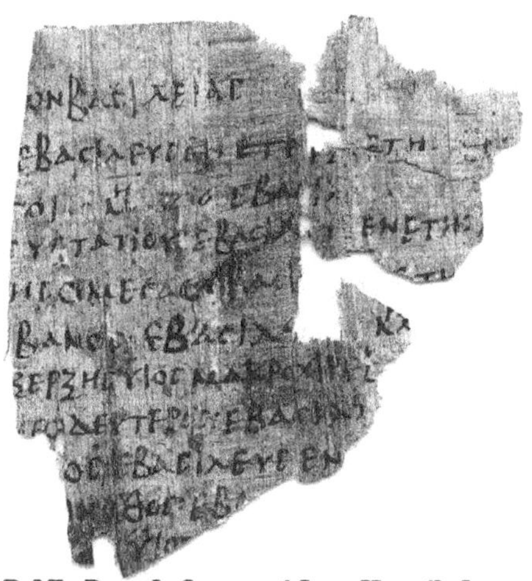

Public Domain fragment from Mantho's "The History of Egypt"

Manetho's *The History of Egypt* is the source for the concept of the various dynasties. Since we no longer have the original, it is reconstructed from various sources. These reconstructions do not always agree with one another. There are many monuments which list the names of kings and their reigns. However, these lists do not match any other record. Many reigns obviously overlapped.

There are also more Egyptian artifacts than artifacts from any other civilization on earth. These can be compared by material, style, and use. There are variations in writing style, materials used such as composition of the inks, and the content of the various documents.

James Breasted did a monumental work of comparing every available record on Egypt and synthesized a comprehensive modern Egyptian chronology. Breasted's chronology is the basis for modern academic chronologies of Egypt. However, this chronology, though popular, does not match any other record. More than one hundred years after the final edition of James Breasted's work, radio carbon dating made a new chronology with much younger dates and shorter reigns. Though a great improvement over Manetho's and Breasted's chronologies, it is still stretched.

4. Carbon-14 dates are younger than Egyptian written records

Many who use radiocarbon dating *assume* that conditions in the past were the same as today. They *assume* that no worldwide catastrophes took place during the practical lifespan of ^{14}C, approximately 60,000 years. They *assume* the timeline of Hebrew History to be incorrect. They do not prove that Hebrew History is incorrect. When we understanding the fact of a worldwide catastrophic flood, then we also understand that ^{14}C dating is less accurate as we move back in time. The stable environment necessary for accurate ^{14}C dating only goes back to the early Roman Period.

The assumption that conditions for the formation of ^{14}C were roughly the same worldwide is probably valid. So even though the ^{14}C testing of Egyptian artifacts from the Pre-Dynastic periods and First Dynasty will still return dates which are older than the actual dates, they are useful for relative dating. That is, even though the actual date is incorrect, ^{14}C will accurately tell us what is older and what is younger.

> The investigators[28] statistically compared the results of radiocarbon testing on 74 new and 112 old specimens from Egypt's Pre-Dynastic periods and First Dynasty with all the other archaeological data collected on those materials. Samples that produced results more than 1,000 years different from those expected were excluded. No result for the Pre-Dynastic periods older than 6500 BC or more recent than 2000 BC was included.
>
> Ignoring Egypt's unifier Menes (aka Narmer, possibly), Aha—the first "official" pharaoh—acceded to the throne, the investigators concluded, around 3100 BC. This date is more recent than those assigned in traditional timelines of ancient Egypt but pretty much in line with the average dates obtained by more recent secular Egyptologists. ... this date is still too early to be compatible with biblical history.

5. Reconciliation of Hebrew history and Egyptian Chronology

Reconciling Hebrew history with Egyptian chronology requires reducing the standard Egyptian timeline. The most likely method of doing this is to understand that there were many co-regencies throughout Egyptian history. David Down and Dr. John Ashton[29] in their book *Unwrapping the Pharaohs* have one possible reconciliation.

H. Indus Valley

Ancient Harappa Civilisation Wikimedia Commons This is a photo of ASI monument number N-PB-32. 16 September 2006 Own work Shefali11011

Like the Clovis people of the Americas, the Harappan civilization of the Indus Valley (modern Pakistan, northwest India) is named for the first location where evidence of their culture was uncovered by modern man. Unlike the Clovis people, the Harappan are one of the oldest civilizations on earth. The Harappan cities are more advanced than Egypt, Akkad, or Sumeria. They also left a written language which has yet to be deciphered. There seem to be centuries of Harappan culture.

Many Harappan cities were built on the banks of now dry rivers. They had sewage systems, dams and locks, harbors for docking ships, fortifications, public water supplies, brick and stone buildings, and many evidences of a very advanced civilization. They had public baths like the Romans, realistic statues, organized labor for making pottery, shipbuilding, stonecutting, markets, jewelry, metalworking and a banking system with standardized weights and measurements.

The civilization included hundreds of cities and at one time millions of people.

Unburied bodies in streets and layers of ash seem to indicate that they were overrun by invaders. The standard interpretation is that Aryan invaders quickly overran and destroyed the Harappan civilization.

Without deciphering their language and cross-referencing their documents with other cultures, we cannot be certain about the Harappan civilization. Artifacts can be very helpful. But artifacts alone are easily misinterpreted.

Collection of seals of the Indus Valley Civilisation. Also showing Swastikas, Britsh Museum 2005 author world imaging creative commons attribution share alike 3.0 unported license

I. Mesopotamia

The term *Hebrew history* includes not only the Bible and ancient Jewish documents, but all documents and artifacts which reference the culture and time period of the Hebrew nation. The Conflict of the Ages series uses Hebrew History as the timeline standard for measuring all other documents and artifacts.

Public Domain image of Mesopotamian king in sphinx form

The word *Mesopotamia* is Greek for "between the rivers," the rivers being the Tigris and Euphrates. The modern phrase "the Fertile Crescent" was popularized by James Breasted in the early 20th century. The Fertile Crescent begins in Egypt, include the lands of Canaan, Syria, Southeast Turkey, and Mesopotamia. Today the term Fertile Crescent usually includes the Indus Valley, though James Breasted did not include the Indus Valley. Satellite images show that riverbeds lie buried underneath the sands of Syria, Jordan, and Saudi Arabia. We do not know how long after the Flood they stopped flowing and turned to sand.

Victory stele of the king Eannatum of Lagash over Umma, called Stele of Vultures. Limestone Sumerian archaic dynasties. Found in 1881 in Girsu (now Tello, Iraq), Mesopotamia, by Édou ard de Sarzec.Eric Gaba (User:Sting), July 2005.GNU Free Documentation License Wikimedia Commons

Victory stele of the King Eannatum of Lagash over Umma, called Stele of Vultures. Limestone Sumerian archaic dynasties. Found 1881 in Girsu (now Tello, Iraq). Mesopotamia by Edou ard de Sarzec Eric Gaba (User:Sting) July 2005 GNU free documentation license Wikimedia commons

The upper cities of Nimrod's kingdom were in a region later known as Assyria. At times the boundaries of Assyria went far into southeast Turkey. Nineveh is the most well-known Assyrian city. To the south and lower in elevation was a region known as Babylonia. Babylonia was divided into the lower Persian Gulf or delta region known as Sumer and Akkad. Akkad was a region with constantly changing boundaries between Assyria and Sumer.

There are detailed chronologies of Sumer and Akkad which go back before the Flood. By understanding that there are errors in these records, they can be corrected and reconciled with Hebrew History. Though they are not perfect, they do establish a reliable standard.

This is possible because they developed an alphabet known as cuneiform. The earliest cuneiform contained symbols known as glyphs. But cuneiform quickly developed into a true alphabet with individual letters. The various cultures throughout the Mesopotamian region had different languages, but they shared the cuneiform alphabet. This is similar to English, Portuguese, Spanish, German, French and other languages sharing a common alphabet today. The most common medium for cuneiform is clay tablets, though cuneiform is inscribed on walls, monuments, and cylinder seals.

Diorite statue (head and body found separately) Believed to be Gudea a ruler (ensi) of the state of Lagash photographer Marie-Lan Nguyen (2011)

Note that this statue's skirt has cuneiform on it.

A scribe with a stick which had one end carved into a shape known today as a wedge would make impressions in the soft clay. When the scribe was finished making impressions in the surface, the clay was baked. The writing process was similar to printing individual letters with a pen or pencil, though slower. A person skilled in reading and writing was known as a scribe. When an official desired to proclaim an edict, a roomful of scribes would all copy the same words at the same time. The tablets would then be baked and the messages distributed. Collections of tablets were kept in libraries.

The various copies of the Sumerian kings list seem to indicate that the antediluvian world, or at least the information which came from Noah, used a decimal numbering system like we use. The Sumerian kings list has clearly different styles of clay tablets for the antediluvian and post-Flood lists.

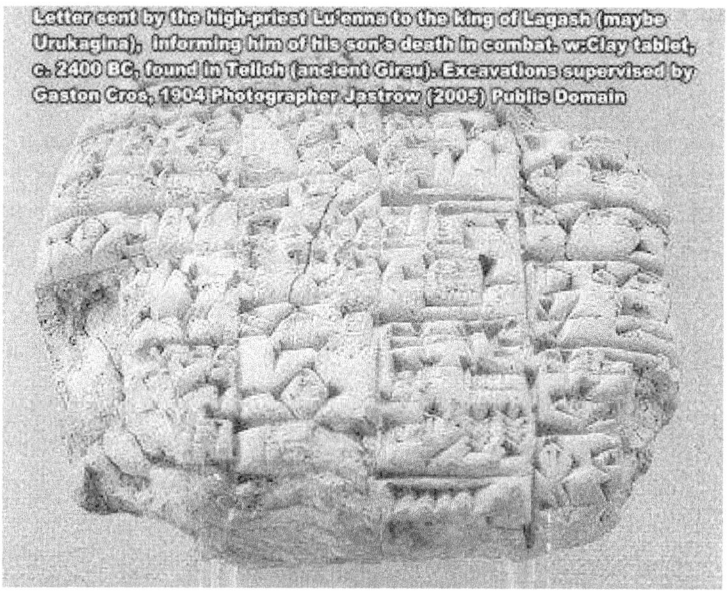

Letter sent by the high priest Lu'enna to the king of Lagash (maybe Urukagina), informing him of his son's death in combat. W: Clay tablet c. 2400 BC, found in Telloh (ancient

Girsu). Excavations supervised by Gaston Cros, 1904 photographer Jastrow 2005 public domain

If Raúl López is correct that "Adam and Noah[30] are not included (as in the King List), and the lives of the patriarchs are similarly rounded to two digits, the sum of the lives has six 103 signs, six 102 signs and six 10 signs. In addition, if the number representing the sum of the ages was wrongly assumed as having been written in the sexagesimal system, the two totals become numerically equivalent." The two totals which are "numerically equivalent" are the antediluvian portions of the Sumerian kings list and the antediluvian genealogies of Genesis.

Sumerian, Akkadian, Babylonian, Assyrian, and Chaldean mathematics used a base sixty numbering system, sexagesimal. Our base ten system is known as a decimal system. The ancient sexagesimal system is still used in timekeeping. The worldwide standard uses sixty minutes in an hour and sixty seconds in a minute. The twelve months in the year is a division of the base sixty numbering system, twelve divided by five. They accurately recorded the movements of the heavens, built enormous buildings with great precision, and built one of the largest systems of canals the world has ever known for both flood control and irrigation of the entire Mesopotamian region.

Ruins in the town of Ur, Southern Iraq 2006 source Flikr author M. Lubinski from Iraq. USA. Creative Commons Attribution share alike 2.0 generic license

This brought an abundance of food and the specialization of labor. They built ships and used standard weights and measures. They traded grains for products they did not produce but needed, such as metals. They produced statues, jewelry, bas reliefs, colored ceramic tiles, pottery with standardized artwork, and organized games.

After the division of languages and the end of the tower of Babel, they also had almost continuous warfare. They continued to build much smaller towers, know as ziggurats. A reasonable explanation is that ziggurats were built by individual cities or small groups of cities.

Unlike China, Europe, Mediterranean cultures further west and the Indus Valley, there are contemporary cuneiform documents as well as artifacts which provide information about the Sumerian and Akkadian cultures. This should not be taken to mean that we have a complete understanding of the Sumerian and Akkadian cultures. While many documents are translated, there are many others waiting to be translated. Since these cities were founded by Nimrod, they are the oldest on earth.

The greatest boaster was Sargon. According to Carl Roebuck;

Public Domain image of Sargon

> "Sargon,[31] the founder of the first large territorial state in Babylonia became a hero of legend after his death, so that it is difficult to separate his historical accomplishments from those with which posterity fictitiously credited him."

The Annals of Sargon[32] are a list of his conquests.

> Sargon who ... marched against the country of Elam and subjugated the men of Elam. ... their

> food he cut off... marched against the country of [Phœnicia], and subjugated the country of Phœnicia. His hand conquered the four quarters (of the world).

The list contains more cities described in similar language. It also includes the astrological signs of the moon he believed to be favorable and the goddess he served, Istar. There is one very interesting phrase:

> "[the countries] of the sea of the setting sun he crossed and for 3 years at the setting sun... [all countries] his hand conquered. Every place to form but one (empire) he appointed. His images at the setting sun he erected. Their spoil he caused to pass over into the countries of the sea."

Sargon made Akkad his capital and founded the Akkadian empire. Matt McClellan dates Sargon after Abraham. The Genesis fourteen record of the battle of four kings against five which Abraham joined would not have been possible after Sargon unified the entire region. The unified Akkadian empire lasted about 150 years, so this is too late for Abraham.

According to Ussher, the events of Genesis fourteen took place "2092 AM, 2802 JP, 1912 BC."

J. The Foundation of Culture

Certain cultural standards were established either by Noah and his immediate family or soon after, certainly before Abraham. Each of the following points have exceptions, but they are also the standard in most cultures.

1. The Family. Usually a husband, wife, and children. Often the extended family lived together; cousins, aunts, uncles, grandparents. Polygamy was common in some cultures and unknown in others. Usually men hunted, traveled, farmed, built, and were in general what we call providers. Women made clothing, educated children, and provided for the home. Sometimes women worked the farm as well.

2. Warfare. The earliest human records, the *Epic of Gilgamesh*, the *Bible* and various Egyptian records such as the *Books of the Dead* not only record warfare, but reference warfare as something older than human writing and memory. The earliest weapons were long spears, shields, knives, and thrown objects such as javelins, darts, atlatls, and rocks. These weapons are depicted in tombs, cave art, and have been uncovered by archeologists. Hunting used the same weapons as and was excellent training for military service.

3. Society. This included laws, structure outside of the family, ceremonies from weddings to parades, social order from slaves (and sometimes poor people worse off than slaves) to kings, division of labor, public meetings, and sanitation.

4. Religion. While no two people believe exactly the same thing, the similarities are more noticeable than the differences. Atheism, Confucianism, Taoism and many similar concepts either did not exist or were not recorded for at least a thousand years. There was Noah and Abraham's worship of one God. All other religions worshiped a pantheon of male and female gods who acted like powerful humans. The gods demanded worship and gave favors to their favorites. While the exact number of gods and goddesses varied, there were usually about a dozen very powerful gods and goddesses who lived on or near earth. There were also about a dozen more who interacted with humans and gods.

Sometimes these were called demigods or children of gods. Pleasing the gods was accomplished through temple worship, offering sacrifices, both animal and grain offerings, and ritual purifications. Sex was closely regulated, usually sanctifying both marriage and temple prostitution. Emotions and events were controlled by various gods whose desires were often in conflict. The trickster god was usually the most powerful or one of the more powerful gods. Attendance at public worship events was required.

Probably the most noticeable similarity is the relationship between the two most powerful gods. In Greece that was Apollo and Zeus. Zeus was the ruler of the gods and the creator god. Apollo was his son and interacted with men. Though the Romans used the Greek gods, they renamed Zeus, calling him Jupiter. Apollo was so important, they did not change his name. With the Norse, Odin and Thor existed in the same relationship. In Egypt the concept of a creator god changed over time, but there was always a creator god and his son. The most powerful creator god was, depending on the time in Egyptian history, Ptah, Amun, Isis, Aten or Ra (Re).

The similarities with Judaism and Christianity are obvious. There is only one question. Did Christianity evolve from these pagan religions? Or was there an original true religion which was corrupted by these many copies?

As Robert Bowie Johnson Jr. says, "Ancient Greek religion,[33] what we call mythology, tells the same story as the book of Genesis, except that the serpent is the enlightener of mankind rather than our deceiver. Athena represents Eve—the reborn serpent's Eve in the new Greek age."

Marduk Iran's heritage in Musee du Louvre 2010 author Ramashhadi public domain

But this did not originate with the Greeks. The all-powerful Marduk of the ancient Babylonians/Akkadians/Sumerians clearly represents Satan and his name can be translated as Bel or Lord. He led the younger gods in rebellion against the old gods. Though he had many symbols, he was especially known by the dragon with the forked tongue. Marduk became ruler of the young gods, earth and humans by slaying Tiamat. Tiamat, was a chaos monster who created the cosmos through water. Marduk slew her and the earth was formed out of the water of her dead body.

Every ancient religion is some form of a reversal of the truths revealed in the Word of God. Good is always shown as evil and evil is portrayed as good.

Hattusa, capital of the Hittite Empire at one point. The Lion Gate at Bogazkale, Turkey. This was one of the two city gates. 2001, user China_Crisis Creative Commons attribution share alike 2.0 Generic license

5. Housing. The earliest house was either a cave or a tent. However, even very wealthy people were still living in tents centuries later. Not only Abraham, but the Greeks in the *Iliad,* in their ten-year siege of Troy, are living in tents. Plato states that Socrates lived much of his life in tents. Spartans only lived in buildings a few months of the year and spent the rest of their lives in tents. Likewise the Mongolians and Bedouins. But the astounding similarity are the houses for thousands of years. Poor people not attached to any family or city have always lived the best they could. But others lived in very similar structures. In the American West, these were wooden army forts. These forts were patterned after British forts, which were patterned after Roman villas, which were patterned after Hittite villages, which are remarkably similar to Mayan, Harappan buildings in the Indus Valley, Xia dynasty structures in China, and even in modern jungle cultures. The building materials might be wood, logs, stone, or brick. Even European castles

follow the same basic structure. The smallest might only house a dozen people while a large structure might hold hundreds. In cities, the specialization of labor allowed for more homes and each house was smaller, sometimes as small as a single room.

An outer wall for protection had a limited number of well-guarded gates, made as secure as possible. Usually the outer wall had few or no windows. Towers were set into the walls. Often another fortified tower stood inside the walls. The center was an open area usually called a courtyard. Rooms around the outside opened inward to the courtyard. Along one wall they built stables for the animals, usually as far from the living quarters as possible. Sometime only a cistern, but usually a well, ensured a water source inside the walls.

Excavated ruins of Mohenjo-daro, with the Great Bath in the foreground and the Buddhist Stupa in the background. Author 2014 Saqib Oayyum Creative Commons attribution share alike 3.0 unported license

If the climate permitted, the cooking area was outside and the fire was kept burning continuously. In poor areas, many people slept in the same room with beds which attached to the wall. Certain areas were designated for different tasks, such as looms for making cloth, tables for dressing animals for meal preparation, shoemaking, blacksmithing, and areas for bathing. Brick Harappan[34] houses using this basic floor plan included indoor plumbing. They looked like they belonged in modern America or Europe.

Ice Age Literature

V. Ice Age Literature

There are thousands of untranslated cuneiform clay tablets. No known method can be used to date them since cuneiform was used from the beginning of writing until the Persian Empire fell to Alexander the Great in 333 BC. Only a very careful study can give approximate dates for many of them. The tablets which have been translated are so generic they could be from any time period. They include legal documents such as title deeds, weddings, tax receipts, letters home, and accounting ledgers.

The British Museum Cuneiform Collection author Mujtaba Chohan Creative Commons attribution share alike 3.0 unported license

The *Epic of Gilgamesh*, the Egyptian *Books of the Dead* (each tomb has a different version) as well as the many other fragments from this time period were written during the Ice Age. Probably the most well-known complete story from this time period is the *Enuma Elish*, the Sumerian/Akkadian/Babylonia creation legend. The title comes from the first three words which mean *When On High* or *When In the Height*. It is part of the *Seven Tablets of Creation.*

The Egyptian Pyramid texts were written about the same time. The oldest are written on the walls of the pyramid at Saqqara. They help us to understand the entire Egyptian culture. The Pyramid texts are a lengthy list of spells. While the priests performing the burial ceremony might have read these aloud, the words were written for the deceased Pharaoh to say to spirits in the underworld. They assumed that he would be able to read what was written on the walls. It is also possible that the pyramids were used as schools to train future priests.

Similar to the later book(s) of the dead and the book(s) of gates, these are instructions to the pharaoh. These are hundreds of pages of not only words the pharaoh was the speak, but detailed instructions as to what he was to do. The Egyptians believed that the pharaoh was to travel through the underworld and then return with eternal life for his subjects. The various feats he was to perform in these texts read like a video game. However, there are a few passages which read like corruptions of passages in the Word of God, especially the Psalms.

The following content is edited to omit crude language passages in portions of these texts.

Egyptian

HYMN TO THE NILE[35]

I

Adoration to the Nile!

Hail to thee, O Nile!
who manifesteth thyself over this land,
and comest to give life to Egypt!

Mysterious is thy issuing forth from the darkness,
on this day whereon it is celebrated!

Watering the orchards created by Ra
to cause all the cattle to live,
thou givest the earth to drink, inexhaustible one!

Path that descendest from the sky,
loving the bread of Seb and the firstfruits of Nepera,
thou causest the workshops of Ptah to prosper!

The River Nile near Aswan, Egypt. 1996 author Alchemica GNU free documentation license version 1.2

II

Lord of the fish, during the inundation,
no bird alights on the crops.

Thou createst the corn, thou bringest forth the barley,

assuring perpetuity to the temples.

If thou ceasest thy toil and thy work,
then all that exists is in anguish.

If the gods suffer in heaven
then the faces of men waste away.

III

Then he torments the flocks of Egypt, and great and small are in agony.

But all is changed for mankind when he comes;
he is endowed with the qualities of Num.

If he shines, the earth is joyous,
every stomach is full of rejoicing,
every spine is happy,
every jaw-bone crushes (its food).

IV

He brings the offerings, as chief of provisioning;
he is the creator of all good things,
as master of energy, full of sweetness in his choice.

If offerings are made it is thanks to him.

He brings forth the herbage for the flocks,
and sees that each god receives his sacrifices.

All that depends on him is a precious incense.

He spreads himself over Egypt,
filling the granaries, renewing the marts,
watching over the goods of the unhappy.

Sobek 2008 God of the Nile and crocodiles Jeff Dahl Creative Commons Attribution Share Alike

V

He is prosperous to the height of all desires,
without fatiguing himself therefor.

He brings again his lordly bark;
he is not sculptured in stone, in the statues crowned with the uræus serpent,
he cannot be contemplated.

No servitors has he, no bearers of offerings!
He is not enticed by incantations!

None knows the place where he dwells,
none discovers his retreat by the power of a written spell.

VI

No dwelling (is there) which may contain thee!
None penetrates within thy heart!

Thy young men, thy children applaud thee
and render unto thee royal homage.

Stable are thy decrees for Egypt
before thy servants of the North!

He stanches the water from all eyes
and watches over the increase of his good things.

VII

Where misery existed, joy manifests itself;
all beasts rejoice.

The children of Sebek, the sons of Neit,
the cycle of the gods which dwells in him, are prosperous.

No more reservoirs for watering the fields!
He makes mankind valiant,
enriching some, bestowing his love on others.

None commands at the same time as himself.

He creates the offerings without the aid of Neit,

making mankind for himself with multiform care.

VIII

He shines when he issues forth from the darkness,
to cause his flocks to prosper.

It is his force that gives existence to all things;
nothing remains hidden for him.

Let men clothe themselves to fill his gardens.
He watches over his works,
producing the inundation during the night.

It is a god Ptah ...

He causes all his servants to exist,
all writings and divine words,
and that which he needs in the North.

IX

It is with the words that he penetrates into his dwelling;
he issues forth at his pleasure through the magic spells.

Thy unkindness brings destruction to the fish;
it is then that prayer is made for the (annual) water of the season;
Southern Egypt is seen in the same state as the North.

Each one is with his instruments of labour,
none remains behind his companions.

None clothes himself with garments,
the children of the noble put aside their ornaments.

The night remains silent,
but all is changed by the inundation;
it is a healing-balm for all mankind.

X

Establisher of justice! mankind desires thee,
supplicating thee to answer their prayers;
thou answerest them by the inundation!

Men offer the first-fruits of corn;
all the gods adore thee!

XI

A festal song is raised for thee on the harp,
with the accompaniment of the hand.

Thy young men and thy children acclaim thee
and prepare their (long) exercises.

Thou art the august ornament of the earth,
letting thy bark advance before men,
lifting up the heart of women in labour,
and loving the multitude of the flocks.

XII

When thou shinest in the royal city,
the rich man is sated with good things,
the poor man even disdains the lotus;
all that is produced is of the choicest;
all the plants exist for thy children.

If thou hast refused (to grant) nourishment,
the dwelling is silent, devoid of all that is good
the country falls exhausted.

XIII

O inundation of the Nile,
offerings are made unto thee,
oxen are immolated to thee,
great festivals are instituted for thee.

Birds are sacrificed to thee,
gazelles are taken for thee in the mountain,
pure flames are prepared for thee.

Sacrifice is made to every god as it is made to the Nile.
The Nile has made its retreats in Southern Egypt,
its name is not known beyond the Tuau.

The god manifests not his forms,

he baffles all conception.

XIV

Men exalt him like the cycle of the gods,
they dread him who creates the heat,
even him who has made his son the universal master
in order to give prosperity to Egypt.

Come (and) prosper! come (and) prosper!
O Nile, come (and) prosper!
[O thou who makest men to live through his flocks
and his flocks through his orchards!
Come (and) prosper, come,
O Nile, come (and) prosper!]

This work has been successfully finished and dedicated to the scribe of the treasury Qaqabu [by the scribe Ennana]

From the *Pyramid Texts*[36]

Pyramid Text in Teti pyramid in Saqqara Egypt 2007 author LassiMU public domain

"All the gods are in exultation; they say: "How beautiful is Neferkarē', with whom his father Geb is satisfied!"

8h. To say by Nut: I unite thy beauty with this body (and with) this *ba,* for life, endurance, joy, health

8i. of Horus, divine apparition, king of Upper and Lower Egypt, Neferkarē' (of the land of) the two goddesses, divine apparition, Neferkarē',

8j. powerful lord (of Ombos), Neferkarē', living eter[nally].

9b. To say: I give to thee thy head; I fasten for thee thy head to (thy) bones.

[This is the first spell in a series of resurrection spells]

10c. To say: He has caused it to be brought to him. One drink of water.

17a. He who goes, goes with his ka: Horus goes with his ka; Set goes with his ka;

17b. Thoth goes with his ka; the god goes with his ka; Osiris goes with his ka;

Detail wall tomb of Pharaoh Horemheb, Osiris, Anubis, and Horus. 2009 author derivative work: A. Parrot Jean-Pierre Dalbera Creative Commons Attribution 2.0 generic license

[the word god in these texts is someone like a human; he is different from Set, Horus, Osiris, Thoth and the other named beings we think of as the Egyptian gods]

72f. To say four times: For Neferkarē, a lifting up of the offering, four times. Food: One loaf, one beer.

[There are hundreds of various offerings, all very specific.]

118b. They have swallowed the 'bright eye of Horus which is in Heliopolis.

118c. The little finger of Neferkarē, draws out that which is in the navel of Osiris.

140a. O Neferkarē,

140b. let thy messengers go; let thine envoys hasten to thy father, to Atum.

140c. Atum, let him ascend to thee; enfold him in thine embrace,

141a. (for) there is no god, (who has become) a star, who has not his companion. Shall I be thy companion?

146. Look (at me); thou hast regarded the form of the children of their fathers,

141c. who know their speech. (They are now) imperishable stars.

153b. "Neferkarē, comes, an imperishable spirit;

153c. if he wills that ye die, you will die; if he wills that ye live, you will live."

164c. Neferkarē comes, he is displeased (?) with the Nine (Bows?), an imperishable spirit.

164d. The Westerners, who are on the earth belong to Neferkarē

164e. Neferkarē comes, he is displeased (?) with the Nine (Bows?) an imperishable spirit.

165a. The Easterners who are on the earth belong to Neferkarē

165b. Neferkarē comes, he is displeased (?) with the Nine (Bows?) an imperishable spirit.

165c. The Southerners who are on the earth belong to Neferkarē

165d. Neferkarē comes, he is displeased (?) with the Nine (Bows?), an imperishable spirit.

166a. The Northerners who are on the earth belong to Neferkarē

166b. Neferkarē comes, he is displeased (?) with the Nine (Bows?), an imperishable spirit.

166c. Those who are in the underworld belong to Neferkarē

166d. Neferkarē' comes, he is displeased (?) with the Nine (Bows?), an imperishable spirit.

394c. Neferkarē' is lord of craftiness, whose name his mother knows not.

395a. The honour of Neferkarē' is in heaven, his might is in the horizon,

395b. like his father, Atum, who begat him. He has begotten him mightier than he.

396a. The *kas* of Neferkarē' are behind him, his maid-servants are under his feet,

396b. his gods are over him, his uraeus-serpents are upon his brow;

396c. the leader-serpent of Neferkarē' is on his forehead, she who perceives the soul (of the enemy), (as) a diadem, a flame of fire;

396d. the might of Neferkarē' is for his protection.

397a. Neferkarē' is the bull of heaven, who (once) suffered want and decided (lit. gave in his heart) to live on the being of every god ...

Tale of the Shipwrecked Sailor[37]

The wise servant said, “Let thy heart be satisfied, O my lord, for that we have come back to the country; after we have been long on board, and rowed much, the prow has at last touched land. All the people rejoice and embrace us one after another. Moreover, we have come back in good health, and not a man is lacking; although we have been to the ends of Wawat [Nubia], and gone through the land of Senmut [Kush], we have returned in peace, and our land---behold, we have come back to it. Hear me, my lord; I have no other refuge. Wash thee, and turn the water over thy fingers; then go and tell the tale to the majesty.”

His lord replied, “Thy heart continues still its wandering words! but although the mouth of a man may save him his words may also cover his face with confusion. Will you do then as your heart moves you? This that you will say, tell quietly.”

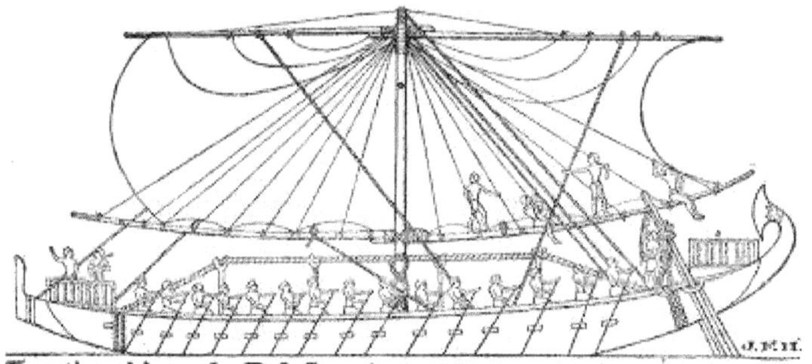

Egyptian ship on the Red Sea, about 1250 BC from Torr's Ancient Ships" Mr. Langton Cole calls attention to the rope truss in this illustration, stiffening the beam of the ship. No other such use of the truss is known until the days of modern engineering. Public Domain

The sailor then answered, “Now I shall tell that which has happened to me, to my very self. I was going to the mines of Pharaoh, and I went down on the sea in a ship of one hundred and fifty cubits long and forty cubits wide, with one hundred and fifty sailors of the best of Egypt who had seen heaven and earth, and whose hearts were stronger than lions. They had said that the wind would not be contrary, or that there would be none. But as we approached the land, the wind arose, and threw up waves eight cubits high. As for me, I seized a piece of wood; but those who were in the vessel perished, without one remaining. A wave threw me on an island, after that I had been three days alone, without a companion beside my own heart. I laid me in a thicket, and the shadow covered me. Then stretched I my limbs to try to find something for my mouth. I found there figs and grain, melons of all kinds, fishes, and birds. Nothing was lacking. And I satisfied myself; and left on the ground that which was over, of what my arms had been filled withal. I dug a pit, I lighted a fire, and I made a burnt offering unto the gods.

"Suddenly I heard a noise as of thunder, which I thought to be that of a wave of the sea. The trees shook, and the earth was moved. I uncovered my face, and I saw that a serpent drew near. He was thirty cubits long, and his beard greater than two cubits; his body was as overlaid with gold, and his color as that of true lazuli. He coiled himself before me. "Then he opened his mouth, while that I lay on my face before him, and he said to me, "What has brought you, what has brought you, little one, what has brought you? If you say not speedily what has brought you to this isle, I will make you know yourself; as a flame you shall vanish, if you tell me not something I have not heard, or which I knew not, before you.'

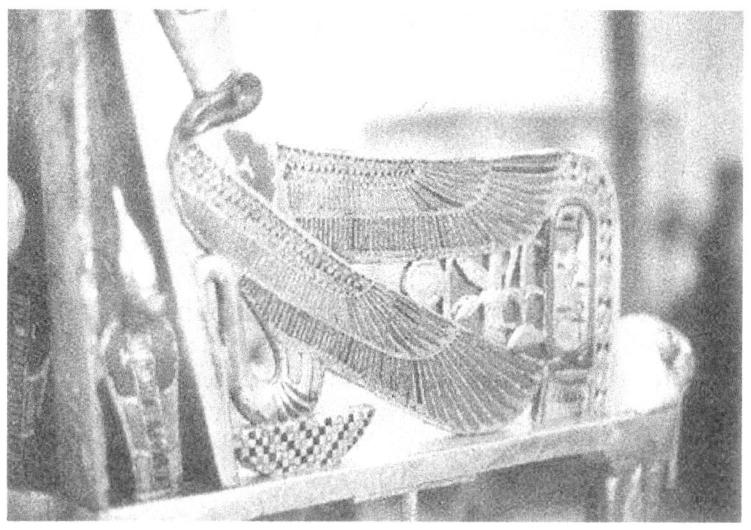

Public Domain image serpent guardian from King Tut's Tomb

"Then he took me in his mouth and carried me to his resting-place, and laid me down without any hurt. I was whole and sound, and nothing was gone from me. Then he opened his mouth against me, while that I lay on my face before him, and he said, "What has brought you, what has brought you, little one, what has brought you to this isle which is in the sea, and of which the shores are in the midst of the waves?'

"Then I replied to him, and holding my arms low before him, I said to him, "I was embarked for the mines by the order of the majesty, in a ship, one hundred and fifty cubits was its length, and the width of it forty cubits. It had one hundred and fifty sailors of the best of Egypt, who had seen heaven and earth, and the hearts of whom were stronger than lions. They said that the wind would not be contrary, or that there would be none. Each of them exceeded his companion in the prudence of his heart and the strength of his arm, and I was not beneath any of them. A storm came upon us while we were on the sea. Hardly could we reach to the shore when the wind waxed yet greater, and the waves rose even eight cubits. As for me, I seized a piece of wood, while those who were in the boat perished without one being left with me for three days. Behold me now before you, for I was brought to this isle by a wave of the sea.'

"Then said he to me, "Fear not, fear not, little one, and make not your face sad. If you have come to me, it is God who has let you live. For it is He who has brought you to this isle of the blest, where nothing is lacking, and which is filled with all good things. See now, you shall pass one month after another, until you shall be four months in this isle. Then a ship shall come from your land with sailors, and you shall leave with them and go to your country, and you shall die in your town.'

"'Converse is pleasing, and he who tastes of it passes over his misery. I will therefore tell you of that which is in this isle. I am here with my brethren and my children around me; we are seventy-five serpents, children, and kindred; without naming a young girl who was brought unto me by chance, and on whom the fire of heaven fell, and burned her to ashes. As for you, if you are strong, and if your heart waits patiently, you shall press your infants to your bosom and embrace your wife. You shall return to your house which is full of all good things, you shall see your land, where you shall dwell in the midst of your kindred.'

"Then I bowed in my obeisance, and I touched the ground before him. "Behold now that which I have told you before. I shall tell of your presence unto Pharaoh, I shall make him to know of your greatness, and I will bring to you of the sacred oils and perfumes, and of incense of the temples with which all gods are honored. I shall tell, moreover, of that which I do now see (thanks to him), and there shall be rendered to you praises before the fullness of all the land. I shall slay asses for you in sacrifice, I shall pluck for you the birds, and I shall bring for you ships full of all kinds of the treasures of Egypt, as is comely to do unto a god, a friend of men in a far country, of which men know not.'

Himet standing before a table of offerings Public Domain

"Then he smiled at my speech, because of that which was in his heart, for he said to me: "You are not rich in perfumes, for all that you have is but common incense. As for me, I am prince of the land of Punt, and I have perfumes. Only the oil which you say you would bring is not common in this isle. But, when you shall depart from this place, you shall never more see this isle; it shall be changed into waves.'

"And behold, when the ship drew near, according to all that he had told me before, I got up into an high tree, to strive to see those who were within it. Then I came and told to him this matter, but it was already known unto him before. Then he said to me, "Farewell, farewell, go to your house, little one, see again your children, and let your name be good in your town; these are my wishes for you.' "Then I bowed myself before him, and held my arms low before him, and he, he gave me gifts of precious perfumes, of cassia, of sweet woods, of kohl, of cypress, an abundance of incense, of ivory tusks, of baboons, of apes, and all kinds of precious things. I embarked all in the ship which was come, and bowing myself, I prayed God for him. Then he said to me, "Behold you shall come to your country in two months, you shall press to your bosom your children, and you shall rest in your tomb.' After this I went down to the shore unto the ship, and I called to the sailors who were there. Then on the shore I rendered adoration to the master of this isle and to those who dwelt therein.

"When we shall come, in our return, to the house of Pharaoh, in the second month, according to all that the serpent has said, we shall approach unto the palace. And I shall go in before Pharaoh, I shall bring the gifts which I have brought from this isle into the country. Then he shall thank me before the fullness of the land. Grant then unto me a follower, and lead me to the courtiers of the king. Cast your eye upon me after that I have both seen and proved this. Hear my prayer, for it is good to listen to people. It was said unto me, "Become a wise man, and you shall come to honor,' and behold I have become such."

This is finished from its beginning unto its end, even as it was found in a writing. It is written by the scribe of cunning fingers, Ameni-amenaa; may he live in life, wealth, and health!

HYMN TO OSIRIS-SOKAR[38]

Behold the lord of fear, who causeth himself to come into being!

Hail, thou whose heart palpitateth not,--take possession of thy city!

Behold the one beloved of gods and goddesses

Hail, thou who causeth the inundation,--take possession of thy temple!

Hail, dweller in the underworld,--take possession of thy offerings!

Hail, thou protector,--take possession of thy temple!

Published by James Wasserman; facsimile made by E. A. Wallis Budge; from the Papyrus of Ani. The syncretized god Sokar-Osiris

Book published 1994; facsimile created 1890; original artwork created c. 1300 BC Scanned from The Egyptian Book of the Dead: The Book of Going Forth by Day by James Wasserman et al.Public Domain

Hail, thou who growest like unto the ape of Tehuti, or to the shining sunlight!

Hail, thou flower honoured of Pharaoh!

Hail, thou who handlest the holy rigging of the Sektet-boat!

Behold the lord of youth,--he becometh old in his shrine!

Behold the excellent souls, which are in the realms of Death!

Behold the sacred designer of north and south!

Behold the mysterious one, lie who is unknown to mankind!

Sumerian/Akkadian/Babylonian documents

ENUMA ELISH[39]*: THE EPIC OF CREATION*

THE FIRST TABLET

When in the height heaven was not named,
And the earth beneath did not yet bear a name,
And the primeval Apsu, who begat them,
And chaos, Tiamut, the mother of them both
Their waters were mingled together,
And no field was formed, no marsh was to be seen;
When of the gods none had been called into being,
And none bore a name, and no destinies were ordained;
Then were created the gods in the midst of heaven,
Lahmu and Lahamu were called into being...

Ages increased,...
Then Ansar and Kisar were created, and over them....
Long were the days, then there came forth.....
Anu, their son,...
Ansar and Anu...

And the god Anu...

Nudimmud, whom his fathers, his begetters.....
Abounding in all wisdom,...'
He was exceeding strong...
He had no rival -
Thus were established and were... the great gods.

But Tiamat and Apsu were still in confusion...
They were troubled and...
In disorder...
Apru was not diminished in might...
And Tiamat roared...
She smote, and their deeds...
Their way was evil...

Then Apsu, the begetter of the great gods,
Cried unto Mummu, his minister, and said unto him:
"O Mummu, thou minister that rejoicest my spirit,
Come, unto Tiamut let us go!
So they went and before Tiamat they lay down,
They consulted on a plan with regard to the gods, their sons.

Tablet said to be "Babylonian Map of Creation" Public Domain

Apsu opened his mouth and spake,
And unto Tiamut, the glistening one, he addressed the word:
...their way...
By day I can not rest, by night I can not lie down in peace.
But I will destroy their way, I will...
Let there be lamentation, and let us lie down again in peace."

When Tiamat heard these words,
She raged and cried aloud...
She... grievously...,

She uttered a curse, and unto Apsu she spake:
"What then shall we do?
Let their way be made difficult, and let us lie down again in peace."

Mummu answered, and gave counsel unto Apsu,
...and hostile to the gods was the counsel Mummu gave:
Come, their way is strong, but thou shalt destroy it;
Then by day shalt thou have rest, by night shalt thou lie down in peace."

Apsu harkened unto him and his countenance grew bright,
Since he (Mummu) planned evil against the gods his sons.
... he was afraid...,
His knees became weak; they gave way beneath him,
Because of the evil which their first-born had planned.
... their... they altered.
... they...,
Lamentation they sat in sorrow...

Then Ea, who knoweth all that is, went up and he beheld their muttering.

[about 30 illegible lines]

... he spake:
... thy... he hath conquered and
... he weepeth and sitteth in tribulation.
... of fear,
... we shall not lie down in peace.
... Apsu is laid waste,
... and Mummu, who were taken captive, in...
... thou didst...
... let us lie down in peace.
... they will smite....
... let us lie down in peace.
... thou shalt take vengeance for them,

... unto the tempest shalt thou...!"

And Tiamat harkened unto the word of the bright god, and said:
... shalt thou entrust! let us wage war!"
... the gods in the midst of...
... for the gods did she create.

They banded themselves together and at the side of Tiamat they advanced;
They were furious; they devised mischief without resting night and day.
They prepared for battle, fuming and raging;
They joined their forces and made war,

Ummu-Hubur [Tiamat] who formed all things,
Made in addition weapons invincible; she spawned monster-serpents,
Sharp of tooth, and merciless of fang;
With poison, instead of blood, she filled their bodies.

Fierce monster-vipers she clothed with terror,
With splendor she decked them, she made them of lofty stature.
Whoever beheld them, terror overcame him,
Their bodies reared up and none could withstand their attack.
She set up vipers and dragons, and the monster Lahamu,
And hurricanes, and raging hounds, and scorpion-men,
And mighty tempests, and fish-men, and rams;
They bore cruel weapons, without fear of the fight.

Her commands were mighty, none could resist them;
After this fashion, huge of stature, she made eleven [kinds of] monsters.
Among the gods who were her sons, inasmuch as he had given her support,
She exalted Kingu; in their midst she raised him to power.

To march before the forces, to lead the host,

To give the battle-signal, to advance to the attack,
To direct the battle, to control the fight,
Unto him she entrusted; in costly raiment she made him sit, saying:
I have uttered thy spell, in the assembly of the gods I have raised thee to power.
The dominion over all the gods have I entrusted unto him.
Be thou exalted, thou my chosen spouse,
May they magnify thy name over all of them the Anunnaki."

She gave him the Tablets of Destiny, on his breast she laid them, saying:
Thy command shall not be without avail, and the word of thy mouth shall be established."

Now Kingu, thus exalted, having received the power of Anu,
Decreed the fate among the gods his sons, saying:
"Let the opening of your mouth quench the Fire-god;
Whoso is exalted in the battle, let him display his might!"

THE SECOND TABLET

Tiamat made weighty her handiwork,
Evil she wrought against the gods her children.
To avenge Apsu, Tiamat planned evil,
But how she had collected her forces, the god unto Ea divulged.

Ea harkened to this thing, and
He was grievously afflicted and he sat in sorrow.
The days went by, and his anger was appeased,
And to the place of Ansar his father he took his way.

He went and, standing before Ansar, the father who begat him,
All that Tiamat had plotted he repeated unto him,
Saying, "Tiamat our mother hath conceived a hatred for us,

With all her force she rageth, full of wrath.
All the gods have turned to her,
With those, whom ye created, they go at her side.

They are banded together and at the side of Tiamat they advance;
They are furious, they devise mischief without resting night and day.
They prepare for battle, fuming and raging;
They have joined their forces and are making war.

Ummu-Hubur, who formed all things,
Hath made in addition weapons invincible; she hath spawned monster-serpents,
Sharp of tooth, and merciless of fang.
With poison, instead of blood, she hath filled their bodies.
Fierce monster-vipers she hath clothed with terror,
With splendor she hath decked them; she hath made them of lofty stature.

Whoever beholdeth them is overcome by terror,
Their bodies rear up and none can withstand their attack.
She hath set up vipers, and dragons, and the monster Lahamu,
And hurricanes and raging hounds, and scorpion-men,
And mighty tempests, and fish-men and rams;
They bear cruel weapons, without fear of the fight.

Her commands are mighty; none can resist them;
After this fashion, huge of stature, hath she made eleven monsters.
Among the gods who are her sons, inasmuch as he hath given her support,
She hath exalted Kingu; in their midst she hath raised him to power.
To march before the forces, to lead the host,
To give the battle-signal, to advance to the attack.

To direct the battle, to control the fight,
Unto him hath she entrusted; in costly raiment she hath made him sit, saying:
I have uttered thy spell; in the assembly of the gods I have raised thee to power,
The dominion over all the gods have I entrusted unto thee.

Be thou exalted, thou my chosen spouse,
May they magnify thy name over all of them
She hath given him the Tablets of Destiny, on his breast she laid them, saying:
'Thy command shall not be without avail, and the word of thy mouth shall be established.'

Now Kingu, thus exalted, having received the power of Anu,
Decreed the fate for the gods, her sons, saying:
'Let the opening of your mouth quench the Fire-god;
Whoso is exalted in the battle, let him display his might!'"

When Ansar heard how Tiamat was mightily in revolt, he bit his lips, his mind was not at peace,
..., he made a bitter lamentation:
... battle,

... thou...
Mummu and Apsu thou hast smitten
But Tiamat hath exalted Kingu, and where is one who can oppose her?
... deliberation
... the ... of the gods, -Nudimmud.

[A gap of about a dozen lines occurs here.]

Ansar unto his son addressed the word:
"... my mighty hero,
Whose strength is great and whose onslaught can not be withstood,
Go and stand before Tiamat,

That her spirit may be appeased, that her heart may be merciful.
But if she will not harken unto thy word,
Our word shalt thou speak unto her, that she may be pacified."

He heard the word of his father Ansar
And he directed his path to her, toward her he took the way.
An drew nigh, he beheld the muttering of Tiamat,
But he could not withstand her, and he turned back.
... Ansar
... he spake unto him:

[A gap of over twenty lines occurs here.]

an avenger...
... valiant
... in the place of his decision
... he spake unto him:
... thy father
" Thou art my son, who maketh merciful his heart.
... to the battle shalt thou draw nigh,
he that shall behold thee shall have peace."

And the lord rejoiced at the word of his father,
And he drew nigh and stood before Ansar.
Ansar beheld him and his heart was filled with joy,
He kissed him on the lips and his fear departed from him.

"O my father, let not the word of thy lips be overcome,
Let me go, that I may accomplish all that is in thy heart.
O Ansar, let not the word of thy lips be overcome,
Let me go, that I may accomplish all that is in thy heart."

What man is it, who hath brought thee forth to battle?

... Tiamat, who is a woman, is armed and attacketh thee.
... rejoice and be glad;
The neck of Tiamat shalt thou swiftly trample under foot.

... rejoice and be glad;
The neck of Tiamat shalt thou swiftly trample under foot.

O my son, who knoweth all wisdom,
Pacify Tiamat with thy pure incantation.
Speedily set out upon thy way,
For thy blood shall not be poured out; thou shalt return again."

The lord rejoiced at the word of his father,
His heart exulted, and unto his father he spake:
"O Lord of the gods, Destiny of the great gods,
If I, your avenger,
Conquer Tiamat and give you life,
Appoint an assembly, make my fate preeminent and proclaim it.
In Upsukkinaku seat yourself joyfully together,
With my word in place of you will I decree fate.
May whatsoever I do remain unaltered,
May the word of my lips never be chanced nor made of no avail."

THE THIRD TABLET

Ansar opened his mouth, and
Unto Gaga, his minister, spake the word.

"O Gaga, thou minister that rejoicest my spirit,
Unto Lahmu and Lahamu will I send thee.
... thou canst attain,
... thou shalt cause to be brought before thee.
... let the gods, all of them,
Make ready for a feast, at a banquet let them sit,
Let them eat bread, let them mix wine,
That for Marduk, their avenger they may decree the fate.

Go, Gaga, stand before them,
And all that I tell thee, repeat unto them, and say:
'Ansar, vour son, hath sent me,
The purpose of his heart he hath made known unto me.
The purpose of his heart he hath made known unto me.

He saith that Tiamat our mother hath conceived a hatred for us,
With all her force she rageth, full of wrath.
All the gods have turned to her,
With those, whom ye created, they go at her side.

They are banded together, and at the side of Tiamat they advance;
They are furious, they devise mischief without resting night and day.
They prepare for battle, fuming and raging;
They have joined their forces and are making war.

Ummu-Hubur, who formed all things,
Hath made in addition weapons invincible; she hath spawned monster-serpents,
Sharp of tooth and merciless of fang.
With poison, instead of blood, she hath filled their bodies.
Fierce monster-vipers she hath clothed with terror,
With splendor she hath decked them; she hath made them of lofty stature.
Whoever beboldeth them, terror overcometh him,
Their bodies rear up and none can withstand their attack.

Public Domain image of scorpion demigod

She hath set up vipers, and dragons, and the monster Lahamu,
And hurricanes, and raging bounds, and scorpion-men,
And mighty tempests, and fish-men, and rams;
They bear merciless weapons, without fear of the fight.
Her commands are mighty; none can. resist them;
After this fashion, huge of stature, hath she made eleven monsters.

Among the gods who are her sons, inasmuch as he hath given her support,
She hath exalted Kingu; in their midst she hath raised him to power.
To march before the forces, to lead the host,
To give the battle-signal, to advance to the attack,
To direct the battle, to control the fight,
Unto him hath she entrusted; in costly raiment she hath made him sit, saying:
I have uttered thy spell; in the assembly of the gods
I have raised thee to power,
The dominion over all the gods have I entrusted unto

thee.

Be thou exalted, thou my chosen spouse,
May they magnify thy name over all of them … the Anunnaki."
She hath given him the Tablets of Destiny, on his breast she laid them, saying:
Thy command shall not be without avail, and the word of thy mouth shall be established."

Now Kingu, thus exalted, having received the power of Anu,
Decreed the fate for the gods, her sons, saving:
Let the opening of your mouth quench the Fire-god;
Whoso is exalted in the battle, let him display his might!"

I sent Anu, but he could not withstand her;
Nudimmud was afraid and turned back.
But Marduk hath set out, the director of the gods, your son;
To set out against Tiamat his heart hath prompted him.

He opened his mouth and spake unto me, saying: "If I, your avenger,
Conquer Tiamat and give you life,
Appoint an assembly, make my fate preeminent and proclaim it.

In Upsukkinaku seat yourself joyfully together;
With my word in place of you will I decree fate.
May whatsoever I do remain unaltered,
May the word of my lips never be changed nor made of no avail."'

Hasten, therefore, and swiftly decree for him the fate which you bestow,
That he may go and fight your strong enemy.
Gaga went, he took his way and
Humbly before Lahmu and Lahamu, the gods, his fathers,
He made obeisance, and he kissed the ground at their

feet.

He humbled himself; then he stood up and spake unto them saying:
"Ansar, your son, hath sent me,
The purpose of his heart he hath made known unto me.
He saith that Tiamat our mother hath conceived a hatred for us,
With all her force she rageth, full of wrath.

All the gods have turned to her,
With those, whom ye created, they go at her side.
They are banded together and at the side of Tiamat they advance;
They are furious, they devise mischief without resting night and day.
They prepare for battle, fuming and raging;
They have joined their forces and are making war.

Ummu-Hubur, who formed all things,
Hath made in addition weapons invincible; she hath spawned monster-serpents,
Sharp of tooth and merciless of fang.
With poison, instead of blood, she hath filled their bodies.
Fierce monster-vipers she hath clothed with terror,
With splendor she hath decked them, she hath made them of lofty stature.

Whoever beboldeth them, terror overcometh him,
Their bodies rear up and none can withstand their attack.
She hath set up vipers, and dragons, and the monster Lahamu,
And hurricanes, and raging hounds, and scorpion-men,
And mighty tempests, and fish-men, and rams;
They bear merciless weapons, without fear of the fight.
Her commands are mighty; none can resist them;
After this fashion, huge of stature, hath she made eleven monsters.

Among the gods who are her sons, inasmuch as he hath given her support,
She hath exalted Kingu; in their midst she hath raised him to power.
To march before the forces, to lead the host,
To give the battle-signal, to advance to the attack,
To direct the battle, to control the fight,
Unto him hath she entrusted; in costly raiment she hath made him sit, saying:
I have uttered thy spell; in the assembly of the gods I have raised thee to power,
The dominion over all the gods have I entrusted unto thee.
Be thou exalted, thou my chosen spouse,
May they magnify thy name over all of them...the Anunnaki.

She hath given him the Tablets of Destiny on his breast she laid them, saving:
Thy command shall not be without avail, and the word of thy mouth shall be established.'

Now Kingu, thus exalted, having received the power of Anu,
Decreed the fate for the gods, her sons, saying:
'Let the opening of your mouth quench the Fire-god;
Whoso is exalted in the battle, let him display his might!'
I sent Anu, but he could not withstand her;
Nudimmud was afraid and turned back.

But Marduk hath set out, the director of the gods, your son;
To set out against Tiamat his heart hath prompted him.
He opened his mouth and spake unto me, saying:
'If I, your avenger,
Conquer Tiamat and give you life,
Appoint an assembly, make my fate preeminent and proclaim it.

In Upsukkinaku seat yourselves joyfully together;

With my word in place of you will I decree fate.
May, whatsoever I do remain unaltered,
May the word of my lips never be changed nor made of no avail.'

Hasten, therefore, and swiftly decree for him the fate which you bestow,
That he may go and fight your strong enemy!

Lahmu and Lahamu heard and cried aloud
All of the Igigi [The elder gods] wailed bitterly, saying:
What has been altered so that they should
We do not understand the deed of Tiamat!

Then did they collect and go,
The great gods, all of them, who decree fate.
They entered in before Ansar, they filled...
They kissed one another, in the assembly...;
They made ready for the feast, at the banquet they sat;
They ate bread, they mixed sesame-wine.

The sweet drink, the mead, confused their...
They were drunk with drinking, their bodies were filled.
They were wholly at ease, their spirit was exalted;
Then for Marduk, their avenger, did they decree the fate.

THE FOURTH TABLET

Public Domain reproduction of image of Marduk defeating Tiamat

They prepared for him a lordly chamber,
Before his fathers as prince he took his place.
"Thou art chiefest among the great gods,
Thy fate is unequaled, thy word is Anu!

O Marduk, thou art chiefest among the great gods,
Thy fate is unequaled, thy word is Anu!
Henceforth not without avail shall be thy command,
In thy power shall it be to exalt and to abase.

Established shall be the word of thy mouth, irresistible shall be thy command,
None among the gods shall transgress thy boundary.
Abundance, the desire of the shrines of the gods,
Shall be established in thy sanctuary, even though they lack offerings.

O Marduk, thou art our avenger!
We give thee sovereignty over the whole world.
Sit thou down in might; be exalted in thy command.
Thy weapon shall never lose its power; it shall crush thy foe.
O Lord, spare the life of him that putteth his trust in thee,
But as for the god who began the rebellion, pour out his

life."

Then set they in their midst a garment,
And unto Marduk,- their first-born they spake:
"May thy fate, O lord, be supreme among the gods,
To destroy and to create; speak thou the word, and thy command shall be fulfilled.

Command now and let the garment vanish;
And speak the word again and let the garment reappear!
Then he spake with his mouth, and the garment vanished;
Again he commanded it, and. the garment reappeared.

When the gods, his fathers, beheld the fulfillment of his word,
They rejoiced, and they did homage unto him, saying, " Marduk is king!"
They bestowed upon him the scepter, and the throne, and the ring,
They give him an invincible weapony which overwhelmeth the foe.

Go, and cut off the life of Tiamat,
And let the wind carry her blood into secret places."
After the gods his fathers had decreed for the lord his fate,
They caused him to set out on a path of prosperity and success.

He made ready the bow, he chose his weapon,
He slung a spear upon him and fastened it...
He raised the club, in his right hand he grasped it,
The bow and the quiver he hung at his side.

He set the lightning in front of him,
With burning flame he filled his body.
He made a net to enclose the inward parts of Tiamat,
The four winds he stationed so that nothing of her might escape;
The South wind and the North wind and the East wind

and the West wind
He brought near to the net, the gift of his father Anu.

He created the evil wind, and the tempest, and the hurricane,
And the fourfold wind, and the sevenfold wind, and the whirlwind, and the wind which had no equal;
He sent forth the winds which he had created, the seven of them;
To disturb the inward parts of Tiamat, they followed after him.

Then the lord raised the thunderbolt, his mighty weapon,
He mounted the chariot, the storm unequaled for terror,
He harnessed and yoked unto it four horses,
Destructive, ferocious, overwhelming, and swift of pace;
... were their teeth, they were flecked with foam;
They were skilled in... , they had been trained to trample underfoot.

.... mighty in battle,
Left and right....
His garment was... , he was clothed with terror,
With overpowering brightness his head was crowned.

Then he set out, he took his way,
And toward the raging Tiamat he set his face.
On his lips he held ...,
... he grasped in his hand.

Then they beheld him, the gods beheld him,
The gods his fathers beheld him, the gods beheld him.
And the lord drew nigh, he gazed upon the inward parts of Tiamat,
He perceived the muttering of Kingu, her spouse.

As Marduk gazed, Kingu was troubled in his gait,
His will was destroyed and his motions ceased.
And the gods, his helpers, who marched by his side,
Beheld their leader's..., and their sight was troubled.

But Tiamat... , she turned not her neck,
With lips that failed not she uttered rebellious words:
"... thy coming as lord of the gods,
From their places have they gathered, in thy place are they! "

Then the lord raised the thunderbolt, his mighty weapon,
And against Tiamat, who was raging, thus he sent the word:
Thou art become great, thou hast exalted thyself on high,
And thy heart hath prompted thee to call to battle.

... their fathers...,
... their... thou hatest...
Thou hast exalted Kingu to be thy spouse,
Thou hast... him, that, even as Anu, he should issue decrees.

Thou hast followed after evil,
And against the gods my fathers thou hast contrived thy wicked plan.
Let then thy host be equipped, let thy weapons be girded on!
Stand! I and thou, let us join battle!

When Tiamat heard these words,
She was like one possessed, she lost her reason.
Tiamat uttered wild, piercing cries,
She trembled and shook to her very foundations.

She recited an incantation, she pronounced her spell,
And the gods of the battle cried out for their weapons.
Then advanced Tiamat and Marduk, the counselor of the gods;
To the fight they came on, to the battle they drew nigh.

The lord spread out his net and caught her,
And the evil wind that was behind him he let loose in her face.
As Tiamat opened her mouth to its full extent,
He drove in the evil wind, while as yet she had not shut

her lips.

The terrible winds filled her belly,
And her courage was taken from her, and her mouth she opened wide.
He seized the spear and burst her belly,
He severed her inward parts, he pierced her heart.

He overcame her and cut off her life;
He cast down her body and stood upon it.
When he had slain Tiamat, the leader,
Her might was broken, her host was scattered.

And the gods her helpers, who marched by her side,
Trembled, and were afraid, and turned back.
They took to flight to save their lives;
But they were surrounded, so that they could not escape.

He took them captive, he broke their weapons;
In the net they were caught and in the snare they sat down.
The ... of the world they filled with cries of grief.
They received punishment from him, they were held in bondage.

And on the eleven creatures which she had filled with the power of striking terror,
Upon the troop of devils, who marched at her...,
He brought affliction, their strength he...;
Them and their opposition he trampled under his feet.

Moreover, Kingu, who had been exalted over them,
He conquered, and with the god Dug-ga he counted him.
He took from him the Tablets of Destiny that were not rightly his,
He sealed them with a seal and in his own breast he laid them.

Now after the hero Marduk had conquered and cast down his enemies,
And had made the arrogant foe even like

And had fully established Ansar's triumph over the enemy
And had attained the purpose of Nudimmud,
Over the captive gods he strengthened his durance,
And unto Tiamat, whom he had conquered, he returned.

And the lord stood upon Tiamat's hinder parts,
And with his merciless club he smashed her skull.
He cut through the channels of her blood,
And he made the North wind bear it away into secret places.

His fathers beheld, and they rejoiced and were glad;
Presents and gifts they brought unto him.
Then the lord rested, gazing upon her dead body,
While he divided the flesh of the ... , and devised a cunning plan.

He split her up like a flat fish into two halves;
One half of her he stablished as a covering for heaven.
He fixed a bolt, he stationed a watchman,
And bade them not to let her waters come forth.

He passed through the heavens, he surveyed the regions thereof,
And over against the Deep he set the dwelling of Nudimmud.
And the lord measured the structure of the Deep,
And he founded E-sara, a mansion like unto it.
The mansion E-sara which he created as heaven,
He caused Anu, Bel, and Ea in their districts to inhabit.

THE FIFTH TABLET

He (Marduk) made the stations for the great gods;
The stars, their images, as the stars of the Zodiac, he fixed.
He ordained the year and into sections he divided it;
For the twelve months he fixed three stars.

After he had ... the days of the year ... images,

He founded the station of Nibir [the planet Jupiter] to determine their bounds;
That none might err or go astray,
He set the station of Bel and Ea along with him.

He opened great gates on both sides,
He made strong the bolt on the left and on the right.
In the midst thereof he fixed the zenith;
The Moon-god he caused to shine forth, the night he entrusted to him.

He appointed him, a being of the night, to determine the days;
Every month without ceasing with the crown he covered him, saying:
"At the beginning of the month, when thou shinest upon the land,
Thou commandest the horns to determine six days,
And on the seventh day to divide the crown.

On the fourteenth day thou shalt stand opposite, the half....
When the Sun-god on the foundation of heaven...thee,
The ... thou shalt cause to ..., and thou shalt make his...
... unto the path of the Sun-god shalt thou cause to draw nigh,
And on the ... day thou shalt stand opposite, and the Sun-god shall...
... to traverse her way.
... thou shalt cause to draw nigh, and thou shalt judge the right.
... to destroy..."

[Nearly fifty lines are here lost.]

The gods, his fathers, beheld the net which he had made,
They beheld the bow and how its work was accomplished.
They praised the work which he had done...

Then Anu raised the ... in the assembly of the gods. He

kissed the bow, saving, " It is...!"
And thus he named the names of the bow, saving,
"'Long-wood' shall be one name, and the second name shall be ...,
And its third name shall be the Bow-star, in heaven shall it...!"

Then he fixed a station for it...
Now after the fate of...
He set a throne...
...in heaven...

[The remainder of this tablet is missing.]

THE SIXTH TABLET

When Marduk heard the word of the gods,
His heart prompted him and he devised a cunning plan.
He opened his mouth and unto Ea he spake
That which he had conceived in his heart he imparted unto him:

"My blood will I take and bone will I fashion
I will make man, that man may
I will create man who shall inhabit the earth,
That the service of the gods may be established, and that their shrines may be built.

But I will alter the ways of the gods, and I will change their paths;
Together shall they be oppressed and unto evil shall they....

And Ea answered him and spake the word:
"... the ... of the gods I have changed
... and one...
... shall be destroyed and men will I...
... and the gods .
... and they..."

Public Domain image of the god Enki

[The rest of the text is wanting with the exception of the last few lines of the tablet, which read as follows.]

They rejoiced...
In Upsukkinnaku they set their dwelling.
Of the heroic son, their avenger, they cried:
" We, whom he succored.... !"

They seated themselves and in the assembly they named him...,
They all cried aloud, they exalted him...

THE SEVENTH TABLET

O Asari, [Marduk] "Bestower of planting," "Founder of sowing"
"Creator of grain and plants," "who caused the green herb to spring up!"
O Asaru-alim, [Mardk] "who is revered in the house of counsel," "who aboundeth in counsel,"
The gods paid homage, fear took hold upon them!

O Asaru-alim-nuna, [Marduk] "the mighty one," "the Light of the father who begat him,"
"Who directeth the decrees of Anu Bel, and Ea!"
He was their patron, be ordained their...;
He, whose provision is abundance, goeth forth...

Tutu [Marduk] is "He who created them anew";
Should their wants be pure, then are they satisfied;
Should he make an incantation, then are the gods appeased;
Should they attack him in anger, he withstandeth their onslaught!

Let him therefore be exalted, and in the assembly of the gods let him... ;
None among the gods can rival him!
Tutu [Marduk] is Zi-ukkina, "the Life of the host of the gods,"
Who established for the gods the bright heavens.

He set them on their way, and ordained their path;
Never shall his ... deeds be forgotten among men.

Tutu as Zi-azag thirdly they named, "the Bringer of Purification,"
"The God of the Favoring Breeze," "the Lord of Hearing and Mercy,"
"The Creator of Fulness and Abundance," " the Founder of Plenteousness,"
"Who increaseth all that is small."

In sore distress we felt his favoring breeze,"
Let them say, let them pay reverence, let them bow in humility before him!

Tutu as Aga-azag may mankind fourthly magnify!
"The Lord of the Pure Incantation," " the Quickener of the Dead,"
"Who had mercy upon the captive gods,"
"Who removed the yoke from upon the gods his enemies,"
"For their forgiveness did he create mankind,"
"The Merciful One, with whom it is to bestow life!"

May his deeds endure, may they never be forgotten ,
In the mouth of mankind whom his hands have made!

Tutu as Mu-azag, fifthly, his “Pure incantation” may their mouth proclaim,
Who through his Pure Incantation hath destroyed all the evil ones!”

Sag-zu, [Marduk] “who knoweth the heart of the gods,” “ who seeth through the innermost part!”
“The evil-doer he hath not caused to go forth with him!”
“Founder of the assembly of the gods,” who ... their heart!”
“Subduer of the disobedient,” “...!”

“Director of Righteousness,” “...,”
“ Who rebellion and...!”
Tutu as Zi-si, “the ...,”
“Who put an end to anger,” “who...!”

Tutu as Suh-kur, thirdly, “the Destroyer of the foe,”
“Who put their plans to confusion,”
“Who destroyed all the wicked,” “...,”
... let them... !

[There is a gap here of sixty lines. But somewhere among the lost lines belong the following fragments.]

Who...

He named the four quarters of the world, mankind he created,

And upon him understanding...

“The mighty one...!”

Agil...

“The Creator of the earth...!”

Zulummu...

“The Giver of counsel and of whatsoever...!”

Mummu, “ the Creator of...!”

Mulil, the heavens...,

"Who for...!"

Giskul, let...,

"Who brought the gods to naught....!"

....

... " the Chief of all lords,"

... supreme is his might!

Lugal-durmah, "the King of the band of the gods," " the Lord of rulers."

"Who is exalted in a royal habitation,"

"Who among the gods is gloriously supreme!

Adu-nuna, " the Counselor of Ea," who created the gods his fathers,

Unto the path of whose majesty

No god can ever attain!

... in Dul-azag be made it known,

... pure is his dwelling!

... the... of those without understanding is Lugaldul-azaga!

... supreme is his might!

... their... in the midst of Tiamat,

... of the battle!

[Here follows the better-preserved ending.]

... the star, which shineth in the heavens.
May he hold the Beginning and the Future, may they pay homage unto him,
Saying, "He who forced his way through the midst of Tiamat without resting,
Let his name be Nibiru, 'the Seizer of the Midst'!

For the stars of heaven he upheld the paths,
He shepherded all the gods like sheep!
He conquered Tiamat, he troubled and ended her life,"
In the future of mankind, when the days grow old,
May this be heard without ceasing; may it hold sway forever!

Since he created the realm of heaven and fashioned the firm earth,
The Lord of the World," the father Bel hath called his name.
This title, which all the Spirits of Heaven proclaimed,
Did Ea hear, and his spirit was rejoiced, and he said:
"He whose name his fathers have made glorious,
Shall be even as I, his name shall be Ea!

The binding of all my decrees shall he control,
All my commands shall he make known! "
By the name of "Fifty " did the great gods
Proclaim his fifty names, they, made his path preeminent.

EPILOGUE

Let them [i.e. the names of Marduk] be held in remembrances and let the first man proclaim them;
Let the wise and the understanding consider them together!

Let the father repeat them and teach them to his son;
Let them be in the ears of the pastor and the shepherd!

Let a man rejoice in Marduk, the Lord of the gods,
That be may cause his land to be fruitful, and that he himself may have prosperity!

His word standeth fast, his command is unaltered;
The utterance of his mouth hath no god ever annulled.
He gazed in his anger, he turned not his neck;
When he is wroth, no god can withstand his indignation.

Wide is his heart, broad is his compassion;

The sinner and evil-doer in his presence...
They received instruction, they spake before him,
... unto...
... of Marduk may the gods...;
... May they ... his name... !
... they took and...

From the Library of Ashurbanipal 7th century BC

The Epic of Gilgamesh

THE ELEVENTH TABLET.

THE FLOOD.

Column I.

(The Cause of the Flood).

Gilgamish unto him spake, to Uta-Napishtim the Distant:
"Uta-Napishtim, upon thee I gaze, (yet) in no wise thy presence
Strange is, (for) thou art like me, and in no wise different art thou;

The Flood tablet in the British Museum. 2010 author photograph by Mike Peel creative commonps attribution share alike 4.0 international license

Thou art like me; (yea) a stomach for fighting doth make thee consummate,
[Aye, and to rest (?)] on thy back thou dost lie. [O tell me (?)], how couldst thou
Stand in th' Assemblage of Gods to petition for life (everlasting)?"

Uta-Napishtim (addressing him thus) unto Gilgamish answer'd:
"Gilgamish, I unto thee will discover the (whole) hidden story,

Aye, and the rede of the Gods will I tell thee.

The City Shurippak –

Hero mastering a lion from palace of Sargon II at Dur Sharrukin (now Khorsabad, near Mossul), 713-706 BC. Louvre Museum

excavated by Paul-Emile Botta 1843-1844 photographer TangLung GNU free documentation license Wikimedia commons

(O 'tis) a city thou knowest!—is set [on the marge] of Euphrates,
Old is this city, with gods in its midst. (Now), the great gods a deluge
Purposed to bring: . . . . . . there was Anu, their sire; their adviser
Warrior Enlil; Ninurta 2, their herald; their leader(?) Ennugi;
Nin-igi-azag—'tis Ea—, (albeit) conspirator with them,

Unto a reed-hut their counsel betray'd he: "O Reed-hut, O Reed-hut!
Wall, wall! Hearken, O Reed-hut, consider, O Wall! O thou Mortal,
Thou of Shurippak, thou scion of Ubara-Tutu, a dwelling

Pull down, (and) fashion a vessel (therewith); abandon possessions,
Life do thou seek, (and) thy hoard disregard, and save life; every creature
Make to embark in the vessel. The vessel, which thou art to fashion,

Apt be its measure; its beam and its length be in due correspondence,
(Then) [on] the deep do thou launch it." And I—sooth, I apprehending,
(This wise) to Ea, my lord, did I speak: '[See], Lord, what thou sayest

Thus, do I honour, I'll do—(but) to city, to people, and elders
Am I, forsooth, to explain?' (Then) Ea made answer in speaking,
Saying to me—me, his henchman!—'Thou mortal, shalt speak to them this wise:
"'Tis me alone (?) whom Enlil so hateth that I in your city

No (more) may dwell, nor turn my face unto the land which is Enlil's.
[I will go] down to the Deep, (there) dwelling with Ea, my [liege] lord,
(Wherefore) [on] you will he shower down plenty, yea, fowl [in great number(?)],
Booty of fish . . . . [and big] the harvest.
. . . . causing a plentiful rainfall (?) to come down upon you."'

[(Then) when something] of morning had dawn'd . . . .

(Five lines mutilated).

Pitch did the children 4 provide, (while) the strong brought [all] that was needful.
(Then) on the fifth day (after) I laid out the 5 shape (of my vessel),
Ten gar each was the height of her sides, in accord with her planning(?),
Ten gar to match was the size of her deck (?), and the shape of the forepart (?)

Did I lay down, (and) the same did I fashion; (aye), six times cross-pinn'd her,
Sevenfold did I divide her . . . ., divided her inwards
Ninefold: hammer'd the caulking within her, (and) found me a quant-pole,

(All) that was needful I added; the hull with six shar of bitumen
Smear'd I, (and) three shar of pitch [did I smear] on the inside; some people,
Bearing a vessel of grease, three shar of it brought (me); (and) one shar
(Out of this) grease did I leave, which the tackling (?) consumed; (and) the boatman

Two shar of grease stow'd away; (yea), beeves for the . . .

I slaughter'd,
Each day lambs did I slay: mead, beer, oil, wine, too, the workmen
[Drank] as though they were water 2, and made a great feast like the New Year,

(Five mutilated lines "I added salve for the hand(s)," "the vessel was finish'd . . . Shamash the great." "was difficult," " . . ? I caused to bring above and below," "two-thirds of it"):

[All I possess'd I] laded aboard her; the silver I laded
All I possess'd; gold, all I possess'd I laded aboard her,
All I possess'd of the seed of all living [I laded aboard] her.
Into the ship I embark'd all my kindred and family (with me),

Cattle (and) beasts of the field (and) all handicraftsmen embarking.
(Then) decreed Shamash the hour: " . . . . (?)
Shall in the night let a plentiful rainfall(?) pour down . . . .
(Then) do thou enter the vessel, and (straightway) shut down thy hatchway."

Came (then) that hour (appointed), ... (?)
Did in the night let a plentiful rainfall(?) pour down . . . . (?)
View'd I the aspect of day: to look on the day bore a horror,
(Wherefore) I enter'd the vessel, and (straightway) shut down my hatchway,
(So, too) to shut down the vessel to Puzur-Amurri (?), the boatman,

Did I deliver the poop (of the ship), besides its equipment.

(Then), when something of dawn had appear'd, from out the horizon
Rose a cloud darkling; (lo), Adad (the storm-god) was rumbling within it,

Nabu and Sharru were leading the vanguard, and coming as heralds
Over the hills and the levels: (then) Irragal wrench'd out the bollards;
Havoc Ninurta let loose as he came, th' Anunnaki their torches

Brandish'd, and shrivell'd the land with their flames; desolation from Adad
Stretch'd to (high) Heaven, (and) all that was bright was turn'd into darkness.

(Four lines mutilated)

"the land like . . .," "for one day the st[orm] . . ., " "fiercely blew . . . . " "like a battle . . . ").

Nor could a brother distinguish his brother; from heaven were mortals
Not to be spied. O, were stricken with terror the gods at the Deluge,
Fleeing, they rose to the Heaven of Anu, and crouch'd in the outskirts,

Cow 'ring like curs were the gods (while) like to a woman in travail
Ishtar did cry, she shrieking aloud, (e'en) the sweet-spoken Lady
(She of the gods): 'May that day turn to dust, because I spake evil

Ishtar holding her symbol terracotta relief early 2nd millennium BC from Eshunna Louvre Marie-Lan Nguyen user Jastrow 2009-01-14 creative commons attribution 2.5 generic license

(There) in th' Assemblage of Gods! O, how could I utter (such) evil
(There) in the Assemblage of Gods, (so) to blot out my people, ordaining
Havoc! Sooth, then, am I to give birth, unto (these) mine own people
Only to glut (with their bodies) the Sea as though they were fish-spawn?'

Gods—Anunnaki—wept with her, the gods were sitting (all) humbled,
(Aye), in (their) weeping, (and) closed were their lips amid(?)]the Assemblage.
Six days, a se'nnight the hurricane, deluge, (and) tempest continued
Sweeping the land: when the seventh day came, were quelléd the warfare,

Tempest (and) deluge which like to an army embattail'd were fighting.
Lull'd was the sea, (all) spent was the gale, assuaged was the deluge,
(So) did I look on the day; (lo), sound was (all) still'd; and all human
Back to (its) clay was return'd, and fen was level with roof-tree.

(Then) I open'd a hatchway, and down on my cheek stream'd the sunlight,
Bowing myself, I sat weeping, my tears o'er my cheek(s) overflowing,
Into the distance I gazed, to the furthest bounds of the Ocean,

Land was uprear'd at twelve (points), and the Ark on the Mountain of Nisir
Grounded; the Mountain of Nisir held fast, nor gave lease to her shifting.
One day, (nay,) two, did Nisir hold fast, nor give lease to her shifting.
Three days, (nay), four, did Nisir hold fast, nor give lease to her shifting,
Five days, (nay,) six, did Nisir hold fast, nor give lease to her shifting.

(Then), when the seventh day dawn'd, I put forth a dove, and released (her),
(But) to and fro went the dove, and return'd (for) a resting-place was not.
(Then) I a swallow put forth and released; to and fro went the swallow,
She (too) return'd, (for) a resting-place was not; I put forth a raven,
Her, (too,) releasing; the raven went, too, and th' abating of waters
Saw; and she ate as she waded (and) splash'd, (unto me) not returning.

Unto the four winds (of heaven) I freed (all the beasts), and an off'ring
Sacrificed, and a libation I pour'd on the peak of the mountain,
Twice seven flagons devoting, (and) sweet cane, (and) cedar, and myrtle,

Sumerian necklace and headgear discovered in the royal (and individual) graves at the tomb of Puabi in Ur, showing the way they may have been worn. Photographer JMiall creative commons attribution share alike 3.0 unported license.

Heap'd up beneath them; the gods smelt the savour, the gods the sweet savour
Smelt; (aye,) the gods did assemble like flies o'er him making the off'ring.
Then, on arriving, the Queen (of the gods) the magnificent jewels
Lifted on high, which Anu had made in accord with her

wishes;
'O ye Gods! I will (rather) forget (this) my necklet of sapphires,

Than not maintain these days in remembrance, nor ever forget them.
(So), though (the rest of) the gods may present themselves at the off'ring,
Enlil (alone of the gods) may (himself) not come to the off'ring,
Because he, unreasoning, brought on a deluge, and therefore my people
Unto destruction consign'd.'

Then Enlil, on his arrival,
Spied out the vessel, and (straightway) did Enlil burst into anger,
Swollen with wrath 'gainst the gods, the Igigi: 'Hath any of mortals
'Scaped? Sooth, never a man could have lived through (the welter of) ruin.'
(Then) did Ninurta make answer and speak unto warrior Enlil,

Saying: 'O, who can there be to devise such a plan, except Ea?
Surely, 'tis Ea is privy to ev'ry design.' Whereat Ea
Answer'd and spake unto Enlil, the warrior, saying: 'O chieftain
Thou of the gods, thou warrior! How, forsooth, how (all) uncounsell'd

Couldst thou a deluge bring on? (Aye,) visit his sin on the sinner
Visit his guilt on the guilty, (but) O, have mercy, that (thereby)
He shall not be cut off; be clement, that he may not [perish].
O, instead of thy making a flood, let a lion come, man to diminish;

O, instead of thy making a flood, let a jackal come, man to diminish;
O, instead of thy making a flood, let a famine occur, that the country

May be [devour'd(?)]; instead of thy making a flood, let the Plague-god
Come and the people [o'erwhelm];
Sooth, indeed 'twas not I of the Great Gods the secret revealéd,
(But) to th' Abounding in Wisdom 2 vouchsafed I a dream, and (in this wise)
He of the gods heard the secret. Deliberate, now, on his counsel'.

(Then) to the Ark came up Enlil; my hand did he grasp, and uplifted
Me, even me, and my wife, too, he raised, and, bent-kneed beside me,
Made her to kneel; our foreheads he touch'd as he stood there between us,
Blessing us; 'Uta-Napishtim hath hitherto only been mortal,
Now, indeed, Uta-Napishtim and (also) his wife shall be equal

Like to us gods; in the distance afar at the mouth of the rivers
Uta-Napishtim shall dwell'. (So) they took me and (there) in the distance
Caused me to dwell at the mouth of the rivers.
But thcc, as for thcc, pray,
Who will assemble the gods for thy (need), that the life which thou seekest
Thou mayst discover? Come, fall not asleep for six days, aye, a se'nnight!"

(But Gilgamish is too mortal to resist even sleep).

(Then), while he sat on his haunches a sleep like a breeze

breathed upon him.
Spake to her, Uta-Napishtim, yea, unto his wife: "O, behold him,
E'en the strong fellow who asketh for life, (how) hath breathéd upon him

Sleep like a breeze!" (Then) his wife unto Uta-Napishtim the Distant
Answer 'd: "O, touch him, and let the man wake, that the road he hath traversed
He may betake himself homeward in peace, that he by the portal
Whence he fared forth may return to his land." Spake Uta-Napishtim,

(Yea), to his wife: "(How) the troubles of mortals do trouble thee also!
Bake then his flour (and) put at his head, but the time he is sleeping
On the house-wall do thou mark it." (So straightway) she (did so), his flour
Baked she (and) set at his head, but the time he was sleeping she noted

On the house-wall. (So), first was collected his flour, (then) secondly sifted,
Thirdly, 'twas moisten'd, and fourthly she kneaded his dough, and so fifthly
Leaven she added, and sixthly 'twas baked; (then) seventh—he touch'd him,
All on a sudden, and (so from his slumber) awoke the (great) fellow!

Gilgamish unto him spake, (yea) to Uta-Napishtim the Distant:
220."(Tell me), I pr'ythee (?), was 't thou, who when sleep was shower'd upon me
All on a sudden didst touch me, and (straightway) rouse

me (from slumber)?"
Uta-Napishtim to Gilgamish [spake, (yea), unto him spake he]:
"Gilgamish, told was the tale of thy meal . . . and (then) did I wake thee:

['One'—was collected] thy flour: [(then) 'two']—it was sifted; (and) 'thirdly'—
Moisten'd: (and) 'fourthly'—she kneaded thy dough [(and) 'fifthly'] the leaven
Added: (and) 'sixthly'—'twas baked: [(and) 'seventh'] —'twas I on a sudden

Touch'd thee and thou didst awake." To Uta-Napishtim, the Distant,

Gilgamish answer'd: "O, [how] shall I act, (or) where shall I hie me,
Uta-Napishtim? A Robber 3 (from me) hath ravish'd my [courage,]
Death [in] my bed-chamber broodeth, and Death is wherever I [listen]."

[Spake] to [him, (yea),] to the boatman Ur-Shanabi Uta-Napishtim:
"'Tis thou, Ur-Shanabi . . . the crossing, will hate thee,
(Sooth), to all those who come to its marge, doth its marge set a limit:
(This) man for whom thou wert guide—are stains to cover his body,
Or shall a skin hide the grace of his limbs? Ur-Shanabi, take him,

Lead him to where he may bathe, that he wash off his stains in the water
(White) as the snow: let him cast off his pelt(s) that the sea may remove (them);
Fair let his body appear: of his head be the fillet renewéd,

Let him, as clothes for his nakedness, garb himself in a mantle,

Such that, or ever he come to his city, and finish his journey,
No (sign of) age shall the mantle betray, but preserve (all) its freshness."
Wherefore Ur-Shanabi took him, and where he might bathe did he lead him,
Washing his stains in the [water] like snow, his pelt(s), [too], discarding,

So that the sea might bear them away; (and) his body appearéd
Fair; [of] his head he [the fillet] renewed, and himself in a mantle
Garb'd, as the clothes for his nakedness, [such that or ever his city
Reach he], or ever he finish his journey, [the mantle betray not

Age, but] preserve [(all) its freshness].
(So) into their vessel embarkéd
Gilgamish, (aye), and Ur-Shanabi, launching (their) craft [on the billow],
They themselves riding aboard (her).
(The magic gift of restored youth).
To Uta-Napishtim, the Distant,
Spake (then) his wife: "Came Gilgamish (hither) aweary with rowing,

What wilt thou give wherewith he return to his land?" and the meanwhile
Gilgamish, lifting his pole, was pushing the boat at the seashore.
(Then answer'd) Uta-Napishtim to him, (yea), [to] Gilgamish [spake he]:
"Gilgamish, (hither) didst come (all) aweary with rowing; (O, tell me),
265.What shall I give thee (as gift) wherewith to return

to thy country?
Gilgamish, I will reveal thee a hidden matter . . . I'll tell thee:
There is a plant like a thorn with its root (?) [deep down in the ocean],
Like unto those of the briar (in sooth) its prickles will scratch [thee],

(Yet) if thy hand reach this plant, [thou'lt surely find life (everlasting)] ."
(Then), when Gilgamish heard this, he loosen'd) [his girdle about him],
Bound heavy stones [on his feet], which dragg'd him down to the sea-deeps,
[Found he the plant]; as he seized on the plant, (lo), [its prickles did scratch him].

Cut he the heavy stones [from his feet] that again it restore him
Unto its shore.

Gilgamish spake to him, (yea), to the boatman Ur-Shanabi (this wise):
"(Nay, but) this plant is a plant of great wonder(?), Ur-Shanabi," said he,
"Whereby a man may attain his desire—I'll take it to Erech,

(Erech), the high-wall'd, and give it to eat [unto . . . .].
'Greybeard-who-turneth-to-man-in-his-prime' is its name and I'll eat it
I myself, that again I may come to my youthful condition."

(The Quest ends in Tragedy).

Broke they their fast at the fortieth hour: at the sixtieth rested.

Gilgamish spied out a pool of cool water, (and) therein

descending
Bathed in the water. (But here was) a serpent who snuff'd the plant's fragrance,
Darted he up [from the water (?)], and snatch'd the plant, uttering malison

As he drew back. Then Gilgamish sate him, (and) burst into weeping.
Over his cheeks flow'd his tears: to the boatman Ur - Shanabi [spake he(?)]
"(Pr'ythee), [for] whom have toiléd mine arms, O Ur-Shanabi, (tell me),

(Pr'ythee), for whom hath my heart's blood been spent? (yea), not for mine own self,
Have I the guerdon achieved; (no), 'tis for an earth-lion (only)
Have I the guerdon secured—(and) now at the fortieth hour
(Such an) one reiveth (it)—O, when I open'd the sluice and . . .ed the attachment,
(Aye), I noted the sign (?) which to me was vouchsafed as a warning,

300.Would I had turn'd and abandon'd the boat at the marge (of the ocean)!"
Broke they their fast at the fortieth hour: at the sixtieth rested,
(So in the end) to the middle of Erech, the high-wall'd, arrivéd.

(The Pride of the Architect).

Gilgamish spake to him, (yea), to the boatman Ur-Shanabi (this wise):
"Do thou, Ur-Shanabi, go up and walk on the ramparts of Erech,
Look on its base, and take heed of its bricks, if its bricks be not kiln-burnt,

(Aye), and its ground-work be not bitumen, e'en seven courses,One shar the city, (and) one shar the gardens, and one shar the
. . . . the Temple of Ishtar, amass'd I three shar and . . . (?) of Erech.

No. 6.—TRANSLATION[40] OF THE ANNALS OF SARGON OF ACCAD AND NARAM-SIN

Public Domain image Victory Stele of Aram-Sin

OBVERSE

1. When the moon at its setting with the colour of a dust-cloud filled the crescent, the moon was favourable for Sargon who at this season

2. marched against the country of Elam and subjugated the men of Elam.

3. Misery (?) he brought upon them; their food he cut off.

4. When the moon at its setting filled the crescent with the colour of a dust-cloud, and over the face of the sky the colour extended behind the moon during the day and remained bright,

5. the moon was favourable for Sargon who marched against the country of [Phœnicia], and

6. subjugated the country of Phœnicia. His hand conquered the four quarters (of the world).

7. When the moon increased in form on the right hand and on the left, and moreover [during] the day the finger reached over the horns,

8. the moon was favourable for Sargon who at this season produced joy (?) [in] Babylon, and

9. [like] dust the spoil of Bab-dhuna was carried away and

10. ... he made Accad a city; the city of ... he called its name;

11. [the men of ... in the] midst he caused to dwell.

12. [When the moon] on the left the colour of fire [on] the left of the planet, and

13. [the moon was favourable to Sargo]n who at this season against the country of Phœnicia

14. [marched and subjugated it]. The four quarters (of the world) his hand conquered.

15. [When the moon] behind the moon the four heads were placed,

16. [the moon was favourable to Sargon who at this season] marched [against] the country of Phœnicia and

17. [subjugated the country of Phœnicia.] His [enemies?] he smote; his heroes

18. in the gate of its rising.

19. [When the moon was fixed?] and a span [the moon was favourable to Sargon] as for whom at this season the goddess [Ishtar]

20. [with favours] filled for him his hand the goddess Ishtar [all countries]

21. caused him to conquer; against Tiri (?) ...

22. [When the moon] appeared [like] a lion, the moon was favourable to Sargon who at this season

23. was [very] exalted and a rival (or) equal had not; his own country was at peace. Over

24. [the countries] of the sea of the setting sun he crossed and for 3 years at the setting sun

25. [all countries] his hand conquered. Every place to form but one (empire) he appointed. His images at the setting sun

26. he erected. Their spoil he caused to pass over into the countries of the sea.

27. [When the moon on] the right hand was like the colour of gall, and there was no finger; the upper part was long and the moon was setting (?),

28. [the moon was favourable for] Sargon who enlarged his palace of Delight (?) by mitkhu, and

29. established the chiefs [in it] and called it the House of Kiâm-izallik.

30. When the moon was like a cloud (?), like the colour of gall, and there was no finger; on the right side was the colour of a sword; the circumference of the left side was visible;

31. towards its face on the left the colour extended; the moon was favourable for Sargon against whom at this season Kastubila of the country of Kazalla rebelled and against Kazalla

32. (Sargon) marched and he smote their forces; he accomplished their destruction.

33. Their mighty army he annihilated; he reduced Kazalla to dust and ruins.

34. The station of the birds he overthrew.

35. When the moon was like a cloud (?), like the colour of gall, and there was no finger; 1 on the right side was the colour of a sword; the circumference of the left was visible;

36. and against its face the Seven 2 advanced; the moon was favourable to Sargon, against whom at this season

37. the elders of the whole country revolted and besieged him in the city of Accad; but

38. Sargon issued forth and smote their forces; their destruction he accomplished.

Reverse

1. Their numerous soldiery he massacred; the spoil that was upon them he collected.

2. "The booty of Istar!" he shouted.

3. When the moon had two fingers, and swords were seen on the right side and the left, [and] might and peace were on the left

4. its hand presented a sword; the sword in its left hand was of the colour of 'sukhuruni; the point was held in the left hand and there were two heads;

5. [the moon] was favourable for Sargon who at this season

6. subjected the men of [the country] of ‘Su-edin in its plenitude to the sword, and

7. Sargon caused their seats to be occupied, and

8. smote their forces; their destruction he accomplished; their mighty army

9. he cut off, and his troops he collected; into the city of Accad he brought (them) back.

10. [When the moon] had two fingers and on the right side it was of the colour of a sword and on the left it was visible;

11. [and against its face] the Seven advanced; (its) appearance was of the colour of gall; the moon was favourable for Naram-Sin

12. [who at] this season marched against the city of Apirak, and

13. [utterly] destroyed it: Ris-Rimmon the king of Apirak

14. [he overthrew], and the city of Apirak his hand conquered.

15. [When the moon] on the right it was of the colour of a sword, and on the left it was visible;

16. [and against its face the Seven advanced?]; the moon was favourable for Naram-Sin who at this season

17. marched [against the country of Mâ]ganna 1 and seized the country of Mâganna, and

18 the king of Mâganna his hand captured.

19. [When against the moon] the Seven were banded, [and] behind it

20. ...... never may there be a son (?) ...

Public Domain image of Sargon 1

VI. Summary

The Ice Age began after Noah and his family left the ark. It lasted approximately 700 years, based on accepting Michael Oard's examination of the evidence. Noah left the ark approximately 2350 BC according to Ussher's chronology. The Ice Age ended approximately 1700 BC. Joseph was vizier of Egypt during the seven years of plenty followed by seven years of famine, which ended the Ice Age.

About a century after the Flood Nimrod formed a government to rebel against God. One aspect of this rebellion was to build a tower to heaven. From the city of Babel, the entire world was divided into languages. As they left Babel, people filled the entire earth with two predominant cultures. Nomadic hunters roamed Africa, the Americas, Australia, Southeast Asia, Oceania and the northern parts of Europe and Asia, including Siberia.

Since the ^{14}C dating of many artifacts of these nomads date in the range of tens of thousands of years, we know that they visited every major continent on earth very quickly after leaving the ark, before the building of the tower of Babel. Perhaps they even visited Antarctica. The oldest nomadic artifacts are dated by ^{14}C to be much older than the ^{14}C dates of artifacts found in the cities. It is possible that these nomads, at least some of them, gathered resources for the cities.

China, Egypt, Europe, the Indus Valley, and Mesopotamia all left evidence of advanced civilization through cities and trade. The lack of a written language, or at least written records which we can decipher today, makes a true and complete understanding of the early Chinese, European, and Indus Valley civilizations impossible. What we do know we learn from other cultures and the artifacts they left behind.

It is highly probable that the Ice Age lasted nearly 700 years after the Flood as Michael Oard suggests. These are all Ice Age cultures. It means that very advanced civilization began at the beginning of the Ice Age. At that time ice covered much of the earth and the sea levels were 400 feet lower than they are today. Men could walk to any continent on earth, with the possible exception of Antarctica.

By the end of the Ice Age there were millions of people in hundreds of very advanced cities. Trade by ship was worldwide, though difficult. The Ice Age ended with very real climate change including rising sea levels. But these civilizations were destroyed by the greed of warfare, not climate change.

Review and Study Section

I. Review Questions

1. What did Noah and his family pass on to their descendants after they left the Ark?

The true history of mankind

2. What is the value of some study of Jewish texts?

Many are based on older works that no longer exist that accurately record Jewish traditions. These are the most accurate records of mankind. The Hebrew texts are more accurate than any of the ancient texts of any other ancient culture. Most ancient texts were designed to deceive, keep tyrants in power, and boast of the tyrant's accomplishments.

3. What is the History of Civilization?

the record of man either yielding to God's will for His glory or struggling to rebel against God.

4. What document is the basis for the US Constitution's First Amendment?

The Magna Carta

5. What is the basis for education?

You can rely on (trust) the observation and experiences of others.

6. What Lycurgus' perspective on oral traditions according to Plutarch?

"None of his laws were put into writing ... the most important and binding principles which conduce to the prosperity and virtue of a city were implanted in the

habits and training of its citizens, they would remain unchanged and secure ..."

7. Artifacts by themselves are not ...

History

8. Why do people today fear to challenge the Secular Humanist Establishment of Religion?

They love the praise of men more than pleasing God.

9. Name at least two beliefs that will result from the belief that the earth is millions of years old.

a. No fall of man or original sin
b. no need for atonement,
c. no need for the death, burial, and resurrection of Christ.

10. People do not reject the Bible because they do not understand it, but because ...

do understand it and they reject what it says

11. Do not be misled by the use of mathematical formulas, archeological evidence, or physics to prove a point. What is the real issue for judging the value of arguments?

Examine the underlying assumptions -- Why they believe what they believe.

12. What is the key to discovering and presenting truth?

Align the scientific testimonies of the eyewitnesses with the historical records contained in the Word of God.

13. In the context of our series here, What is a synonym for the word assumption?

belief

14. Why do secularists try to divide fields of study?

So that Bible study can be put in a separate category and divorced from "academic" studies. They are attempting to make their religion superior to the Word of God.

15. Name at least two of the foundations of science found in the Word of God.

a. The order of the universe,
b. the methods God commands men to use for investigation, and
c. the purpose of the universe is found in the Word of God and is foundational to science.

16. What is the foundational belief needed for rejecting the Bible as accurate Science and History?

Deep Time (self will or rebellion are also foundational, but they are not a belief)

17. Name at least two areas of scientific study that unbelievers make assumptions about to use as evidence for the age of the earth and the universe.

a. Astronomy,
b. the geologic column,
c. radiometric dating,
d. dendrochronology, and
e. ice age(s)

18. The Flood occurred approximately how many years after Adam was thrown out of the garden?

1,656

19. What does Anno Mundi mean?

in the year of the world (Jewish Calendar)

20. What was different about the post-Flood population of the world?

Changes in topography and climate favored the adaptation of different organisms compared to the antediluvian world. There was a lower lifespan, and at first little or no death so populations exploded.

21. What climate conditions resulted from the mountains rising and sea levels falling constantly after the Flood?

"A moving temperate zone, falling in elevation" is a correct answer. Answers may vary but should also include some of the following:

Mountains rose (Mountains rise up and valleys sink to the place you have ordained for them. Psalm 104:8, ISV), massive snowstorms covered the mountaintops with snow which did not melt during the summers. Mountains continued to rise and sea levels continued to fall until at their lowest point the sea levels were 400 feet lower than today. This caused a moving temperate zone, falling in elevation.

22. The passing on of Noah's shipbuilding skills and the entire earth being connected by land made what possible?

Men could, and did, travel everywhere on earth, on foot, by ship, riding on animals or using animals to pull carts and wagons.

23. Approximately how long, according to Michael Oard, did this ice age condition last?

700 years

24. Write a brief essay describing conditions that necessitated a nomadic lifestyle after the Flood.

Answers may vary but should include some of the following:

Ice sheets formed, advanced, and retreated rapidly. Flooding would be a constant, serious threat. The continually falling sea level would require constant moving, at least at first. Pasturelands alternated between being marshlands, usable grasslands, and too dry, requiring a constant movement of animals.

25. The real problem with ^{14}C is not that the truth about its use lies somewhere in the middle, but that...

Both sides present accurate scientific information to support their positions. However, some, usually believers in deep time, ignore the equally valid scientific information from the other side.

26. What mistake, according to Dr. Andrew Snelling, have conventional archaeologists made concerning radiocarbon levels in the atmosphere and biosphere? What does that lead to?

a. They have always been the same as they are today.
b. Erroneously estimating much older dates for early human artifacts.

27. What two calendars does the COA series rely on?

Gregorian and Jewish AM (Anno Mundi)

28. What are the three most important events in human history?

Creation (approx. 4000 BC), the Flood (2350 BC), and the death, burial, and resurrection of Jesus Christ.

29. Write a brief essay listing at least five other important events in history and give reasons why they should be included.

Answers may vary but should include some of the following:

Once you have this basic time frame memorized, you can add other important events: Israel moves his family to Egypt, 1700 BC; the Exodus from Egypt, 1450 BC; Solomon begins building the temple, 970 BC; the fall of Jerusalem to Nebuchadnezzar, 585 BC; the Battle of Thermopylae, 480 BC. From this point, dating is more certain: the fall of Rome, AD 476,; defeat of Muslims in Europe at the battle of Tours, AD 732; death of Genghis Khan, founder of the Mongolian Empire, the largest empire in the world, AD 1227; Columbus discovers America, AD 1492; Martin Luther nails the 95 thesis to the church door in Wittenberg, AD 1517. They are spaced out in intervals designed to provide an overview of human history.

Main Text

30. Briefly contrast the secularist view of history with the observable evidence of population, civilization, and technological growth.

Answers may vary but should include some of the following:

Secularism teaches a very long, slow progress for humans. They believe that the discovery of fire, the wheel, and how to domesticate animals took millennia. With much trial and error, one culture very slowly evolved into another. The evidence, however, shows a very rapid, sudden, even explosive growth of population, civilization, and advanced technology from the very beginning.

31. Write a brief essay about the dispersion of people spread out after the Flood apart from the confusion of languages.

Answers may vary but should include some of the following:

Nimrod likely hunted down and forced people to build the tower, as well as stealing their tools, weapons, and other technology. People fled to escape this conscription of labor. They may have had to dwell in caves and use primitive tools until they found a stable environment and had time to settle and build again. Warfare following the confusion of languages resulted in further dispersion and the sudden appearance of civilizations on distant continents.

32. Briefly summarize how Joseph's seven years of plenty and famine could coincide with the end of the Ice Age.

Answers may vary but should include some of the following:

Using a seven-hundred-year period for the end of the Ice Age, we look for an event to indicate the end of this time period. The seven years of plenty in Egypt began in 1715 BC [Ussher] when Joseph was vizier of Egypt. That was about 635 years after the Flood ended, according to Ussher's dating. While there is nothing which says that the seven years of famine ended the ice age, it was a worldwide famine and the timing fits. The people of all the earth came to Egypt to buy grain from Joseph, because the famine was severe in all the earth. (Genesis 41:57 NASB) It is a reasonable assumption that Egypt, which depends on the flooding of the Nile, would experience greater harvests as the rapidly melting ice caps added more soil and nutrients and increased the areas flooded. It is another reasonable assumption that the areas formerly covered by ice in central Africa, which had supplied the Nile with annual floodwater, would become bare and unable to retain both rainwater and water from the annual snow thaws. These areas, which were barren because they were covered by ice, needed time to grow vegetation. The vegetation would keep the melted snow from immediately rushing down the Nile and out to sea and so maintain Egypt's annual floods. It is also possible that this is the time Lake Victoria formed. Whatever the reason, at the end of seven years of drought, the Nile River returned to annual flood cycles. These are assumptions, but they are reasonable assumptions based on the facts.

33. What well-known scientist wrote The Chronology of Ancient Kingdoms Amended to refute exaggerated and incorrect records of ancient times?

Sir Isaac Newton

34. Briefly summarize the everlasting covenant and give the Scripture reference where it is found.

Genesis 9:1-7 Answers may vary but should include some of the following: Man should faithfully spread godly control and responsibility throughout the world. Permission for man to eat meat, and fear of man instilled in animals. No eating of living things or blood. Capital punishment for deliberate murder.

35. Where is the Table of Nations found?

Genesis 10 (and 11)

36. What is a) the secularist explanation for, and b) a more reasonable explanation for, the so-called "solar ships" found in Egypt?

a) ceremonial or religious objects (for example, designed to carry the Pharaoh into the afterlife) b) Actual sailing vessels from the time period used for a variety of purposes such as carrying settlers from Mesopotamia

37. What does the name Nimrod mean?

"we will revolt"

38. According to Josephus, how did Nimrod seek to turn men from the fear of God?

"bring them into a constant dependence on his [Nimrod's] power"

39. What is a likely theory that explains the common ancient literature story of a king with godlike powers around the world?

Nimrod invented Gilgamesh and publicized in various cities to convince people that he was descended from gods and had supernatural powers. Other cultures continued with the legends because the false religious system was useful in controlling people and supporting the government.

40. How does the *Book of Jubilees* say that Canaan came to possess “the land of Lebanon to the river of Egypt”? How does his father respond to his taking this land?

Canaan saw that the land was good, and went there, instead of to the land he was given by his father. Ham, his father, told him he would bring a curse on the land by his sedition.

41. Jewish tradition states that the earth was physically divided...

The physical earth was divided near the death of Peleg.

42. When do modern Creationist geologists believe the physical division took place?

As a continuation of the flood, completed in no more than a few decades.

43. How long does the *Book of Jubilees* say work continued on the Tower of Babel?

43 years

44. How does Ussher interpret the meaning of Peleg’s name (divided)?

He says that Noah divided the earth among his children.

45. What does one theory propose concerning the lifespans of people who went through the Flood?

If Noah’s daughters-in-law were very young when they married, it is possible that the generation led by Joshua into Canaan were the first without any opportunity to talk to a person who had survived the Flood.

46. What is the name of one of the oldest complete written works?

The Epic of Gilgamesh

47. Write a brief essay summarizing the basics of using Carbon 14 dating.

Answers may vary but should include some of the following:

Assuming a constant rate of ^{14}C formation, the best test equipment can only detect ^{14}C for a maximum of 60,000 years. The decay rate is accurate but rate of formation is not. It does not measure time. It measures amount of ^{14}C available in the sample today. All dating methods work based on known, existing conditions. Assumptions are made that existing conditions can be applied to the sample for the entire life of the sample. Those assumptions are applied to modern samples to formulate a date. Any Catastrophes in the past make radiocarbon dates less and less accurate. In former times there were lower amounts of ^{14}C than there are in the present. Timelines have to be adjusted as they approach any event, such as a catastrophe like the flood, which altered the rate of ^{14}C formation. The accuracy of the date of an event depends on the true age of the artifact not the assumptions of biased observers.

48. What is the translation of the name Mizraim elsewhere in the Bible?

Egypt

49. What is the foundational assumption of ^{14}C dating?

^{14}C results for a given sample are, with significant exceptions, the same worldwide. This assumes that

conditions were roughly same throughout the world at the same time.

50. Dates for the time period before, during, and shortly after the Flood are unreliable because

The environment was dramatically different and changed rapidly.

51. What are the two parts to the Chinese Mandate of Heaven?

a) A Ruler has the authority of heaven but
b) power can be transferred to another if he is not just. (It is the right to rebel against unjust authority.)

52. What type of buildings are found throughout Europe and why were they made that way?

"pile dwellings" Frequent flooding caused cities to be built on wooden pilings to keep them above the highest flood level.

53. List at least three ancient cultures from the Ice Age time period.

a) Minoans (on modern Crete), b) Philistines, c) Phoenicians, d) Trojans e) Hittites

54. Write a brief essay explaining in your own words what Solon was told by the Egyptian priest about mythology and the past.

Answers may vary but should include some of the following: The myth of Phaëthon, for example, was symbolic of times when something, possibly a meteor or comet, caused some fiery catastrophe that wiped out a large portion of the population living in mountains or other high elevations. At other times floods might destroy low-lying places. These disasters sometimes result in a loss of knowledge of history and people were unaware of a cycle of such catastrophes, and also possible losses of knowledge, civilization, and technology.

55. Why are Breasted's works still relied upon when they are known to contain many errors?

He had access to sources that no longer exist and some of the information in his works is not available anywhere else.

56. What does Josephus say that Abraham taught the Egyptians?

Arithmetic [Mathematics] and astronomy

57. Based on Mizraim being the settler of Egypt, using Ussher's dating, what year is the earliest possible date for building the oldest of the pyramids?

2100 BC (probably later, possibly 1975 BC based on Abraham's timeline, if Abraham taught them the necessary skills)

58. List at least three sources for Jewish History.

Hebrew History includes not only the a) Bible, but everything written by and about the Hebrews, such as the b) Talmud, the c) Book of Jubilees, d) The Book of Enoch, e) the Apocrypha, f) the Seder Olam, g) Josephus, h) Philo. *There are other possible correct answers.*

59. What Egyptian author and work is credited with being the source of the concept of the dynasties of Egypt?

Manetho's The History of Egypt

60. What is the problem with Manetheo's work, Breasted's and the physical evidences of many kings' lists that have been found?

None of them agree or correlate with each other, and none correlate with Hebrew history.

61. How is Harappan civilization different from many other civilizations? What prevents us from learning more about them?

More advanced than Egypt, Akkad, or Sumeria. Language has not been deciphered.

62. What region did Breasted not include (but should have) when he coined the term Fertile Crescent?

Indus Valley where the Harappan civilization existed.

63. Briefly explain the importance of Cuneiform in ancient languages.

It was a common alphabet for many civilizations. The earliest cuneiform contained symbols known as glyphs. But cuneiform quickly developed into a true alphabet with individual letters. The various cultures throughout the Mesopotamian region had different languages, but they shared the cuneiform alphabet. This implies that cuneiform is older than the division of languages at the tower of Babel.

64. What structure echoed, on a smaller scale, the rebellion of the tower of Babel?

The Ziggurat

65. Why is it important to note that the Genesis 14 battle of the four kings against five in which Abraham participated took place before Sargon's rule?

Sargon unified the entire region. Separate kingdoms would not have existed in his time.

66. Write a brief essay explaining in your own words the five basic cultural standards established soon after the Flood, or choose one of the four points to expand on. In either case, include more detail based on research from at least two outside sources.

Answers may vary but need to include Family, Warfare, Society, Religion, and Housing and some of the points in the text related to each, as well as substantive quotes from outside sources, or sufficient detail if the student elects to concentrate on only one of the five standards.

67. What is true of every ancient religion?

Every ancient religion is some form of a reversal of the truths revealed in the Word of God. Good is always shown as evil and evil is portrayed as good.

68. What feature of Harappan houses made them different from and better than other Fertile Crescent dwellings?

Indoor plumbing

69. Why is it difficult or impossible to date most cuneiform tablets?

Their generic content refers to events that could have taken place at any time. The actual letters were produced the same way for over 1500 years.

Optional essays/projects

1. Students should choose two of the included literary works and create one visual and one written project that gives commentary, especially from a biblical perspective, on truth or error that can be found in the portion of the work included here.

2. Compare or contrast elements of the selections with Scripture passages that may have similar or contrasting content.

3. Cite evidence about how these works fit into the plans of rulers to convince their people of their power and godlike status.

4. Visual projects can include Creating computer presentations, or physical displays, collages, or dioramas, depending on student ages and abilities. Students might illustrate the scenes described in the works, and include depictions of the gods or people and how they looked and dressed, their transportation, and other aspects of culture. Students can also try to reproduce hieroglyphics, cartouches, and other visuals based on artifacts with paint, clay, or other media.

5. Research the types of plant products or animals used in sacrifices and offerings. Compare or contrast them to those used in the Scripture. Comment on similar or contrasting purposes.

II. Vocabulary

NOTE: THESE ARE SUGGESTIONS ONLY

THE TEACHER SHOULD ADJUST THE NUMBER OF WORDS TO THE STUDENT'S NEED.

THE STUDENT SHOULD SPELL CORRECTLY AND KNOW THE PROPER DEFINITION FOR THE WORD THE TEACHER SELECTS.

As the teacher, you may use any method you believe is best for your students. We have found the following suggestions to be helpful.

1) Require the student to write his answers on a piece of paper. This provides the opportunity to develop handwriting skills as well as answer the question correctly.

2) More frequent, smaller assignments seem to allow students a better grasp of the material.

3) Tests, however, are necessary at regular intervals to validate the teaching method. We recommend at least one test per month, using different methods such as fill in the blank and matching. However, requiring an essay using the words properly is a valid test method. It also allows you, the teacher to see if the student grasps the material.

4) We recommend a quiz of five words daily which includes both spelling and comprehension. Reading the words and definitions out loud aids in learning.
5) Ask the student to write an original sentence using some of the vocabulary words in the proper context. This should not take more than 5 minutes.
6) Make the vocabulary list the student is responsible for cumulative.
7) Only add 1 to 3 words per day to the list. Ten new words per week seems like a small number, but at that rate, the total will still be over 300 words per year. Advanced students can handle many more, but remember that you will be responsible for grading those words in a final examination at the end of the school year.

1. Descendants

"When Noah's family left the Ark they passed on the true history of mankind to their descendants."

Children, grandchildren, great-grandchildren, etc. Those born after the family founder and related to him by blood.

2. Thesis

"Beginning with the introductory book *Antidisestablishmentarianism,* this is the thesis of the entire Conflict of the Ages series."

Statement of the main argument, purpose, or point of a work.

3. Mantra

"The mantra of many historians is 'chronology is the backbone of history'."

Statement repeated to focus attention or concentration.

4. Stele

"The well-known stele of Hammurabi's Law Code teaches us dating is not as certain as Secularists would have us believe."

Pillar of stone carved as a sign or notice; permanent record of a message displayed in a public place.

5. Conclude

"That evidence will lead us to honestly conclude that the earth is much less than one million years old."

Make a final decision based on investigation and analysis of evidence.

6. Rebellion

"The *Conflict of the Ages* series includes worldwide literature, geology, physics, biology, archaeology, and art which gives the greatest possible glory to God or points out the most significant rebellion against Him."

Taking action against a ruler to depose or destroy his power over you.

7. Maintain

"For when they maintain this, it escapes their notice that by the word of God the heavens existed long ago and the earth was formed out of water and by water, through which the world at that time was destroyed, being flooded with water."

Insist that something is true.

8. Materialistic

"This belief permits not only a rejection of a universe designed, created, and controlled by God, but also is a belief in an entirely materialistic universe."

No supernatural origin or nature; entirely physical

9. Disguise

"Since evolution is impossible in 6,000 years, the evidence for a young Earth and a catastrophic, worldwide flood must be lied about, disguised, and deliberately distorted."

Hidden by false statements, interpretations, or assumptions

10. Impossible

"Evolution is impossible without vast amounts of time, which they call deep time."

Cannot occur

11. Climate

"The climate had permanently changed."

Total weather, temperature, and atmospheric conditions

12. Topography

"There was a population explosion, but the changes in topography and climate favored the adaptation of different organisms compared to the antediluvian world."

Physical characteristics of the land

13. Temperate

"This caused a moving temperate zone, falling in elevation."

Moderate climate with no extremes of heat, cold, dryness, or wetness

14. Current

"When the oceans stabilized approximately four hundred feet lower than the current sea level, the entire earth was connected by land."

Present time; now

15. Generation

"Assuming very little mortality for the first 350 years, thirty years per generation, and large families, means that the earth's population was in the millions, including women and children, by the time the tower of Babel was attempted."

From the birth to the maturity of new descendants

16. Maritime

"After this they were dispersed abroad, on account of their languages, and went out by colonies every where; and each colony took possession of that land which they light upon, and unto which God led them; so that the whole continent was filled with them, both the inland and the maritime countries."

Along seacoasts; connected with the sea

17. Evidence

"Though it is called Khufu's solar boat, there is no direct evidence of a connection with Khufu."

Things that can be studied, investigated, or otherwise used to establish facts or draw conclusions about something.

18. Savannah

"If the Nile region was, as Herodetous records, a marsh with a high water table and the region to the west vast savannahs filled with game, then these were likely very common ships throughout the Ice Age."

Subtropical grasslands on relatively level ground

19. Imperial

"There sprang from Cush *Nimrod*, the founder of the first imperial kingdom"

Related to an empire – A system for ruling larger population areas than a small geographic area or more limited region.

20. Tyrant

"Noah's great-grandson Nimrod was the world's first tyrant."

Someone who seeks to completely control and force dependence over as many people as possible

21. resistance

"The name itself, *Nimrod* ... 'we will revolt,' points to some violent resistance to God."

Opposition; refusal to submit or obey

22. Revolt

"The name itself, *Nimrod* ... "we will revolt," points to some violent resistance to God."

Turn against a ruler

23. Difference

"The differences of these various demigods are overshadowed by their similarities."

Characteristics that distinguish one thing from another; not the same

24. Territory
"Canaan's territory began in Sidon, and extended to the edge of his brother Mizraim, that is Egypt's territory."

Physical land controlled by a person or persons

(The following sentence contains the words listed in 25-28 below.)

"This is a clear reference to the division of languages and the forced divisions of mankind when God scattered mankind by dividing people into different languages at the tower of Babel."

25. Reference

Statement that directs attention to a particular event

26. Scatter

Widely separate; force apart; disperse by force

27. Language

Concepts that may be written, spoken, or consist of gestures or signs (groupings of letters, syllables, sounds, symbols, etc.) that allow people to communicate

28. Division

Splitting into different segments; separating

29. Movement

"That means the continents stopped their rapid movement and settled in approximately their current locations decades after the flood."

Changing position; relocating from one place to another

30. Confusion

"The historical record of Babel (Confusion) is the beginning of what we call civilization."

Make unclear; creating inability to understand

31. Accomplishment

"The history of Civilization is usually a lengthy praise of man's accomplishments."

Tasks or goals completed; good things done

32. Imagine

"Behold, the people is one, and they have all one language; and this they begin to do: and now nothing

will be restrained from them, which they have imagined to do."

Think up in the mind; plan or decide to do something

33. Location

"The location is not certain."

Where something is

(The following sentence contains the words listed in 34-35 below.)

"According to Ussher, it was under construction for thirteen years when the Lord God intervened."

34. Construction

Process of building

35. Intervene

Change an outcome or prevent something from being accomplished or cause something which otherwise would not have happened

36. Decide

"Instead of accepting this division, men decided to start building the tower of Babel."

Reason out a course of action

37. Passage

"This passage from the *Book of Jubilees* clearly states that the tower of Babel was north of the city of Babylon, because Asshur is the land of Assyria."

Part of a written document, usually distinguished by being about a single subject

38. Opportunity

"This would make the generation led by Joshua into the land of Canaan the first generation without the opportunity to talk to a person who lived before the flood."

Ability to do something; chance to carry something out

39. Meteorologist

"The meteorologist Michael Oard concludes based on the evidence that the length of the Ice Age was approximately 700 years."

Person recognized as an expert in the field of weather forecasting, climate, and atmospheric conditions

(The following sentence contains the words listed in 40-42 below.)

"The oldest surviving artifacts are found in protected environments; tombs, buried ruins and caves."

40. Survive

Continue to exist; remain; not be destroyed

41. Artifact

Surviving physical remnant of the past

42. Environment

Surrounding physical conditions

43. Decipher

"The oldest written documents are written in cuneiform, hieroglyphs, and languages which today cannot be deciphered."

Translated; made understandable

44. Complete

"One of the oldest complete works of literature is the *Epic of Gilgamesh.*"

Not in partial form; containing the whole work

45. normal

"This 7th century version is the version which is normally translated into English."

Usual; regular; in most cases

46. Impossible

"Dating the oldest human artifacts is difficult at best and often impossible."

Cannot be done

47. Usefulness

"We do have some tools, though their usefulness is far more limited than skeptics would like us to believe."

Value for correctly or accurately performing or accomplishing a task

48. Formation

"Radiocarbon (^{14}C) dating assumes a constant rate of Carbon-14 formation for at least 60,000 years."

composing or putting together necessary elements to produce something

49. Archaeologist

"Frankly, among archaeologists, carbon dating is a big joke."

Person who is considered an expert in the study of ancient human history

50. Benefit

"Radiocarbon dating has benefits in spite of its problems."

Positive or helpful features

(The following sentence contains the words listed in 51-52 below.)

"While any scientific procedure is capable of error, the ^{14}C dates for the DSS conform to other documents, artifacts and match the known history of the region for that time period."

51. Procedure

Set of steps followed or actions completed to attain a desired result

52. Conform

Follow similar patterns; agree with

53. Limitation

"Hebrew History helps us understand both the benefits and limitations of ^{14}C dating."

What something is unable to accomplish

54. Papyrus

"J. T. Milik dated the MUR 17 papyrus fragment as 8th century B.C."

Paper-like substance made from the internal "pulp" of the Papyrus reed mixed with water, flattened, and dried

55. Function

"This layer of the city of Jericho had both a functioning spring and grain stored from a recent harvest (Joshua 3:15)."

Working; something that does what is needed

56. Protracted

"It means that the city was prepared for a protracted siege."

Lengthy; long in duration

57. Utensils

"The fire includes houses and utensils in the homes which were considered valuable."

Tools or other items used to perform tasks

58. Fortifications

"The bricks of the outer fortifications are piled on top of each other (they fell down flat)."

Walls, towers, or other structures designed to protect something from attack or prevent entry

59. Collapse

"There is one section of the wall, wide enough for a house, which did not collapse at the same time the rest of the wall collapsed."

Fall down; lose structural integrity

60. Calculate

"Since ^{14}C dates are primarily calculated from artifacts found in tombs or buried in the destruction of a city, the accuracy of the ^{14}C dates depends on the age of the material (often wood) used in making the artifact."

Arrived at by mathematical processes

61. Assumption

"It is a reasonable assumption that all ^{14}C dates older than 3100 BC (^{14}C tested date) are actual dates from 2200 to 2350 BC."

A conclusion reached based on comparing different kinds of evidence but not definitely known to be the final truth about the matter due to possible conflicting factors

(The following sentence contains the words listed in 62-63 below.)

"Understand that in addition to the potential problems listed in this section there are many highly technical issues which must be taken into account to make a radiocarbon date accurate."

62. Potential

Things that may come to pass and affect an outcome

63. Technical

Based on or relying on detailed, difficult elements to accomplish a purpose

64. Exception

"^{14}C results for a given sample are, with significant exceptions, the same worldwide."

Something that does not follow a normal rule or keep within an expected set of conditions

65. Elongate

"Lower amounts of environmental ^{14}C 'stretch' or elongate ^{14}C dates."

Cause to be more lengthy

66. Equilibrium

"Even today, the environmental ^{14}C is not in complete equilibrium."

Stable; not varying or subject to change

67. Correlate

"Understanding these limits, these relative dates can be used to correlate artifacts worldwide."

Establish relationships, similarities, or connections between

68. Contemporaneous

"All of the cultures described in this section were contemporaneous."

Existing during the same time period

69. Nomadic

"Based on ^{14}C evidence, some nomadic groups traveled throughout the earth just decades after leaving the Ark."

Traveling periodically or constantly to seek food for themselves or livestock, or generally more favorable living conditions

70. Outcast

"Perhaps they were outcasts."

Driven away from society for unknown reasons

71. Occupation

"Like Australia, Oceania, and the Americas, there are abundant fragments of human occupation in Sub-Saharan Africa which date from this period."

Living in a certain place

72. Technology

"There is considerable disagreement whether the distinctive Clovis spearhead represents a unified people or a technology adopted by many different peoples."

Using experience, knowledge, and tools to create things

(The following sentence contains the words listed in 73-75 below.)

"Unlike Africa, the Americas, Australia, and Oceania there are remains of agricultural implements, animals which were domesticated, buildings, structures, clothing, plumbing with pipe and thousands of other objects."

73. Agricultural

Related to controlling, cultivating, and improving living and growing things – plants and/or animals

74. Implement

Device that makes work easier – tool or equipment

75. Domesticated

Animals trained and conditioned from a wild to a tame state and serving some purpose such as providing companionship, performing work, or providing food

76. Dynasty

"The Yellow Emperor might have ruled over the Xia dynasty."

Cultural division defining a certain type of rule – a single family or group following similar practices or evidencing a unified government distinct from earlier or later governments

77. Transfer

"If he is not a just ruler, then *The Mandate of Heaven* is transferred to someone else who is responsible to be a just ruler."

Taken from one person and given to another

78. Tribal

"Like the Indus Valley, Mesopotamia, Egypt, and Europe, there were many tribal wars."

Groups of people who are usually related by blood or marriage banding together for mutual benefit or in opposition to other such groups

79. Monument

"Large monuments, buildings, farm implements, canals, and many other evidences of civilization exist throughout Europe for very early civilizations."

Structures set up to communicate some type of message – e.g., honor a ruler, commemorate an event, or display information or laws

80. Warfare

"This shows that the concept of warfare is as old as civilization."

Battling for control of land or people or against theft or subjugation

(The following sentence contains the words listed in 81-84 below.)

"Now, this has the form of a myth, but really signifies a declination of the bodies moving around the earth and in the heavens, and a great conflagration of things upon the earth recurring at long intervals of time: when this happens, those who live upon the mountains and in dry and lofty places are more liable to destruction than those who dwell by rivers or on the sea-shore; and from this calamity the Nile, who is our never-failing savior, saves and delivers us."

81. Conflagration

Large burning; fire

82. Declination

Irregular movements of heavenly bodies adversely affecting the earth

83. Calamity

Disaster, castastrophe

84. Liable

likely

(The following sentence contains the words listed in 85-86 below.)

"When, on the other hand, the gods purge the earth with a deluge of water, among you herdsmen and shepherds on the mountains are the survivors, whereas those of you who live in cities are carried by the rivers into the sea; but in this country neither at that time nor at any other does the water come from above on the fields, having always a tendency to come up from below, for which reason the things preserved here are said to be the oldest."

85. Purge

Process designed to get rid of impurities (in this context the gods are punishing or destroying people for being wicked or otherwise polluting the earth)

86. Tendency

Inclination to do things a certain way

(The following sentence contains the words listed in 87-89 below.)

"And whatever happened either in your country or in ours, or in any other region of which we are informed--if any action which is noble or great, or in any other way remarkable has taken place, all that has been written down of old, and is preserved in our temples; whereas you and other nations are just being provided with letters and the other things which States require; and then, at the usual period, the stream from heaven descends like a pestilence, and leaves only those of you who are destitute of letters and education; and thus you have to begin all over again as children, and know nothing of what happened in ancient times, either among us or among yourselves."

87. Remarkable

Worthy of notice or preservation

88. Pestilence

Widespread deadly disease

89. Destitute

Having nothing; completely without (in this context it refers to being illiterate)

90. Regard

“Secular historians regard Egyptian records as the oldest and most reliable in the history of the world.”

Consider, think of

91. Inconsistencies

“Egyptologists began to realize traditional chronology had serious issues when inconsistencies with Assyrian and Hittite discoveries surfaced.”

Things that could not be reconciled; disagreements

92. Astronomical

“Egyptian chronology also contradicts astronomical records.”

Based on stars or celestial references

93. Inquiry

“History is the Greek word for inquiry.”

Asking questions or investigating

94. Linguistic

“This does not rule out that they are the same man, just that there is no direct linguistic connection.”

Based on language; meaning or grammatical structure

95. Comparison

“Since God did not give us a chronology of Mizraim (Egypt), the lifespan of Arphaxad is used as a rough comparison by generation.”

Examining two or more things for similarities

(The following sentence contains the words listed in 96-98 below.)

“The Egyptians were formerly addicted to different customs, and despised one another’s sacred and accustomed rites, and were very angry one with another on that account, Abram conferred with each of them, and, confuting the reasonings they made use of, every one for their own practices, demonstrated that such reasonings were vain and void of truth: whereupon he was admired by them in those conferences as a very wise man, and one of great sagacity, when he discoursed on any subject he undertook; and this not only in understanding it, but in persuading other men also to assent to him."

96. Addict

Unable to stop doing something

97. Demonstrate

Showed and convinced by example

98. Conference

Talking to a group on subjects important to all members

(The following sentence contains the words listed in 99-100 below.)

"When king Al-Aziz Othman, son of [Saladdin] succeeded his father, he let himself be persuaded by some people from his Court, who were devoid of good sense, to demolish the pyramids.

99. Devoid

Empty; having none

100. Demolish

Completely destroy

101. Expensive

"... As they are the most expensive monuments in human history, we do not know why they were built."

Costing a great amount of money

102. Magnified.

"But beginning with the Persian period and moving backwards in time, these differences are increasingly magnified."

Become greater in size or significance

103. Variation

"There are variations in writing style, materials used such as composition of the inks, the content of the various documents."

Differences; things that are not alike

(The following sentence contains the words listed in 105-106 below.)

"James Breasted did a monumental work of comparing every available record on Egypt and synthesized a comprehensive modern Egyptian chronology."

104. Monumental

Huge; very large in scope and significance

105. Synthesize

Combined separate elements to make a cohesive whole

106 reliable

"Though they are not perfect, they do establish a reliable standard."

Something that can be depended on

107. Impression

"A scribe with a stick which had one end carved into a shape known today as a wedge would make impressions in the soft clay."

Dent or mark

108. Abundance

"This brought an abundance of food and the specialization of labor."

Great quantity

109. Reference

"The earliest human records, the *Epic of Gilgamesh*, the *Bible* and various Egyptian records such as the *Books of the Dead* not only record warfare, but reference warfare as something older than human writing and memory."

Talk about; describe as

110. Symbol

"Though he had many symbols, he was especially known by the dragon with the forked tongue."

Something that represents, characterizes, or stands for something else

111. Structure

"The smallest might only house a dozen people while a large structure might hold hundreds."

Man-made building

112. Cistern

"Sometime it was only a cistern, but usually a well."

Large cup-shaped construction that catches rainwater

113. Ceremony

"While the priests performing the burial ceremony might have read these aloud, the words were written for the deceased Pharaoh to say to Spirits in the underworld."

Ritual or specific set of practices followed for a specific reason; in this case, to honor and lay to rest the dead

III. References, Endnotes, Expanded Study and Appendix Materials

A. References to Outside Sources

Notes to the Reader (Teacher Edition only notes are marked by letters of the alphabet, and student edition notes by numbers.)

a. *The Book of Jubilees* (link to the text note "Source of Jubilees Authority") translated by R. H. Charles, published by the Society for Promoting Christian Knowledge, London, 1917.
(Note: To return to the text, just click the link in the "footnote/reference above.)
http://wesley.nnu.edu/index.php?id=2127
The *Book of Jubilees* from "The Apocrypha and Pseudepigrapha of the Old Testament" R.H. Charles Oxford: Clarendon Press, 1913

b. More Information on the *Book of Jasher*
Also called *Sepher HaYasher* Referenced Joshua 10:13, 2 Samuel 1:18, and 2 Timothy 3:8 (The reference to Jannes and Jambres as Egyptians who withstood Moses is also made in the *Book of Jasher*)
Copyright Ken Johnson 2013 Biblefacts Edition
http://biblefacts.org/creation/Jasher_intro.pdf
Also;

Salt Lake City, J.H. Parry and Company, 1887. http://www.sacred-texts.com/chr/apo/jasher/

We intentionally provide multiple sources for The *Book Jasher*. See the *Jewish Encyclopedia* 1906 edition http://www.jewishencyclopedia.com/articles/8526-jasher-book-of for a history of various editions of The *Book of Jasher*. Ken Johnson takes the position that it is the actual book referenced in the OT, whereas the Jewish Encyclopedia accepts it simply as ancient Jewish tradition to which the name "*Book of Jasher*" was later appended. This latter is the position of the *Conflict of the Ages* series in referencing the *Book of Jasher*.

The *Book of Jasher* is quoted in many ancient sources. It is not inspired and contains errors, so it must be read with caution. It contains ancient Jewish traditions on the same order as Josephus' *Antiquities of the Jews*, the *Sedar Olam, the Cave of Treasures, The Book of the Bee,* and the *Book of Jubilees*. It is probably more reliable than the *Talmuds, the Book of Enoch,* or the *Midrash,* because it is older. It is almost certainly not the *Book of Jasher* quoted in the Old Testament.

The following is from the introduction of Ken Johnson's 2013 edition of the *Book of Jasher*.

> How can we be sure this is the real *Jasher* and not a forgery from the Middle Ages?
>
> There have been at least two forgeries. One is an ethical treatise from the Middle Ages and does not exist in English currently, as far as I know. It is somewhat Gnostic in style beginning with a section on the mystery of creation. A second forgery was published in AD 1829, supposedly translated by Flaccus Albinus Alcuinus. These two are nowhere near the caliber of this *Book of Jasher* and both are missing the information that Scripture tells us is in the real *Book of Jasher*. This is the only *Jasher* that corresponds to what Scripture says it contains. Much of the extra information contained in *Jasher* can also be found in the Babylonian Talmud, the Mishna, and Ginzberg's *Legends of the Jews*. There are numerous quotes showing Rabbi Eliazar used this *Book of Jasher* extensively in the first century AD. The Mishna was completed about AD 200, and the Talmud about AD 800. We can know for a fact that the Mishna and Talmud used this *Book of Jasher* as a source document and not the other way around. Also, since the Ancient Seder Olam was written in about AD 169 and references Jasher, we know the *Book of Jasher* was used by other historians in the second century AD.
>
> "Now as Jannes and Jambres withstood Moses, so do these also resist the truth: men of corrupt minds,

reprobate concerning the faith. But they shall proceed no further: for their folly shall be manifest unto all men, as theirs also was." 2 Timothy 3:8-9

"And when they had gone Pharaoh sent for Balaam the magician and to Jannes and Jambres his sons, and to all the magicians and conjurors and counsellors which belonged to the king, and they all came and sat before the king... And Aaron hastened and threw the rod out of his hand before Pharaoh and before his servants, and the rod turned into a serpent." Jasher 79:27,36

The Ancient Seder Olam is another Hebrew history book (not mentioned by Scripture) that dates from about AD 169. It records that Rabbi Eliezer was the most accurate when figuring dates and festivals because he used the Ancient *Book of Jasher* as the best source for his history. This tells us Jasher was in use and very well known in the first century AD. See chapter 4 of Ancient Seder Olam for details.

What is the history behind the *Book of Jasher*?

According to rabbinic legend, the *Book of Jasher* and several other ancient non-biblical Hebrew texts were brought from Jerusalem to Spain after the fall of Jerusalem in AD 70. One of the officers of Titus, Sidrus by name, was a believer in the God of the Hebrews. He made sure several sacred texts made it out of Jerusalem and into the Spanish city of Sevilia for safe keeping. The Sephardic rabbinate kept the texts safe. In the year AD 1613, the first official printed Hebrew copy of the *Book of Jasher* was published in Venice, Italy. The first translation from the Hebrew version of *Jasher* into English was completed in AD 1840.

Has the text been corrupted over the centuries?

The ancient scrolls of this book were in poor condition when the book was printed in Hebrew in 1613.

It is true that the Mormon publishing house, *J. H. Parry and Company,* first published the 1840 English translation of Jasher in 1887.

Mormonism has long been fascinated with the *Book of Jasher*, but it is not officially recommended because some portions of *Jasher* contradict Mormon teaching. http://biblefacts.org/creation/Jasher_intro.pdf

The reviewer who stated that the "*Book of Jasher* is not authentic. What is being cited is an 18th century forgery..." provided the following link. http://www.gotquestions.org/book-of-Jasher.html

The first four paragraphs of this link are very helpful and filled with useful information. That is followed by dogmatic, unsupported, gratuitous assertions. It simply asserts without any evidence that "It is an eighteenth-century forgery that alleges to be a translation of the "lost" *Book of Jasher* by Alcuin, an eighteenth-century English scholar."

The *Jewish Encyclopedia* 1906 edition frequently quotes from the *Book of Jasher*. It is often quoted with the *Book of Enoch*.

> "In the compiling of the work the following sources were made use of, namely: the Babylonian Talmud; Bereshit Rabbah; Pirke R. Eliezer; the Yalkut; the Chronicle of Moses; Yosippon; Midrash Abkir; and various Arabic legends. As to the place and time of the work's origin various legendary accounts are given in the preface of the first edition (Naples, 1552).
>
> Modern Translations:
>
> In 1750 the London printer Thomas Ilive issued an English translation of the work, asserting that he had published the real "Book of Yashar" mentioned in the Bible; and in 1828 the London "Courier" (Nov. 8) reported that a man from Gazan in Persia, by name Alcurin (Noah has "Alcuin"), had discovered the book named after Joshua, and brought it with him to London. Eleven days later (Nov. 19) a Jew of Liverpool named Samuel reported in the same paper that he was working on a translation of this work, which he had obtained in North Africa. Zunz thereupon found himself compelled to assert, in the "Berliner Nachrichten" of Nov. 29, 1828, that the work mentioned was the same as that published in Naples in 1552 or 1613; and in his "Gottesdienstliche Vorträge," 1832, the same author declared that the book originated in Spain in the twelfth century. That Italy, however, was the land of its origin seems evident from the author's knowledge of Italian names, as Tuscany, Lombardy, and the Tiber (x. 7-36), and also from the description of the rape of the Sabines (xvii. 1-14). The appearance of Arabic names, such as Sa'id, Allah, Abdallah, and Khalif, only tends to show that the book was written in southern Italy, where Arabic influence was strongly felt even in the eleventh century.

The "Yashar" has appeared in the following editions: Naples, 1552; Venice, 1625; Cracow, 1628; Prague, 1668; Frankfort-on-the-Main, 1706; Amsterdam, 1707; Constantinople, 1728; Fürth, 1768; Koretz, 1785; Frankfort-on-the-Oder, 1789; Grodno, 1795; Lemberg, 1816 and 1840; Warsaw, 1846; Wilna, 1848; Lemberg, 1850; Wilna, 1852; Warsaw, 1858. It was translated into Judæo-German by Jacob ha-Levi, and published with various annotations and Arabic glosses (Frankfort-on-the-Main, 1674; Sulzbach, 1783). A Latin version by Johann G. Abicht appeared in Leipsic in the middle of the eighteenth century under the title "Dissertatio de Libro Recti." The work was first translated into English by Thomas Ilive, as mentioned above, and later by M. M. Noah under the title "The Book of Yashar" (New York, 1840). http://www.jewishencyclopedia.com/articles/15067-yashar-sefer-ha

c. *Civilization Past and Present* (Both quotes are from the prologue.) Single volume Fourth edition T. Walter Wallbank Emeritus Professor of History, University of Southern California Alastair M. Taylor Professor of Political Studies and Geography, Queen's University Nels M. Bailkey Professor of History, Tulane University Copyright 1962, 1967, 1971 Scott, Foresman and Company Glenview, Illinois

d. [credit for graphic quote] Tharpar, Romila. *Frontline* magazine Volume 18, Issue 19, Sep. 15-28, 2001.

e. From Plato's Dialogue *Phaedrus,* Translated by Benjamin Jowett, 1871.

f. Plutarch, from his *Life of Lycurgus,* translated by John Dryden and others, 1683.

g. New Advent article: "Hammurabi"
http://www.newadvent.org/cathen/07125a.htm

h. 101 evidences for a young age of the earth and the universe by Don Batten Published: 4 June 2009
http://creation.com/age-of-the-earth
The 10 Best Evidences from Science that Confirm a Young Earth September 6, 2012; last featured October 2, 2012
https://answersingenesis.org/evidence-for-creation/the-10-best-evidences-from-science-that-confirm-a-young-earth/
See also Ch 14 What Does the Scientific Evidence Prove? At the end of the book.

i. *Special Note: Wikipedia* is easily the most common online source. One of our reviewers said, "*Wikipedia* is not a scholarly source, and it is always in a state of flux. So I strongly recommend against citing. Students who rely on your work for school projects will be penalized if they cite *Wiki.*"

While this is true, it is only one side of the coin. *Wikipedia* is first and foremost an encyclopedia and an encyclopedia is a poor source for citing in a paper. But encyclopedias are an excellent place to begin your research. Here is what one well-respected secular source, *livescience,* said about *Wikipedia.*

> "In 2005, the peer-reviewed journal *Nature* asked scientists to compare *Wikipedia's* scientific articles to those in *Encyclopaedia Britannica* "the most scholarly of encyclopedias," according to its own Wiki page. The comparison resulted in a tie; both references contained four serious errors among the 42 articles analyzed by experts.
>
> And last year, a study published in the *Journal of Clinical Oncology* found that *Wikipedia* had the same level of accuracy and depth in its articles about 10 types of cancer as the *Physician Data Query*, a professionally-edited database maintained by the National Cancer Institute.
>
> The self-described "free encyclopedia that anyone can edit" has fared similarly well in most other studies comparing its accuracy to conventional encyclopedias, including studies by *The Guardian, PC Pro, Library Journal, the Canadian Library Association*, and several peer-reviewed academic studies.
>
> Still, because anyone can edit *Wikipedia* entries, they "can easily be undermined through malice or ignorance," noted *BBC* technology commentator Bill Thompson. http://www.livescience.com/32950-how-accurate-is-wikipedia.html

j. 1999 online lecture at http://www.hawking.org.uk/does-god-play-dice.html and transcribed in *The Nature of Space and Time* (1996) by Stephen Hawking and Roger Penrose, p. 26

k. *Scientific Naturalism as Science* by Larry Vardiman, Ph.D. *Larry Vardiman, Ph.D. 1997. Scientific Naturalism as Science. Acts & Facts. 26 (11).* http://www.icr.org/article/422/
(Dr. Vardiman is Chairman of the Astro/Geophysics Department at ICR.)

l. *Rules For Interpretation,* Dr. David L. Cooper, *Biblical Research Monthly* 1947, 1949 http://www.biblicalresearch.info/page7.html This common quote might be older, but it is the oldest source we could find.

m. *Rightly Dividing the Word of Truth,* Michael J. Findley, *August 6, 2012,* from our blog *Elk Jerky for the Soul.* https://findleyfamilyvideopublications.com/2012/08/06/rightly-dividing-the-word-of-truth/

n. *The Orthodox Jewish Bible*, completed by Phillip Goble in 2002, is an English language version that applies Yiddish and Hasidic cultural expressions to the Messianic Bible. Copyright Information: The Orthodox Jewish Bible fourth edition, OJB. Copyright 2002,2003,2008,2010, 2011 by Artists for Israel International. All rights reserved. http://www.biblegateway.com/versions/Orthodox-Jewish-Bible-OJB/

o. Michael Oard, *Frozen in Time: The Wooly Mammoth, The Ice Age and the Bible,* Green Forest, AR: Master Books, Inc., 2004.

p. The North Ronaldsay sheep pictured in the main text are important for two reasons: 1. The Wikimedia Commons captioning on the photo claims the following: "The sheep are a special breed which has evolved to eat seaweed. All access to the shore is fenced to stop them getting onto pastures as their digestive systems cannot cope with grass." Millions of living things have adapted to local living conditions but there is no evolution taking place. No new species has emerged. These sheep have simply changed to eat what is available to them. 2. The seaweed these sheep eat has a much higher ^{13}C content than grass. This likely means that upon death the ^{14}C in their bodies will be different from grass-eating sheep, and therefore yield different results should the remains be tested. This is just one evidence that ^{14}C dating requires correction and caution if it is used as a dating method.

q. Example article for more ^{14}C dating information https://answersingenesis.org/geology/carbon-14/carbon-14-dating/

r. Example article of Dendrochronology problems http://creation.com/tree-ring-dating-dendrochronology

s Lower amount of ^{14}C in the past https://answersingenesis.org/geology/carbon-14/doesnt-carbon-14-dating-disprove-the-bible/

t. Dating the founding of Carthage http://www.varchive.org/nldag/carthage.htm

u. Johannes van der Plicht1 • Hendrik J Bruins2 • Albert J Nijboer3 THE IRON AGE AROUND THE MEDITERRANEAN: A HIGH CHRONOLOGY PERSPECTIVE FROM THE GRONINGEN

RADIOCARBON DATABASE RADIOCARBON, Vol 51, Nr 1, 2009, p 213–242 © 2009 by the Arizona Board of Regents on behalf of the University of Arizona Celebrating 50 Years of Radiocarbon

v.
http://en.wikipedia.org/wiki/Chronology_of_the_ancient_Near_East
This general *Wikipedia* article contains a brief statement of a well-know fact. "Radiocarbon dates run one or two centuries earlier than the dates proposed by archaeologists." It is usually more verbose in academic journals, but it is the same fact. In this case *Wikipedia* accurately states the problem.

w. Carbon dating shows ancient Egypt's rapid expansion 00:01 04 September 2013 by Jo Marchant
http://www.newscientist.com/article/dn24145-carbon-dating-shows-ancient-egypts-rapid-expansion.html#.U4d5y_ldUjo

x. ^{14}C dates for flood fossils
https://answersingenesis.org/geology/carbon-14/7-carbon-14-in-fossils-coal-and-diamonds/

y. A three-part series by Dr. Snelling
http://www.answersingenesis.org/articles/am/v5/n4/carbon-dating
http://www.answersingenesis.org/articles/am/v6/n1/carbon-14

z. Radiocarbon level assumption dating
http://www.answersingenesis.org/articles/am/v6/n2/creationist-puzzle
Dendrochronology and ^{14}C
http://creation.com/tree-ring-dating-dendrochronology
Carbon-14 Dating explained in everyday terms
http://creation.com/carbon-14-dating-explained-in-everyday-terms
http://creation.com/much-inflated-carbon-14-dates-from-subfossil-trees-a-new-mechanism
http://www.icr.org/article/young-earth-creation-flood-14¢
http://www.icr.org/article/carbon-14-evidence-for-recent-global/

3. Main Text

1. The Annals of the World "The Origin of Time, and Continued to the Beginning of the Emperor Vespasian's Reign and the Total Destruction and Abolition of the Temple and Commonwealth of the Jews." by James Ussher 1650. From the Internet Sacred Text Archive, managed by John Bruno Hare.

2. Flavius Josephus *Antiquities of the Jews , Book I,* Translated by William Whiston, 1737. From the Internet Sacred Text Archive, managed by John Bruno Hare.

3. Ice Age timeline https://answersingenesis.org/environmental-science/ice-age/where-does-the-ice-age-fit/

4. (emphasis added), *The Chronology of Ancient Kingdoms Amended* printed posthumously by J. Tonson, J. Osborn and T. Longman. 1728, London, England

5 From Ussher: "The Second Age of the World: 1657a AM, 2366 JP, 2348 BC by James Ussher, Archbishop of Armagh Church of Ireland, printed in London 1658

6. Josephus on Genesis 10 http://www.answersingenesis.org/articles/aid/v4/n1/josephus-and-genesis-chapter-ten

7. Josephus *Antiquities* 5:1

8. Giza Boat excavations http://www.bluffton.edu/~sullivanm/egypt/giza/boat/boat.html

9. *Clark's Foreign Theological Library* Keil and Delitszch (Multivolume Series) 1867ff Edinburgh T and T Clark, George Street Keil & Delitzsch Commentary on the Old Testament Johann (C.F.) Keil (1807-1888) & Franz Delitzsch (1813-1890)

10. (Josephus Antiquities 4:2)

11. Graphic of Nimrod's influence on the god-king myth contains reduced images that are sourced where they appear larger in other locations throughout the work.

12. The *Book of Jubilees,* x:28-34, translated by R. H. Charles, published by the Society for Promoting Christian Knowledge, London, 1917.

13 *Seder Olam* or *Seder Olam Rabbah* (The Hebrew words mean "The Great Order of the World") Tradition says that Rabbi Yose ben Halafta wrote the *Seder Olam* approximately 160 AD. Written in Hebrew, it begins with Creation and ends with Alexander the Great. The exact dates are not certain. English Translation of the *Seder Olam*
http://www.betemunah.org/sederolam.html

14 Clary, T. 2013 "Hot Mantle Initiated Flood Beginnings." Acts&Facts 42(8):15

15. "Computer Modeling of the Large Scale Tectonics Associated With the Genesis Flood" John R. Baumgardner, Ph.D. 1965 Camino Redondo Los Alamos, NM 87544 Presented at the Third International Conference on Creationism Pittsburgh, PA, July 18-23, 1994

16. Tower of Babel Location https://answersingenesis.org/tower-of-babel/where-in-the-world-is-the-tower-of-babel/

17. Archaeologists on ^{14}C dating http://creation.com/timing-is-everything "Timing is everything" A talk with field archaeologist David Down by Tas Walker, Steve Cardno and Jonathan Sarfati Archaeological Diggings (Australia) for publishing details, editor@diggings.com.au

18. A Guide to the Dead Sea Scrolls and Related Literature. By Joseph A. Fitzmyer 2008 Wm. B. Eerdmans Publishing, Grand Rapids Michigan

19. Walls of Jericho http://creation.com/the-walls-of-jericho

20. Diamond, Coal, and Fossil dating http://creation.com/diamonds-a-creationists-best-friend https://legacy-cdn-assets.answersingenesis.org/assets/pdf/am/v7/n4/Thousands-Not-Billions-ch3-carbon14.pdf

21. *Timaeus* by Plato Written 360 B.C.E Translated by Benjamin Jowett

22. Egyptian radiocarbon dating https://answersingenesis.org/archaeology/ancient-egypt/radiocarbon-dating-shortens-the-timeline-for-ancient-egypt/

23. Sothic Theory https://answersingenesis.org/archaeology/ancient-egypt/fall-of-the-sothic-theory-egyptian-chronology-revisited/

24. An Account of Egypt by Herodotus being the second book of his histories called Euterpe translated by G.C. Macaulay, New York, 1890.

25. Beginning of Egyptian History https://answersingenesis.org/archaeology/ancient-egypt/doesnt-egyptian-chronology-prove-bible-unreliable/

26. Josephus *Antiquities* Book 1:8:2

27. transl. SACY, Description de l'Egypte IX, 468 [French linguist and orientalist Antoine-Isaac Silvestre de Sacy (1758-1838) wrote Description of Egypt in French, from which this description is taken.

.28. Shortened timeline https://answersingenesis.org/archaeology/ancient-egypt/radiocarbon-dating-shortens-the-timeline-for-ancient-egypt/

http://dendro.cornell.edu/articles/manning2006a.pdf

29. Reconciling Egyptian timeline https://answersingenesis.org/archaeology/ancient-egypt/a-correct-chronology/

30. Patriarchs and Sumerian kings list https://answersingenesis.org/bible-history/the-antediluvian-patriarchs-and-the-sumerian-king-list/

31. The World of Ancient Times, Carl Roebuck 1966 Charles Scribner and Sons New York, NY

32. Abraham and the Chronology of Ancient Mesopotamia https://answersingenesis.org/bible-timeline/abraham-and-the-chronology-of-ancient-mesopotamia/

33. by Robert Bowie Johnson Jr. https://answersingenesis.org/bible-characters/adam-and-eve/athena-and-eve/

34. Ancient Harappan cities and houses http://mrholmes.pbworks.com/w/page/23951472/Alec-Jake-Ancient%20indian%20architecture

Appendix material

35. Oliver J. Thatcher, ed., Translated by Rev. F. C. Cook (1901) The Library of Original Sources (Milwaukee: University Research Extension Co., 1907), Vol. I: The Ancient World, pp. 79-83.

36. The Pyramid Texts Translation by Samuel A. B. Mercer Professor Emeritus of Semitic Languages and Egyptology Trinity College in the University of Toronto LONGMANS, GREEN & CO.NEW YORK, LONDON, TORONTO 1952 from Internet Sacred Texts Archive. http://www.sacred-texts.com/index.htm

37. Tale of the Shipwrecked Sailor Source: Eva March Tappan, ed., The World's Story: A History of the World in Story, Song and Are, (Boston: Houghton Mifflin, 1914), Vol. III: Egypt, Africa, and Arabia, trans. W. K. Flinders Petrie, pp. 41-46. Scanned by: J. S. Arkenberg, Dept. of History, Cal. State Fullerton. Prof. Arkenberg has modernized the text. Read more: http://www.touregypt.net/shipwreckedsailor.htm#ixzz37OjicVQl

38. *The Burden of Isis*: Being the Lament of Isis and Nephthys translated from the Egyptian with an introduction by James Teackle Dennis London: John Murray, Albemarle Street, W. 1st Edition March 1910 Reprinted July 1918 Scanned at sacred-texts.com, May

2002, J.B. Hare, redactor. This text is in the public domain.

39. *Enuma Elish: The Epic of Creation* L. W. King, Translator (from The Seven Tablets of Creation, London 1902) Scanned at sacred-texts.com, May 2002, J.B. Hare, redactor. This text is in the public domain.
A more complete etext of the Seven Tablets of Creation is also available here: http://www.gutenberg.org/files/9914/9914-h/9914-h.htm

40. Sargon inscription
http://www.sacred-texts.com/ane/rp/rp201/rp20111.htm

Bibliography

———— answersingenesis.org (various unsigned articles)

———— www.bluffton.edu

———— creation.com (various unsigned articles)

———— newadvent.org

———— pbworks.com

———— http://www.sacred-texts.com

———— varchive.org

———— wikipedia.org

Batten, Don. *101 Evidences for a Young Age of the Earth and the Universe* 4 June 2009 http://creation.com/age-of-the-earth

Baumgardner, John R. Ph.D. "Computer Modeling of the Large Scale Tectonics Associated With the Genesis Flood" 1965 Camino Redondo Los Alamos, NM 87544 Presented at the *Third International Conference on Creationism* Pittsburgh, PA, July 18-23, 1994 Creation Science Fellowship, Inc. Pittsburgh, PA

ben Halafta, Yose, Rabbi *Seder Olam* or *Seder Olam Rabbah* (The Hebrew words mean "The Great Order of the World") trad. date approximately 160 AD. English Translation of the Seder Olam http://www.betemunah.org/sederolam.html

Charles, R. H., trans. *The Book of Jubilees*. Society for Promoting Christian Knowledge, London, 1917. Also *The Book of Jubilees* from "The Apocrypha and Pseudepigrapha of the Old Testament" R.H. Charles Oxford: Clarendon Press, 1913

Clark, T and T, and George Street. *Clark's Foreign Theological Library, Keil and Delitszch* (Multivolume Series) 1867ff Edinburgh Keil & Delitzsch Commentary on the Old Testament Johann (C.F.) Keil (1807-1888) & Franz Delitzsch (1813-1890)

Clary, T. 2013 "Hot Mantle Initiated Flood Beginnings." *Acts&Facts* 42(8):15

Cooper, Dr. David L. "Rules For Interpretation." *Biblical Research Monthly* 1947, 1949 http://www.biblicalresearch.info/page7.html

de Sacy, Antoine-Isaac Silvestre. *Description de l'Egypte IX,* 468 [French linguist and orientalist Antoine-Isaac Silvestre de Sacy (1758-1838)

Dennis, James Teackle, trans., intro. *The Burden of Isis: Being the Lament of Isis and Nephthys* London: John Murray, Albemarle Street, W. 1st Edition March 1910 Reprinted July 1918 Scanned at sacred-texts.com, May 2002, J.B. Hare, redactor. This text is in the public domain.

Dryden, John and others, trans. Plutarch, from his *Life of Lycurgus,* 1683.

Findley, Michael J., "Rightly Dividing the Word of Truth." August 6, 2012, *Elk Jerky for the Soul.* https://findleyfamilyvideopublications.com/2012/08/06/rightly-dividing-the-word-of-truth/

Fitzmyer, Joseph A. *A Guide to the Dead Sea Scrolls and Related Literature.* Wm. B. Eerdmans Publishing, Grand Rapids Michigan, 2008.

Goble, Phillip. *The Orthodox Jewish Bible* completed 2002. Fourth edition, OJB. Copyright 2002,2003,2008,2010, 2011 by Artists for Israel International. All rights reserved. http://www.biblegateway.com/versions/Orthodox-Jewish-Bible-OJB/

Hawking, Stephen, Roger Penrose. "Does God Play Dice With the Universe?" 1999 online lecture at http://www.hawking.org.uk/does-god-play-dice.html and transcribed in *The Nature of Space and Time* (1996).

Johnson, Ken. *The Book of Jasher* (Also called Sepher HaYasher) Copyright Ken Johnson 2013 Biblefacts Edition http://biblefacts.org/creation/Jasher_intro.pdf also Salt Lake City, J.H. Parry and Company, 1887. http://www.sacred-texts.com/chr/apo/jasher/

Josephus Flavius. *Antiquities of the Jews, Book I,* Trans. William Whiston, 1737. From the Internet Sacred Text Archive, managed by John Bruno Hare.

Jowett, Benjamin, trans. Plato's Dialogue *Phaedrus,* 1871.

King, L. W. Translator. *Enuma Elish: The Epic of Creation* (from *The Seven Tablets of Creation,* London 1902) Scanned at sacred-texts.com, May 2002, J.B. Hare, redactor. This text is in the public domain. A more complete etext of the Seven Tablets of Creation is also available here: http://www.gutenberg.org/files/9914/9914-h/9914-h.htm

Marchant, Jo. "Carbon dating shows ancient Egypt's rapid expansion." 00:01 04 September 2013 by http://www.newscientist.com/article/dn24145-carbon-dating-shows-ancient-egypts-rapid-expansion.html#.U4d5y_ldUjo

Mercer, Samuel A. B., trans., *The Pyramid Texts* (Professor Emeritus of Semitic Languages and Egyptology Trinity College in the University of Toronto) LONGMANS, GREEN & CO.NEW YORK, LONDON, TORONTO 1952 from Internet Sacred Texts Archive.

Oard, Michael. *Frozen in Time: The Wooly Mammoth, The Ice Age and the Bible,* Green Forest, AR: Master Books, Inc., 2004.

Roebuck, Carl. *The World of Ancient Times.* Charles Scribner and Sons New York, NY, 1966.

Snelling, Andrew. 3-Part Series on Carbon-14 Dating *Answers Magazine* September 14, 2010; last featured March 30, 2011.

_____. "Evidence of the Continental Divide." http://www.icr.org/ecp/

Tappan, Eva March ed. "Tale of the Shipwrecked Sailor." *The World's Story: A History of the World in Story, Song and Are,* (Boston: Houghton Mifflin, 1914), Vol. III: Egypt, Africa, and Arabia, trans. W. K. Flinders Petrie, Scanned by: J. S. Arkenberg, Dept. of History, Cal. State Fullerton. Prof. Arkenberg has modernized the text. http://www.touregypt.net/shipwreckedsailor.htm#ixzz37OjicVQl

Tharpar, Romila. *Frontline magazine* Volume 18, Issue 19, Sep. 15-28, 2001.

Thatcher, Oliver J., ed., Translated by Rev. F. C. Cook (1901) *Vol. I: The Ancient World. The Library of Original Sources* (Milwaukee: University Research Extension Co., 1907).

Thompson, Bill, BBC technology commentator."How Accurate Is Wikipedia?" *LiveScience.* http://www.livescience.com/32950-how-accurate-is-wikipedia.html

Tonson, J., J. Osborn, and T. Longman. *The Chronology of Ancient Kingdoms* Amended printed posthumously 1728, London, England

Ussher, James. *The Annals of the World* "The Origin of Time, and Continued to the Beginning of the Emperor Vespasian's Reign and the Total Destruction and Abolition of the Temple and Commonwealth of the Jews." 1650. From the Internet Sacred Text Archive, managed by John Bruno Hare.

van der Plicht, Johannes Hendrik J Bruins Albert J Nijboer. THE IRON AGE AROUND THE MEDITERRANEAN: A HIGH CHRONOLOGY PERSPECTIVE FROM THE GRONINGEN RADIOCARBON DATABASE. *RADIOCARBON*, Vol 51, Nr 1, 2009, p 213–242 © 2009 by the Arizona Board of Regents on behalf of the University of Arizona Celebrating 50 Years of Radiocarbon

Vardiman, Larry Ph.D. "Scientific Naturalism as Science." *Acts & Facts*. 26 (11), 1997. http://www.icr.org/article/422/

Walker, Tas, Steve Cardno, and Jonathan Sarfati. "Timing is everything" A talk with field archaeologist David Down *Archaeological Diggings* (Australia) for publishing details, editor@diggings.com.au.

Wallbank, T. Walter Emeritus Professor of History, University of Southern California Alastair M. Taylor Professor of Political Studies and Geography, Queen's University Nels M. Bailkey Professor of History, Tulane University. *Civilization Past and Present* Single volume Fourth edition Copyright 1962, 1967, 1971 Scott, Foresman and Company Glenview, Illinois.

B. Articles from Elk Jerky For The Soul

1. “What Did Scalia Say and Why Did He Say It?”

“The United States Supreme Court has held that secular humanism is a religion. Belief in evolution is a central tenet of that religion.” Antonin Scalia, in the case Edwards v. Aguillard, U.S. Supreme Court, 1987

This is one of the most hated, denied, and attacked statements on our entire blog. We used it in our *book Antidisestablishmentarianism* in the section “What Is Secular Humanism?” Both are available on Amazon for those interested in the context we provided. For those not interested in reading our book to find out the full context, this blog is a brief explanation of why this statement by Justice Scalia is an accurate statement.

http://www.amazon.com/Antidisestablishmentarianism-Michael-Findley-ebook/dp/B0040V4DOE

http://www.amazon.com/Secular-Humanism-Antidisestablishmentarianism-Serial-Version-ebook/dp/B0087GA7TI

First, here is a link to the entire case *Edwards v Aguillard*. It is available many places. This is just one possibility. It is large and requires a lot of bandwidth.

http://www.law.cornell.edu/supremecourt/text/482/578#writing-USSC_CR_0482_0578_ZD

Second, Justice Scalia wrote a dissenting opinion in this case. If you understand how the SCOTUS works, you will understand that this quote is in the background section of his decision. This is not, in and of itself, either Justice Scalia’s ruling or an opinion. He is simply stating historical background.

Third, Justice Scalia took notes on testimony of Senator Keith. These may or may not be the exact words of Senator Keith. They might be the words of another witness or they might simply be the words of Justice Scalia. They are the notes of Justice Scalia which Justice Scalia entered into the official record. This notes section begins with the following words: “Senator Keith and his witnesses testified essentially as set forth in the following numbered paragraphs:” I have no doubt that both Senator Keith and Justice Scalia believe these words.

Fourth, here is the paragraph in full so that the reader may understand the complete context.

“(5) The censorship of creation science has at least two harmful effects. First, it deprives students of knowledge of one of the two scientific explanations for the origin of life, and leads them to believe that evolution is proven fact; thus, their education suffers, and they are wrongly taught that science has proved their religious beliefs false. Second, it violates the Establishment Clause. The United States Supreme Court has held that secular humanism is a religion. Id. at E-36 (Sen. Keith) (referring to Torcaso v. Watkins, 367 U.S. 488, 495, n. 11 (1961));1 App. E-418 (Sen. Keith); 2 id. at E-499 (Sen. Keith). Belief in evolution is a central tenet of that religion. 1 id. at E-282 (Sen. Keith); id. at E-312 – E-313 (Sen. Keith); id. at E-317 (Sen. Keith); id. at E-418 (Sen. Keith); 2 id. at E-499 (Sen. Keith). Thus, by censoring creation science and instructing students that evolution is fact, public school teachers are now advancing religion in violation of the Establishment Clause. 1 id. at E-2 – E-4 [p625] (Sen. Keith); id. at E-36 – E-37, E-39 (Sen. Keith); id. at E-154 – E-155 (Boudreaux paper); id. at E-281 – E-282 (Sen. Keith); id. at E-313 (Sen. Keith); id. at E-315 – E-316 (Sen. Keith); id. at E-317 (Sen. Keith); 2 id. at E-499 – E-500 (Sen. Keith).”

Emphasis added.

Fifth, Here is the *Torcaso v. Watkins*, 367 US 488 – Supreme Court 1961 case which was referenced by Justice Scalia.

It reads in part:

“The appellant Torcaso was appointed to the office of Notary Public by the Governor of Maryland but was refused a commission to serve because he would not declare his belief in God. He then brought this action in a Maryland Circuit Court to compel issuance of his commission, charging that the State’s requirement that he declare this belief violated “the First and Fourteenth Amendments to the Constitution of the United States . . . ."[1] The Circuit Court rejected these federal constitutional contentions, and the highest court of the State, the Court of Appeals, affirmed...”

The important part is the last words of this next paragraph:

“Appellant also claimed that the State’s test oath requirement violates the provision of Art. VI of the Federal Constitution that “no religious Test shall ever be required as a Qualification to any Office or public Trust under the United States.” Because we are reversing the judgment on other grounds...” (Emphasis added)

You may look up the case for yourself, but the important part is that SCOTUS did not rule on the basis of “no religious test” but instead found Secular Humanism (not using those exact words) to be a religion.

Here is the exact wording of the 1961 ruling;

"This Maryland religious test for public office unconstitutionally invades the appellant's freedom of belief and religion and therefore cannot be enforced against him."

The exact words of SCOTUS;

a refusal to "declare his belief in God" is "the appellant's freedom of belief and religion."

Torcaso v. Watkins, 367 US 488 – Supreme Court 1961

http://scholar.google.com/scholar_case?case=17484916405561277413&q=torcaso+v.+watkins+367+u.s.+488&hl=en&as

Sixth: ""Among religions in this country which do not teach what would generally be considered a belief in the existence of God are Buddhism, Taoism, Ethical Culture, Secular Humanism, and others." *Torcaso v. Watkins*, United States Supreme Court, 1961

This is the same case quoted in point five.

Seventh: Justice Black based his comments on the 1957 case of Fellowship of Humanity v. County of Alameda. In this case an organization of humanists sought a tax exemption on the ground that they used their property "solely and exclusively for religious worship." The court ruled that the activities of Fellowship of Humanity entitled it to an exemption. These activities included weekly Sunday meetings. The Fellowship of Humanity case used the word humanism, not secular humanism.

Eighth: *Torcaso v. Watkins* is just one of hundreds of cases, most of them on state and local court (magistrate) levels. However, the most remarkable feature is the amount of agreement with *Torcaso v. Watkins.*

Ninth: Many Secular Humanist organizations have organized as religions and been granted 501c3 (charitable organization), as a religion.

http://www.irs.gov/Charities-&-Non-Profits/Charitable-Organizations/Exemption-Requirements-Section-501(c)(3)-Organizations

Examples of such organizations are the First Church of Atheism, http://firstchurchofatheism.com/

The American Humanist Association http://americanhumanist.org/

The Church of Reality
http://www.churchofreality.org/wisdom/humanism/

There are many other secular organizations with legal religious status with the IRS. Here are a few of the more well known "statements of belief" or creeds or manifestos. These are not recommended reading, but they are easy to find if you so choose.

A Secular *Humanist Manifesto I, II and III;* Humanist Declaration by CODESH (Council for Democratic Secular Humanism);

A Secular Humanist Manifesto

To repeat:

"The United States Supreme Court has held that secular humanism is a religion. Belief in evolution is a central tenet of that religion." Antonin Scalia, in the case *Edwards v. Aguillard*, U.S. Supreme Court, 1987

As President John Adams said,

"Facts are stubborn things; and whatever may be our wishes, our inclinations, or the dictates of our passion, they cannot alter the state of facts and evidence."

https://findleyfamilyvideopublications.com/2014/04/18/what-did-scalia-say-and-why-did-he-say-it/

The Problem with Dates in History: Hammurabai's Law Code

In 1901-1902 AD a French team excavating in Susa, one of the ancient Capitals of Elam, then Persia, now modern Iran, discovered pieces of a basalt stele. It was completely reconstructed and now sits in the Louve, in Paris. The head of the French team, M. de Morgan used the surroundings where it was found to date the stele, the now famous Law Code of Hammurabi around 1100-1200 BC.

An American/German team headed by the German born American Hermann Hilprecht was excavating in Nippur at the same time. Nippur is in ancient Mesopotamian, an area ruled over by the Assyrians, Babylonians, Persians, Greeks, Ottoman Turks and is now modern Iraq. They found a kings list with the name Hammurabi on it. This list made Hammurabi a ruler in the 24th century, BC. Hermann Hilprecht immediately (January 1903) proclaimed the Hammurabi stele as the oldest law code ever found in a lecture at the University of Pennsylvania.

A book entitled The Oldest Code of Laws in the World, by Hammurabi, King of Babylon was immediately published in early 1903 and is available as an ebook through Project Gutenberg. It proclaims that Hammurabi ruled from 2285-2242 B.C. The forward is by C.H.W. Johns, M.A. of Cambridge. The book was printed in Edinburgh.

Since 1903, several other Sumerian kings lists were discovered. A rather brief but thorough article in the Roman Catholic online encyclopedia New Advent describes the major positions mainstream archeologists take on the time Hammurabi actually ruled. Most 21st century archaeologists hold to some type of a "middle" position, that Hammurabi ruled around 1700 B.C.

It is very important to Liberals and Secular Humanists that the law code of Hammurabi be older than the Law Code of Moses. They insist that the Mosaic Code "evolved" from the lower Hammurabi Code, and that our laws today have "evolved" beyond the Mosaic Code. Since the Law was divinely given by God, it makes no difference if Hammurabi wrote his Law Code before God gave Moses the Law on Sinai. Since God revealed His Law to Noah, Hammurabi's Law code is still a corruption of God's revealed Law. God saw that man had corrupted His Law and needed to reveal it once more in writing to Moses.

If the 1700 date for Hammurabi is correct, then Hammurabi ruled while the Children of Israel were slaves in Egypt. They would remain slaves for another 250+ years before Moses would lead them out.

However, if the original date of M. de Morgan is correct, then Hammurabi's Law Code was written about 250 years after God revealed His Law to Moses on Sinai. While this seems to make very little difference, it is anathema to Evolutionists.

The important point is how can the uncertain date of Hammurabi's Law Code be a "backbone" on which to base history? "Human history has become too much a matter of dogma taught by professionals in ivory towers as though it's all fact. Actually, much of human history is up for grabs. The further back you go, the more that the history that is taught in the schools and universities begins to look like some kind of faerie story." (Graham Hancock Fingerprints of the Gods.

3. Building the Pyramids of Egypt According to Herodotus — post by Michael J. Findley https://findleyfamilyvideopublications.com/2014/07/20/building-the-pyramids-of-egypt-according-to-herodotus-post-by-michael-j-findley/

Image courtesy of Ricardo Liberato – All Gizah Pyramids from Wikimedia Commons.

The Greek Herodotus wrote a book in the 5th century BC he called *Inquiries* or *To Know By Searching Out.* We transliterate the letters *Histories.* Though written more than 1,600 years after the pyramids of Giza were built, the diligent inquiries of Herodotus are the most reliable records we have for the construction of the Egyptian pyramids. Herodotus inquired of the Egyptians alive in his day, who related this record to him. It is neither a primary nor a secondary source, yet it is the most accurate information available to us. Herodotus himself begins the section on Egypt with this disclaimer: "These Egyptian stories are for the benefit of whoever believes such tales: my rule in this history is that I record what is said by all as I have heard it."

Those who, like myself, would like to know why the pyramids were built will find this disappointing. It only gives one version of one possible way the pyramids might have been constructed. Here is link to the complete work, *The History of Herodotus* parallel English/Greek English translation: G. C. Macaulay, (pub. Macmillan, London and NY) [1890] http://www.sacred-texts.com/cla/hh/ And here is a link to the section on the building of the pyramids. http://www.cheops-pyramide.ch/khufu-pyramid/herodotus.html

"Down to the time when Rhampsinitos was king, they told me there was in Egypt nothing but orderly rule, and Egypt prospered greatly; but after him Cheops became king over them and brought them to every kind of evil." Cheops is his Greek name. He had several

Egyptian names, but the most well know is Khufu. He enslaved the entire country and made "all the Egyptians work for him." The description made by Herodotus makes Khufu seem like a crazed, power-mad maniac.

The individual stones were cut upstream and loaded onto a ship called a "baris." Once the stone was unloaded, the barge was dragged upstream from the shore back to the place of stone cutting. The construction of the barges are described in detail.

The Egyptians "worked by a hundred thousand men at a time, for each three months continually. Of this oppression there passed ten years while the causeway was made by which they drew the stones, which causeway they built, and it is a work not much less, as it appears to me, than the pyramid; for the length of it is five furlongs and the breadth ten fathoms and the height, where it is highest, eight fathoms, and it is made of stone smoothed and with figures carved upon it. For this, they said, the ten years were spent, and for the underground chambers on the hill upon which the pyramids stand, which he caused to be made as sepulchral chambers for himself in an island, having conducted thither a channel from the Nile. For the making of the pyramid itself there passed a period of twenty years; and the pyramid is square, each side measuring eight hundred feet, and the height of it is the same. It is built of stone smoothed and fitted together in the most perfect manner, not one of the stones being less than thirty feet in length."

From this description, most historians have dismissed this entire account because pulling these stones up any kind of causeway is impossible, as many have demonstrated. However, nothing in this says that the causeway was uphill. If the stones were pulled downhill, even on a slight grade, and they had some type of lubricant, the stones could be moved. The great pyramid has an estimated 2.3 million stones.

The three pyramids were built in a total of 106 years. "This Cheops, the Egyptians said, reigned fifty years; and after he was dead his brother Chephren succeeded to the kingdom. This king followed the same manner as the other, both in all the rest and also in that he made a pyramid, not indeed attaining to the measurements of that which was built by the former (this I know, having myself also measured it), and moreover there are no underground chambers beneath nor does a channel come from the Nile flowing to this one as to the other, in which the water coming through a conduit built for it flows round an island within, where they say that Cheops himself is laid: but for a basement he built the first course of Ethiopian stone of divers colours; and this pyramid he made forty feet lower than the other as regards size, building it close to the great pyramid. These stand both upon the same hill, which is about a hundred feet high. And Chephren they said reigned fifty and six years. Here then they reckon one hundred and six years, during which they say that there was nothing but evil for the Egyptians..."

The Egyptians who labored on the pyramids where fed, housed, clothed, and given medical attention. But they were not paid. Even so, the cost bankrupted the country. "On the pyramid it is declared in Egyptian writing how much was spent on radishes and onions and leeks for the workmen, and if I rightly remember that which the interpreter said in reading to me this inscription, a sum of one thousand six hundred talents of silver was spent; and if this is so, how much besides is likely to have been expended upon the iron with which they worked, and upon bread and clothing for the workmen, seeing that they were building the works for the time which has been mentioned and were occupied for no small time besides, as I suppose, in the cutting and bringing of the stones and in working at the excavation under the ground?"

"Cheops moreover came, they said, to such a pitch of wickedness, that being in want of money he caused his own daughter to sit in the stews, [the wages of prostitution] and ordered her to obtain from those who came a certain amount of money (how much it was they did not tell me); but she not only obtained the sum appointed by her father, but also she formed a design for herself privately to leave behind her a memorial, and she requested each man who came in to her to give her one stone upon her building: and of these stones, they told me, the pyramid was built which stands in front of the great pyramid in the middle of the three, each side being one hundred and fifty feet in length." The third pyramid was built by Mykerinos, son of Cheops. "This king also left behind him a pyramid, much smaller than that of his father, of a square shape and measuring on each side three hundred feet lacking twenty, built moreover of Ethiopian stone up to half the height."

The important point which has puzzled many is the actual assembly of the stones once they were on site. The description of Herodotus leaves much to the imagination. "This pyramid was made after the manner of steps, which some call "rows" and others "bases": and when they had first made it thus, they raised the remaining stones with machines made of short pieces of timber, raising them first from the ground to the first stage of the steps, and when the stone got up to this it was placed upon another machine standing on the first stage, and so from this it was drawn to the second upon another machine; for as many as were the courses of the steps, so many machines there were also, or perhaps they transferred one and the same machine, made so as easily to be carried, to each stage successively, in order that they might take up the stones; for let it be told in both ways, according as it is reported. However that may be, the highest parts of it were finished first, and afterwards they proceeded to finish that which came next to them, and lastly they finished the parts of it near the ground and the lowest ranges."

While the traditional view is that the stones could not be put in place this way, there are several possibilities. First, there was water surrounding the pyramid. The lower stones are much larger and a dike could have been constructed to make a moat or pond and float the larger stones into place. When they were too high to add more water, the "machines" took over. Levers can raise stones inches at a time. Since Herodotus uses the word machine, there were likely a series of levers. But it would be difficult to move the stone laterally, that is sideways. So the stone would require precise placement before the machine began lifting it.

The details Herodotus leaves with us certainly make the building of the pyramids by this method seem unlikely, though possible. As I began this piece, we still do not know why they were built.

4. A Simple Overview of the Mechanisms Which Caused the Flood.

https://findleyfamilyvideopublications.com/2014/10/26/a-simple-overview-of-the-mechanisms-which-caused-the-flood-post-by-michael-j-findley/

1) There is more water under the seas than in the seas. The exact amount is not important. It is important to understand that this is

considerably more than enough water for a worldwide flood.

2) At the beginning of the Flood, the single antediluvian continent ripped apart rapidly. This had two important results.

3) The antediluvian mountains collapsed. So covering the mountains with water did not require as much water as flood deniers claim.

4) Rifts opened up between the continents. As the rifts widened, they were flooded by ocean water. These rift are now on the sea floor. Today, we know of more than 66,000 km of ridges in the oceans. Modern mountain chains, such as the Cascades (the Cascades are just one example) were also formed by volcanic activity at this time. They are not included in the 66,000 km of rifts (now ridges) from the Atlantic and the Pacific Rim. There are other ridges worldwide, in addition to these ridges and volcanic mountain chains When the rifts are built up with magma, they become mountain ridges.

5) We can measure the eruptive force of the known Mt St Helens eruption. The Yellowstone caldera erupted with 2,500 times the force Mt St Helens either during the Flood or soon after. The ocean rifts were millions of times the force and size of the Yellowstone caldera.

6) Most volcanic activity though starting on land, was quickly flooded by seawater and continued undersea. As depth increases, the ocean water pressure requires greater steam pressure for an eruption to occur. The amount of steam released by undersea volcanic activity increases with depth.

7) The heat from the volcanic activity turns the ocean water which comes into contact with it into steam. This steam saturated the atmosphere, causing rain.

8) Moisture would rise in the atmosphere to the point where it would cool and condense as rain. This rain would cool the lower atmosphere and create a continuous rain cycle. This is a more extreme hydrologic cycle than we know today.

9) Aquatic life and life on the ark survived because they were not in the areas of great volcanic activity. The most extreme volcanic activity was regional, not global. The rifts where the most extreme volcanic activity occurred are the divisions of the new continents, where the continents broke apart.

10) The steam released by undersea volcanic activity was either cooled by the surrounding ocean water or if it reached the surface, it eventually turned to rain. On a miniature scale, modern undersea volcanoes do the same thing.

11) There are tens, perhaps hundreds of thousands of volcanic cones

today. There are hundreds just on the north rim of the Grand Canyon alone.

12) At the end of the Flood, the valleys sank down and the mountains arose.

13) These forces can easily produce a global flood in 40 days.

14) What do you chose to believe?

https://findleyfamilyvideopublications.com/2014/10/26/a-simple-overview-of-the-mechanisms-which-caused-the-flood-post-by-michael-j-findley/

C. Evidence Lists for a Young Earth

1. Ten Best Evidences by Answers In Genesis
http://www.answersingenesis.org/articles/am/v7/n4/ten-best-evidences

2. Age of the earth: 101 evidences for a young age of the earth and the universe
http://creation.com/age-of-the-earth

(Point 3 is Chapter 14, "What Does the Scientific Evidence Prove?" and follows the next two excerpts.)

Material from *Antidisestablishmentarianism*

Prologue and Introduction to Antidisestablishmentarianism

Preface:
Disestablishmentarianism
... When they knew God,
they glorified him not as God,
neither were thankful;
but became vain in their
imaginations, and their foolish
heart was darkened.
Professing themselves to be wise,
they became fools...
Romans 1:21,22

Preface: Disestablishmentarianism

... When they knew God, they glorified him not as God, neither were thankful; but became vain in their imaginations, and their foolish heart was darkened. Professing themselves to be wise, they became fools...
Romans 1:21, 22

The most religious people on earth are those who claim not to have any religion. Dogmatic, intolerant, and bigoted, they refuse to allow anyone to so much as speak their opposition. Yet these same people demand political power and tax support. The mildest opposition, such as the mere mention of Intelligent Design (not God), has blacklisted tenured professors. Just two parents in a middle school in Texas made the national news by objecting to Gideon Bibles placed, without comment, on a table outside the school office.[1] Such people dishonestly claim that they are not religious and "religion" is a group of mythologies. The truth is that they are the ones promoting mythology. In every aspect of life they promote this mythology with unproven dogmatic assertions under the guise of "Science" vocabulary. After hijacking the word "Science," they use the courts to elevate their misuse of the term to an established religion.

Science is the study of the world around us, the use of the experimental method and the improvement of our lives through the application of technology. It is divided into various academic disciplines such as Chemistry, Physics, Mathematics and Biology. However, what the federal courts, the Academic community and the mainstream Western media mean by science is uniformitarianism. It is the cosmological foundation of the religion of Secular Humanism. "Since the fathers fell asleep, all things continue as they were from the beginning of the creation" (II Peter 3:4). This concise description of Uniformitarianism clearly shows that it is completely and entirely a religious belief in antiscientific myths.

Secular Humanists use words which have been in the English language for hundreds of years but give them "new" meanings. However, "there is no new thing under the sun" (Ecclesiastes 1:9, KJV). The words believe, faith and trust are all historic judicial terms and they also form the foundation of the true scientific method. What

Secular Humanists promote as their version of the scientific method consists of preconceptions, presuppositions and assumptions. It is the opposite of an open mind.

A true open mind is founded in belief, faith and trust. The historic meaning of believe is to perceive or understand with the mind and then make an informed decision.[2] The most basic use of the word believe which the average American would understand is that of a juror in court. Which witness do you believe? Which piece of evidence is believable? A synonym would be the word credible. When we believe something or someone and then act on that belief, that is faith. The active part of belief is faith. The passive part of belief is trust. Suppose your brother says that he will drive you to the doctor. If you believe him, then you understand what he says and you make a decision to get ready. If you get in the vehicle with him, that is faith. You act on your belief. When you sit in the vehicle as he drives, that is trust, a passive reliance on what you have proven true. You trust in his driving skills. You trust in the vehicle. You trust the roads, etc. Everything we do is a combination of belief, faith or trust. By restoring their historic definitions, belief, faith and trust re-emerge as the clear language of true experimental science. These terms were deliberately segregated from science to deceive people into believing Secular Humanism.

Liberals, Secular Humanists and materialists, however, use the word "belief" as a synonym for a philosophical position, just an opinion. Faith and trust to them are metaphysical words which mean different things to different people. And this is just the tip of an enormous iceberg. Secular Humanists have redefined hundreds of words to support their religion, such as sin, judgment and anthropology. A conversation with them can be very difficult since they use historical English words but mean something entirely different.

The traditional role of religion is to place priesthood as intermediary between God and man. The traditional role of an establishment of religion places the government in that intermediary role between God and man. In the Middle Ages the Roman Catholic Church put itself between man and God, as other religions have in the past. Johann Tetzel, a "professional pardoner," sold indulgences representing forgiveness for sins in Germany. Indulgences were based on the "storehouse" of good works believed to exist because of the sacrifice of Christ and the good deeds and prayers of past saints. Tetzel was said to promise that, "As soon as a coin in the coffer rings, a soul from purgatory springs."[3]

Selling indulgences was the final act of many which brought on the Reformation. People wouldn't have bought them if they hadn't believed the Catholic Church alone could placate God on their behalf.

Martin Luther convinced the princes of Germany that they did not need to send their money to Rome because they could go to God directly. Rome sent armies to collect the money. Even Modern Roman Catholics who do not believe that their church today claims to stand between them and God have to admit that the medieval Roman Catholic Church did.

The combined power of Church and State restricted personal worship, scientific study and access to historical truth. Today Secular Humanism has done the same by removing foundational truths from education. It excludes study and discovery that contradicts uniformitarianism. It rewrites history to undermine morality and freedom of expression.

The union between the medieval Romanist church and the state came to an end in two ways. In Southern Europe during the Renaissance, art, architecture, literature, and learning opened up to all men, not just those who were part of the church and state system. The Renaissance left the power intact, however. In Northern Europe, the Reformation abolished the need for a church like Rome through the great affirmations of the Reformation: The Scriptures are the absolute authority; Justification is by faith alone apart from works; and every believer is his own priest with direct access to God. The Reformation made a special priesthood class unnecessary because men could pray directly to God and read His Word on their own.

The medieval Roman Catholic Church kept the Scriptures almost exclusively in Latin to prevent ordinary people from studying them, forcing people to come to the priest. The priest would not only tell them what the Scriptures said, but he also mingled that with the church's interpretation. In order for ordinary people who did not know Latin to read the Bible for themselves, the Scriptures had to be translated into the language of the ordinary people. Translation work by Reformers was essential to enable ordinary men to read the Scriptures for themselves, even though it was punishable by death under the Church-State system. The Renaissance and the Reformation worked together in the development of moveable type to make printing and distribution of translations of the Scriptures easier. Renaissance scholars revived interest in studying forgotten manuscripts and making translations into the vernacular. Erasmus's Greek New Testament provided a basis for more accurate translations of the Scriptures.

The Medieval Romanist Church-State system took away freedom by forcing man to rely on and accept its teachings. The Renaissance and the Reformation restored freedom by returning art, science, and all forms of learning to ordinary people. In particular the people were able to worship God as the Scriptures taught, without Church-State control. Modern western culture, and American culture in particular, was founded on this religious freedom. American culture is more Christian than European cultures, but neither of these cultures can survive if the foundation of religious freedom is destroyed.

It is this Christian foundation of religious freedom which is the real target of Secular Humanists. These Secular Humanists have taken outrageous liberties in their unrelenting quest to replace religious freedom with their established religion of Secular Humanism, which they incorrectly call science or Natural Law. Their major tool is the US court system. Sympathetic US courts have consistently supported Secular Humanism by using every possible opportunity to replace the word religion with the ancient concept of Natural Law. However, since Natural Law has been used so many different ways, the courts had to standardize the term Natural Law. Their version of Natural Law goes back to Plato's *Republic*. Though Plato never used the phrase "natural law" in his *Republic,* translator Benjamin Jowett's notes state that, "Plato among the Greeks, like Bacon among the moderns, was the first who conceived a method of knowledge... "[4] Plato's *Republic* is at least the foundation of modern Natural Law, if not the detailed finished product. Together with Aristotle, Plato is supposed by secularists to have laid the foundation for learning and development of the Sciences. This is really is essence of Natural Law.

Jowett goes on to say that Plato provided for a means to spread his method of acquiring knowledge. "In the ideal State which is constructed by Socrates, the first care of the rulers is to be education."[4] Jowett makes it clear that Socrates meant to impart much more than mere academic knowledge, just as Natural Law means to teach more than mere Science. Socrates promoted "the conception of a higher State, in which 'no man calls anything his own,' and in which there is neither 'marrying nor giving in marriage,' and 'kings are philosophers' and 'philosophers are kings;' and there is another and higher education, intellectual as well as moral and religious, of science as well as of art, and not of youth only but of the whole of life."[4]

Many know that Plato in his *Republic* based his state on a philosopher/king. Few, however, are aware that he believed in communism and free love and that these two "natural" principles were to be foundational principles of the state.

Though the preceding condensation by Benjamin Jowett is an excellent job, as you can read for yourself, the actual words of Socrates, as quoted by Plato, are much longer and more difficult to understand. "None of them will have anything specially his or her own." "... Their legislator, having selected the men, will now select the women and give them to them [the legislator gives selected women to selected men]... they must live in common houses and meet at common meals ... they will be together ... And so they will be drawn by a necessity of their natures to have intercourse with each other..." "... Until philosophers are kings, or the kings and princes ... have the spirit and power of philosophy, and political greatness and wisdom meet in one ... cities will never have rest from their evils."[5]

The philosopher/king, according to Socrates, was to lay these foundational ideas through education. Though he did not use the phrase "establishment of religion," Plato clearly advocated an established religion. It was to be put in place by a philosopher/king through education based on a state where "no man calls anything his own" and where there is neither "marrying nor giving in marriage." Though this education would begin with children, it would continue throughout a person's entire life. This is the Natural Law which the US Court system has imposed.

The US needs to disestablish its Establishment of Religion and reestablish religious freedom. In the 1800's churches which tried to break away from the Church of England were called disestablishmentarians. The people who fought against the disestablishment of those churches within the Church of England in the 1800s were called Antidisestablishmentarians. Today, the mainstream media, liberal politicians, the academic community, the liberal courts and all others who file lawsuits, blacklist, fire, refuse to hire, tax, legislate against, libel, slander and do whatever is necessary to maintain their positions of privilege and power are modern Antidisestablishmentarians.

---

1 (No author) "Parents Fuming as Texas Schools Let Gideons Provide Bibles to Students," Tuesday, May 19, 2009, *Fox News.com*. "A spokeswoman for the school district said that a number of materials are made available to students this way, including newspapers, camp brochures and tutoring pamphlets. College and military recruitment information is available all year long. The Gideon Bibles were made available for just one day. 'We have to handle this request in the same manner as other requests to distribute non-school literature – in a view-point neutral manner,' Shana Wortham, director of communications for the district, wrote in an e-mail to *FoxNews.com*.

2 Alexander Hamilton, in an 1802 letter to James Bayard. "I have carefully examined the evidences of the Christian religion, and if I was sitting as a juror upon its authenticity I would un-hesitatingly give my verdict in its favor. I can prove its truth as clearly as any proposition ever submitted to the mind of man."

3 Philip Schaff, *History of the Christian Church,* Volume 7, "The Reformation," Charles Scribner's Sons, 1910.

4 Plato, *The Republic* (c. 360 B.C.), translated by Benjamin Jowett over a period of 30 years until his death in 1893, completed posthumously by Lewis Campbell. (Introductory material (in double quotes) and paraphrases of Plato's ideas (in single quotes) were written by Jowett.)

5 Plato, *The Republic*, Book Five Dialogue excerpts among Socrates, Adeimantus, Glaucon and Thrasymachus have been placed in parentheses within Jowett's introductory material.

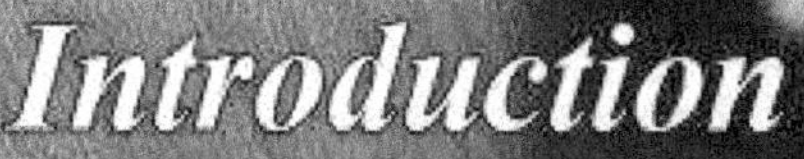

"Facts are stubborn things;
and whatever
may be our wishes,
our inclinations,
or the dictates of our passion,
they cannot alter
the state of facts and evidence."
John Adams

Introduction

Facts are stubborn things; and whatever may be our wishes, our inclinations, or the dictates of our passion, they cannot alter the state of facts and evidence.[1]
John Adams

Sometime in the early twentieth century, Secular Humanist indoctrination convinced almost everyone in the United States that "an establishment of religion" in the first phrase of the first amendment of the United States Constitution is vague and can mean just about anything. "The state of the facts and evidence," as John Adams so eloquently put it, is the exact opposite.

Section One of this work documents what the founders meant by the phrase "an establishment of religion." The Founding Fathers made as clear a statement as the English language permitted. The Constitution of the United States is founded on English law and to a lesser extent, various European laws, especially German and Dutch. In each of these countries, an Establishment of Religion was the collection of taxes to support education, welfare and public worship. The various governments appointed the teachers, welfare workers and pastors and expected these people to support the government in turn.

The original state constitutions not only permitted, but openly encouraged establishments of religion, especially in the areas of welfare and education. The foundation of the US Constitution is the fact that federal government was to have no control whatsoever in these areas. Their concept of a separation of Church and State was the exact opposite of what the courts have rammed down our throats for the past hundred years. The church should have the right to pray and teach without any federal intervention whatsoever. Judges should have the right to post any Scriptures they want. The courts should have no authority whatsoever to comment. Removing a state judge from office for posting the Ten Commandments is not merely an Establishment of Religion. It is the Inquisition.

Section Two documents the foundations of Secular Humanism and how it grew to become America's Establishment of Religion. The words "Secular Humanism" come from various groups in the 1950's. The phrase "Secular Humanist" is found in court documents to describe this set of beliefs. Secular Humanism is as old as civilization, but the primary foundation of twenty first century Secular Humanism is Plato's *Republic*. In America, Secular Humanism can be said to have originated with Thomas Paine. Secular Humanism has specific beliefs which are written down in various manifestos. Like Christianity, Islam and Judaism, Secular Humanism has many variations. Though Secular Humanists do not like the term, the most accurate words to describe these variants are "sects" or "denominations." Like Christians, Muslims and Jews, many Secular Humanist denominations do not get along with one another. Therefore, we have attempted to point out the beliefs which have the greatest agreement.

Section Three defines science, since Secular Humanists claim that science separates them from all other religions. Since true science is founded in the belief, faith and trust of the Bible, all of these words are defined carefully and in detail. In the Bible, belief, faith and trust are legal terms. Believe means to examine the evidence and come to a reasoned conclusion. Action taken on that belief is faith. Trust is the passive version of faith.

The Scientific Method is the biblical version of belief, faith and trust applied to the material world which God created for us. In the Bible, the Scientific Method recognizes that God is the creator, that we are required to be responsible managers of the material world God has given us, and that there is a final judgment after death which will include how well we managed the gifts God allowed us to use.

Our book concludes with Section Four, the results of having Secular Humanism as an Establishment of Religion. With the exception of America's founding documents and the ancient documents such as Plato, Plutarch and Genesis, hundreds of other quotes could easily be substituted for the quotes that appear here. There is nothing new or unique in this book. It is a combination of what used to be common knowledge in America before Secular Humanism took over and destroyed the education system and current events. If we were to start over today, we would pull different stories from the daily news. Though the individual stories would be different, the points would be the same. "There is nothing new under the sun" (Ecclesiastes 1:9). Or to state the same thing another way, the more things change, the more they stay the same.

America's Established Religion is Secular Humanism. This work is dedicated to exposing, defining and disestablishing it.

---

1 John Adams, "Argument in defence of the [English] soldiers in the Boston Massacre trial," December 1770.

2 "Alabama's Judicial Ethics Panel removed Chief Justice Roy Moore from office Thursday for defying a Federal judge's order to move a ten commandments monument from the State Supreme Court building." Friday, November 14, 2003. Posted 6:56 AM Eastern time. *CNN.com*

3. What Does the Scientific Evidence Prove?

14. What Does The Scientific Evidence Prove?

"I am quite conscious that my speculations run quite beyond the bounds of true science."
Charles Darwin[1]

"Facts are stubborn things; and whatever may be our wishes, our inclinations, or the dictates of our passion, they cannot alter the state of facts and evidence."
John Adams[2]

"In the space of one hundred and seventy-six years the Mississippi has shortened itself two hundred and forty-two miles. Therefore ... in the Old Silurian Period the Mississippi River was upward of one million three hundred thousand miles long ... seven hundred and forty-two years from now the Mississippi will be only a mile and three-quarters long. ... There is something fascinating about science. One gets such wholesale returns of conjecture out of such a trifling investment of fact."
Mark Twain[3]

Samuel Johnson said, "Integrity without knowledge is weak and useless, and knowledge without integrity is dangerous and dreadful."[4] Christians often believe that science is an enemy. They think this way because most who use the word "science" have completely abandoned Johnson's demand that integrity go hand-in-hand with knowledge. Uniformitarians replace truth with selective evidence which supports preconceived conclusions. Christians should neither develop an antagonism toward true science, nor should they ignore the very real contributions of true science. True scientists should not ignore the very real foundation of science in Christianity. Dennis Prager, author, columnist, radio show host and historian, laments the unthinking reliance on pseudo-science in today's society.

"In much of the West, the well-educated have been taught to believe they can know nothing and they can draw no independent conclusions about truth, unless they cite a study and 'experts' have affirmed it. 'Studies show' is to the modern secular college graduate what 'Scripture says' is to the religious fundamentalist."[5]

In everyday life, probably the greatest area of conflict between Christianity and those who misuse the word science is moral relativism. This came about because of the dishonest use of the word relativity. The theories of relativity (special and general) neither support nor have any reference to moral relativism. The similarity in the sound of the words is simply a propaganda technique. Neither do the moral absolutes of the Word of God belittle true science. However, since the established religion of Secular Humanism teaches just the opposite, the following list of scientific facts can help us understand that true science can only be explained by the world as described in the Bible. None of these scientific facts prove the Bible. Each does prove the religious belief in deep time to be a scientific impossibility.

"I am quite conscious that my speculations run beyond the bounds of true science."
Charles Darwin

"Facts are stubborn things; and whatever may be our wishes, our inclinations, or the dictates of our passion, they cannot alter the state of facts and evidence."
John Adams

"In the space of one hundred and seventy-six years the Mississippi has shortened two hundred and forty-two miles. In the Old Silurian Period [it] was one million three hundred thousand miles long. [In]Seven hundred and forty- two years [it] will be only 1 and 3/4 miles long. There is something fascinating about science. One gets such wholesale returns of conjecture out of such a trifling investment of fact.
Mark Twain

Sun Energy Source

Until shortly after WWII, the majority of scientists believed the sun shrank by an average of .01 percent per year. They concluded, based on 400 years' worth of scientific observations, that this was proof that the sun was powered by gravitational collapse. In the late 1800s the Kelvin-Helmholtz Contraction Theory was developed to explain both the observed contraction and how the sun was powered.[6]

In the 1930s religious Secular Humanists, understanding the consequences of this theory, proposed nuclear fusion as the energy source for the sun. In 1928 George Gamow published a paper proposing a theory. The Gamow theory included what came to be known as the Gamow factor.[7] This was the first serious step toward the idea that stars are powered by nuclear fusion. General acceptance was slow. Gamow's ideas were further explored in the 1930s. This exploration grew into Hans Bethe's theory of Stellar Nucleosynthesis.[8] Bethe won a Nobel Prize for this work in 1967. The detonation of the atomic bombs actually did more to convince people than the theoretical papers. According to the Kelvin-Helmoltz Contraction Theory, with gravitational collapse powering the sun, the sun would have been so large and hot around 50,000 years ago that it would have boiled all the water out of all the oceans on the earth. A mere million years ago the orbit of the earth would have been inside the sun.[9]

These are not just creationist rantings. While we might disagree about the exact numbers, there is no questioning the basic principle. Here are the words of very committed uniformitarians.

"But Kelvin-Helmholtz contraction cannot be the major source of the Sun's energy today. If it were, the Sun would have had to be much larger in the relatively recent past. Helmholtz's own calculations showed that the Sun could have started its initial collapse from the solar nebula no more than about 2.5 million years ago. But the geological and fossil record shows that the earth is far older than that, and so the Sun must be as well. Hence, this model of a Sun that shines because it shrinks cannot be correct."[10]

Why is the Kelvin-Helmholtz contraction incorrect? Because they *believe* "that the earth is far older than that."

"While the early faint Sun paradox does not tell us that the Solar System is only thousands of years old, it does seem to rule out the age being billions of years."

Dr. Danny R. Faulkner

Secularists' religious belief that life on earth has existed for billions of years required the sun to be billions of years old. So they eagerly accepted that the sun was powered by nuclear fusion. It is also true that the sun's surface is not static, as is the case with water, rock, or ice on a planet's surface, so a consistent measurement of the sun's diameter is not possible. Two different measurements on the same day might yield different diameters because of massive fluctuations on the sun.

The sun's life cycle in this theory would be 9.2 billion years. At 4.6 billion years the sun would be roughly half way through its life cycle. The problem with this theory is that the sun would have been too cool; forty percent of its present brightness, 4.6 billion years ago, and the earth would have been a frozen wasteland. This is also known as the early faint sun paradox.

Project *SOHO*, launched in 1995, has provided us with more information about the sun. Unwilling to change their belief about the age of the sun and life on earth, some Secular Humanists now believe that the sun is powered by a perfect balance of different types of nuclear fusion combined with gravitational collapse, which has produced a uniform temperature for life on earth for the last 4.6 billion years. The best way to describe this kind of balance is "miraculous."[11]

NASA's Solar Dynamics Observatory Satellite, or SDO, was launched in February 2010 and chief scientist Dean Pesnell said it has already reshaped our theories of how the star works.[12]

ScienceBlogs.com contributor Ethan Siegal, PhD in theoretical astrophysics at the University of Florida, writes a blog called "Starts with a Bang." In a post titled, "How the Sun works, from the inside out", originally written August 12, 2011 he has included crossed out and updated information, indicating how rapidly information changes. Theories about the sun must be changed, updated, and corrected to match the most up-to-date information.[13]

Many who insist on billions of years agree that 4.6 billion years is just a rough estimate. They explain that the 9.2 billion year figure is correct, but that they simply are not certain how far our sun is into its 9.2 billion year lifecycle. With such rapid changes in information, how is it possible to state dogmatically that the sun has a lifespan of 9.2 billion years?

Radiohalos and Radiometric Dating

The 4.6 billion year figure comes from radiometric dating. The most common radiohalos are found in zircons. Zircons are found all over the earth and range in size from microscopic to the size of rocks. Zircons are crystals of zirconium silicate. Zircons can be of gemstone quality and large zircons are often used as substitutes for diamonds (cubic zirconia is a close man-made synthetic). Most zircons, however, are around the size of very small grains of sand. Though the wide range of impurities creates an enormous variety of zircons, the most important geological use for zircons is radiometric dating. Zircons contain trace amounts of uranium and thorium. Tiny zircons are sliced open to examine fission tracks produced by decaying uranium.

Zircons are sliced open to examine fission tracks produced by decaying Uranium. These methods have dated zircons as old as 4.404 billion years. Helium diffusion dating of the same samples returns a date of 6,000 years ± 2,000 years.

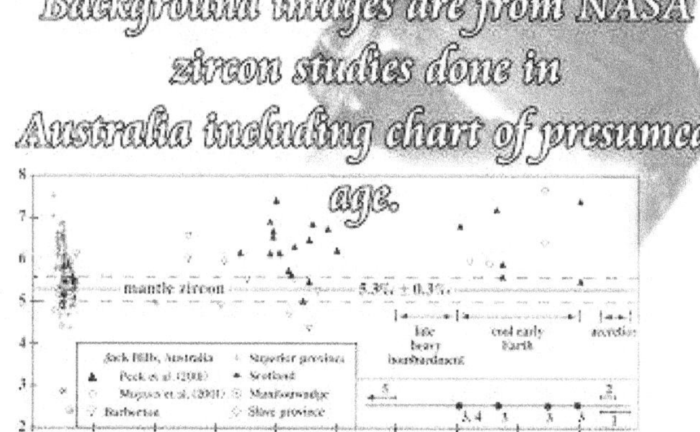

These fission tracks and the UPb (Uranium to lead) methods of radiometric dating have dated zircons as old as 4.404 billion years.[14]

This means, according to uniformitarian assumptions, that the original crystal formation of these tested zircon samples occurred 4.404 billion years ago. As with all radiometric samples, there is no scientific way of knowing the original condition of the sample tested.

The same zircons also contain helium, which provides another dating method. Helium retention rates in these zircons have a date range beginning as young as 4000 years.[14] While there are a tremendous number of articles attacking this date as too young, most of these articles read like tabloids reporting on British royalty, not honest science. A true scientist would look for an explanation that accounted for both the uranium radiohalos and helium retention. It is far easier to come up with an explanation for the radiohalos' presence if the rocks have a young age. It is nearly impossible to explain the retained helium if the rocks are ancient. One possible explanation for young radiohalos is that they were created at the same time the earth was created.

Another possible answer is that a massive thermonuclear event such as the sun exploding and losing an outer layer sent thermonuclear radiation through the entire planet. Since such an event would have destroyed all non-aquatic life on earth, this would have happened around 2350 BC, at the time of the Flood.

Whatever the trigger, the most likely scenario is accelerated nuclear decay during the Flood. The accelerated nuclear decay during the Flood is the only explanation we are aware of which properly balances all the existing evidence.

Dating Rock Formations

Travel anywhere and you will see signs proclaiming various rocks or layers of rocks to be millions or even billions of years old. "The Little Willow Formation consists primarily of contorted quartz schist and gneiss; at 1.7 billion years old, it is the oldest rock in the Salt Lake City area."[15] This religious belief in the myth of great ages is proclaimed in textbooks, school classrooms, museums, and, most importantly, by employers, who will either refuse to hire or actually fire anyone who refuses to openly support this religious myth. Though many supposed scientific facts are used to support these dates, radiometric dating is the foundation for all dating methods.[16]

Since fossils have no direct methods of dating, such as radiometric dating, how is the age of a particular fossil determined? It is compared to other fossils of a "known" age or it is dated according to strata where it was found. How is the age of the other fossils or the strata determined? The usual answer is more fossils of a "known" age or strata of a "known" age. This circular reasoning is standard textbook content. Radiometric dating is the only dating method that does not rely on a comparison with something else already dated. Radiometric dating is not valid on fossils. Radiometric dating must be used on the rocks in the surrounding strata.

Every form of radiometric dating always depends on an unstable radioactive isotope deteriorating (decaying) to a stable isotope at a known, stable rate. K–>Ar (Potassium to Argon) and U–>Pb (^{235}U to Lead) are just two examples of isotopes used as radiometric clocks. All radioactive isotopes used as radiometric clocks work the same way. A sample is taken and analyzed. The result is always a ratio of radioactive isotope to the stable final element. The ratio can be found on a chart because the rate of decay is stable, that is, unaffected by any known outside influence.

Everyone who uses radioactive isotopes as clocks must, however, rely on three invalid religious assumptions. The first is the unscientific religious leap of faith that the sample being tested had no daughter material when it was formed. For radiometric clocks to work, it is an absolutely essential scientific necessity to know the original condition of the sample. If the original condition of the sample is less than one hundred percent radioactive, then the date is less than the published date. These widely publicized dates, however, assume that the tested sample began its existence (at the time it was formed) one hundred per cent radioactive with no daughter element present. In reality, the only scientific information we learn from these radiometric tests is the current ratio of radioactive material to nonradioactive material. The published dates are always the upper possible date of a range of possible dates.

The second assumption is that nothing contaminated the sample during its existence. It is impossible to know the conditions of the sample during its existence. Simply to assume that contamination never occurred is not science. It is especially bad science when the very people claiming the accuracy of radiometric dating also claim that the earth underwent a series of what they call extinction events which catastrophically changed the surface of the earth.

The third assumption is that nothing changed the decay rate. While the second assumption is something changed the individual sample or the immediate environment of the sample, this assumption is worldwide or throughout the universe. In other words, is the present really the key to the past? How can we know that?

If there was a sample with a known date, other samples could be calibrated against it. Not only do such calibration samples not exist, without a time machine to go back in time and obtain a calibration sample, it is not possible to have a calibration sample. With very few exceptions, the published dates of tens of thousands to billions of years are based purely on mythological religious assumptions.

There are a few exceptions, however. Thermoluminescence is used to date pottery. Thermoluminescence is based on the time the pottery was fired, a known event. ^{14}C is another one of these exceptions. The radioactive isotope ^{14}C is integrated into the tissue of living organisms throughout the lifetime of that organism. At the time of death that amount of ^{14}C becomes a fixed amount and begins to radioactively decay into ^{14}N. That amount of ^{14}C at the time of death is equal to the amount of ^{14}C in the atmosphere at the time of death. The ratio of ^{14}C in the sample tested at the time of death compared to the assumed amount of ^{14}C in the atmosphere at the time of death should be an almost perfect radiometric clock. However, certain conditions can alter that ratio. If the ratio is in some way tampered with, that tampering is normally leaching. That particular sample will then test to be older than it really is. ^{14}C dates older than 1000 B.C. also assume atmospheric amounts of ^{14}C and absorption rates of ^{14}C similar to current absorption rates. That is almost certainly an invalid assumption, making many, if not all ^{14}C dates for items dated older than 1000 B.C. older than they actually are.

Finally, radiometric dating never gives an absolute date. It only tells us the upper limit of a range of possible dates. One of the most important but rarely published conclusions by secularists about ^{14}C dating is that even they admit that after approximately 60,000 years, the remaining ^{14}C is such a small amount that it is difficult to test for it. They have also concluded that ^{14}C disappears entirely after a little more than 100,000 years. Though fossils which are pronounced older than 100,000 years are rarely tested for ^{14}C, those few which have been tested usually have some trace of ^{14}C.

"Carbon-14 (^{14}C) dating of multiple samples of bone from 8 dinosaurs from Texas, Alaska, Colorado, and Montana revealed that they are only 22,000 to 39,000 years old."

"After the AOGS-AGU conference in Singapore, the abstract was removed from the conference website by two chairmen because they could not accept the findings. Unwilling to challenge the data openly, they erased the report from public view without a word to the authors or even to the AOGS officers, until after an investigation. It won't be restored.

The researchers presented their findings at the 2012 Western Pacific Geophysics Meeting in Singapore, August 13-17, a conference of the American Geophysical Union (AGU) and the Asia Oceania Geosciences Society (AOGS)."[17]

Lunar Recession

"Scotty, I need power now!" pleads a desperate Captain Kirk, on *Star Trek* the original series, only to hear his Chief Engineer reply, "He's turned the engines off. Completely cold. Thirty minutes to startup. I canna change the laws of physics, Captain!" The only hope of pulling out of a decaying orbit and saving the *Enterprise* is a restart of her engines.

Why? The Earth is surrounded by nonpowered satellites. Why does the *Enterprise* need power? The *Enterprise* needs to remain in a slow orbit as near the planet as possible while maintaining a fixed point over it. The only way to accomplish that is to keep the engines powered up to constantly change the orbit and counter the pull of gravity. The closer a satellite is to the object it is orbiting, the faster it has to travel to maintain a stable orbit without engine power. Mercury is the fastest-traveling planet orbiting the sun. Venus, Earth and Mars are all progressively slower at their greater distances.

For a given velocity there is only one stable orbit around (distance from) a planet (or sun). The closer the satellite (or starship) is to the object it is orbiting, the faster it needs to travel (without power or thrust). Otherwise it needs power (thrust) to maintain the orbit.

All orbiting objects have one of three types of orbits.

1) The orbit is a decaying orbit (being pulled into the planet),

2) A stable orbit (no change in orbit over time) or

3) A receding orbit (moving away from the planet).

The closer the satellite (or starship) is to the object it is orbiting, the faster it must travel or the more power (thrust) it must use to counteract the attraction of gravity.

The laser reflectors left by the Apollo missions on the lunar surface have been hit with lasers from earth many times. It proves the moon is moving away from the earth at a rate of about 1.5 inches per year.[18] Assuming the Moon has not changed mass, velocity or direction of orbit, sometime in the past it would have possessed a stable orbit closer to the Earth. Even closer to the earth, inside that stable orbit, the moon's orbit with no change in mass, velocity, or orbital direction, would have decayed.

The important point is the stable or equilibrium orbit.

At the current rate of recession, the moon is receding from the earth at a rate of approximately one mile every 42,240 years. If the Moon were to remain unchanged in mass, velocity and rate of recession, just over 42 million years ago, the moon would be more than one thousand miles closer to the earth. With no change in its mass and velocity, in far less than 42 million years the moon's orbit would be a decaying orbit, not a receding orbit. The moon would be drawing closer to the Earth and not moving away from the earth as it is now. Just like the *Enterprise,* the moon would have a decaying orbit.

Since the lunar orbit is receding, not decaying, it means that the existing lunar orbit is, geologically speaking, very young. If you reject the conclusion that this indicates a recent creation, you are left with only two choices:

1) The Moon is a very recent addition to the Earth or

2) Some sort of catastrophe has relatively recently altered the Moon's orbit. This catastrophe would have required far more energy than what could be produced by the simultaneous detonation of all the nuclear weapons on Earth.

That catastrophic event would have occurred quite recently, even according to uniformitarians. Any catastrophe powerful enough to alter the moon's orbit would also have catastrophically affected the Earth as well.

Geomagnetic Field Decay

The earth's magnetic field seems to have a half-life of around 1400 years. Assuming that to be correct, just 11,200 years ago the earth's magnetic field would have been 256 times stronger than it is now. 14,000 years ago the earth's magnetic field would have been 1024 times stronger than it is now. That would make animal life impossible.[19]

Dr. Russell Humphreys has continued to work in this field. He believes that a strict linear half-life is unlikely and concludes his article with the following: "These ideas weigh heavily against the idea that there is currently a "dynamo" process at work in the core that would ultimately restore the lost energy back to the field. Without such a restoration mechanism, the field can only have a limited lifetime, in the thousands of years. So the clarity of this new fit, especially the exponential part, is further evidence that the earth's magnetic field is young."[20]

The *dynamo process* Dr. Humphreys references is the theory that instead of continually decaying, earth's magnetic field is continually rebuilding or restoring itself. Its existence would make the entire life cycle of the earth's magnetic field much more stable and therefore much, much older.

Many articles purport to "debunk" these observations. They usually begin with personal attacks on the original authors. Even if the "debunkers" are correct that the half-life of the earth's magnetic field is longer than 1,400 years, for life to exist hundreds of millions years ago, the half-life must be hundreds of times larger. Instead of making personal attacks, detractors should present data supporting a much longer half-life. Instead, they use data based on the presupposition that the earth is millions of years old to insist that the earth's magnetic field must have a large half-life.

An excellent response to these uniformitarian proposals is Jonathan Sarfati's article, *The Earth's Magnetic Field: Evidence That the Earth Is Young*. After including many detailed examples, it concludes, "The clear decay pattern shows the earth could not be older than about 10,000 years."[21]

A key element of the decay of the earth's magnetic field is the evidence of magnetic field reversals found in cooled lava flows. "Lava flows in Nevada's Sheep Creek Range may have preserved evidence that the planet's magnetic field rapidly changed direction." Other evidence in the paleomagnetic lava flow at Steens Mountain in Oregon shows that the earth's magnetic field reversed its polarity in just over two weeks. This is in line with a magnetic field half-life of 1,400 years, but entirely unexplainable with a magnetic field hundreds of millions or billions of years old. Also, the sun reverses the polarity of its magnetic field every eleven years. [22]

The earth's magnetic field has a half-life of 1,400 years. Just 14,000 years ago the earth's magnetic field would have been ten times stronger than it is now. 1.4 million years ago the earth's magnetic field would have been 1,000 times stronger than it is now. That would make animal life impossible.

Paleomagnetic lava flow at Steens Mountain in Oregon

Mount Saint Helens Canyon Formation

Though the eruption of this volcano was observed by millions via television, internet and print media, few are aware of the significance. It carved another "Little Grand Canyon" similar to the Grand Canyon

in

The eruption of Mount Saint Helens also carved another "Little Grand Canyon" similar to the Grand Canyon in Arizona in days or perhaps only hours.

Arizona in days or perhaps only hours. Millions witnessed this event. We saw it happening live or on video in real time. To those who understand, the evidence is so overwhelming that even some evolutionists are admitting it, though quite grudgingly. They still believe, without any evidence, that the catastrophe creating most other prominent geologic sites happened millions of years ago. But the evidence has forced them to admit that the Grand Canyon's formation was rapid, created with massive amounts of water.[23]

Varves

Paint brush shows scale.

Photo Information/Credit[24]

Mount Saint Helens produced more scientifically observable evidence, in the form of something remarkably like varves. According to most dictionaries, a varve is a layer of alternating fine and course (light and dark) silt at the bottom of a pond or lake. Counting varves used to be considered a very important method of dating. Each layer has two parts, one lighter and the other darker. One part is the time of year when water moves quickly and brings many deposits. The other part is the time of year when water is stationary, perhaps even stagnant, such as the winter when the lake is covered in ice. All honest scientists admit that there might be more than one varve per year. A core sample, which counts varves to determine the age of a lake, might give a date older than the actual date. The assumption that conditions in the past were similar to the present is an assumption that the difference in dates is slight. Though the varve count might be slightly older than the actual date, it is still assumed to be reliable.

The eruption of Mt. St. Helens discredited the use of varves as a dating method (based on the assumption that one mud/silt layer equals one year). Ash and mud sandwiched together in thin light and dark layers, just like varves, accumulated up to twenty-five feet thick with thousands of layers and within hours, perhaps only minutes.

The eruption of Mount St. Helens on May 18, 1980 scientifically proved that assumption to be in error. Ash and mud up to twenty-five feet thick with thousands of layers filled the region. Though these layers are never called varves, they display the same characteristics as varves, a thin light and dark layer sandwiched together. These thousands of layers, put down in a matter of hours, perhaps minutes, completely discredit the concept of using layers for dating. People who use varves for dating never acknowledge or even mention this.25

Lake Titicaca

Catastrophes change the shape of the land where they occur forever. Few places have been changed more dramatically than Lake Titicaca. It rises 12,500 feet (3,800 meters) above sea level in South America between Bolivia and Peru. Fresh water rivers and streams feed the lake now, but the salt content is about five-and-a-half parts per thousand, classifying the lake as brackish. No current conditions explain the salt content of the lake. The most likely explanation is that Lake Titicaca was once at or below sea level and that a catastrophic uplift moved a lake full of seawater almost two and a half miles above sea level. Marine fossils are preserved around the lake. The current salt level of Lake Titicaca is about fifteen percent of the Pacific Ocean off Peru, where the Pacific Ocean varies from 34 to 37 parts per thousand.

"In the heart of the Andes ... is Lake Titicaca." [Its saltiness and the present fauna (It contains sea horses)] strongly suggested that the present fauna of Lake Titicaca has survived from a time when the lake communicated directly with [was connected to] the ocean."[26]

Theories other than uplift have been postulated. These theories, however, require completely speculative processes that have never been observed. That is not a scientific process. Some evolutionists believe the uplift theory because the scientific evidence is so overwhelming, but say that the catastrophe occurred millions of years ago. A past waterline is slanted in relation to the current waterline.

At one time Lake Titicaca had more water than it does now, and this waterline is much higher at one end of the lake, proving that a catastrophe tipped the lake in the past.

"The strandline [near Lake Titicaca] was carefully surveyed for a length of about 375 miles [603 km]. And then it was established that it is not 'straight.' ... Its level showed a slant of a most peculiar character in relation to the present ocean-level, or, which amounts to the same, relative to the present level of Lake Titicaca."[27]

Past irrigation and buildings in and around the lake prove an ancient civilization built the port city of Tiahuanaco. It is approximately 800 feet higher than the current lake surface. Tiahuanaco was a harbor, but is now twelve miles south of the lake, and the ship berths are of a size most likely built for ocean-going vessels. The lake "is large, 3,261 square miles. It contains sea horses, suggesting that this region or its water were once below sea level. On the mountain sides ... are terraces of ancient corn fields going up to 17,000 feet. Yet corn will not germinate [sprout] above 11,500 feet!"[20]

A catastrophic upthrust during the time of civilized habitation is the only explanation for the presence of a former seaport city and corn terraces up to 17,000 feet surrounding Lake Titicaca, which is situated 12,500 feet above sea level.

There is also a building beneath the lake, about 660 feet long, with a road running to it and roads and steps leading down into deeper water. It is twice the size of a modern soccer field and modern archaeologists believe it to be a temple.[28]

Himalayan Yellow Band Ammonites

Geological features suddenly and catastrophically created by water can be found all over the world. Near the top of the Himalayan Mountains, reaching up to 29,029 feet (8,848 m) above sea level, is a layer of rock known as the yellow band. This yellow band is filled with marine fossils called ammonites. "Marine fossils are also found high in the Himalayas, the world's tallest mountain range, reaching up to 29,029 feet (8,848 m) above sea level. For example, fossil ammonites (coiled marine cephalopods) are found in limestone beds in the Himalayas of Nepal. All geologists agree that ocean waters must have buried these marine fossils in these limestone beds. "[29] Ammonites are common fossils found all over the earth and are similar to a modern marine creature known as the Nautilus. These fossilized marine creatures lived in oceans, not a freshwater lake. All of the Himalayan mountain chain had to have been under seawater. This many fossilized ammonites were not transported somehow after the mountains were formed. Sometime in the past either the entire Himalayan Mountain chain was five miles lower than it is now or the entire planet had more than twice the water volume than it has now.

The eruption of Mount St. Helens on May 18, 1980 scientifically proved that assumption to be in error. Ash and mud up to twenty-five feet thick with thousands of layers filled the region. Though these layers are never called varves, they display the same characteristics as varves, a thin light and dark layer sandwiched together. These thousands of layers, put down in a matter of hours, perhaps minutes, completely discredit the concept of using layers for dating. People who use varves for dating never acknowledge or even mention this.[25]

Also, these ammonite fossils are not crushed. They were moved by a catastrophic (sudden) event while the entire layer was plastic (mud). The ammonites had to be protected to keep them from being crushed. The only scientific answer is that the surrounding mud protected them. A slow uplift over a long period of time would have dried out the surrounding mud. Instead of protecting the ammonites, the hardened rock would have ground the ammonites to powder. Since water weighs approximately eight pounds per gallon, the energy necessary to create the Himalayan Mountains was thousands of times greater than all the nuclear weapons in all the nuclear arsenals in every country on earth detonating at the same time.

On a much smaller scale, highway engineers have carved into mountains all over the earth. Thousands of mountains at every possible elevation all over the earth show bent, folded and twisted layers intact without cracks. These layers had to be plastic [mud] when they were put in place. This is the only way these mountains could have formed.

Thousands of mountains at every possible elevation all over the earth show bent, folded and twisted layers intact without cracks.

Catastrophic Fossil Formation

Fossils like the ammonites of the yellow band were formed in a catastrophic event. Even evolutionists have to admit that. Insects, microbes and weathering combine to destroy everything except bones in less than one hundred years, often in less than a week. Tissue deteriorates too rapidly for fossilization without a catastrophe. The question is: When did this catastrophe occur? Once again, the only available scientific evidence indicates a more recent event. Since fossils were bones, they once contained ^{14}C. If a standard test for ^{14}C discovered any ^{14}C, the tested sample would scientifically prove a date less than 60,000 years old.

Since the religion of Secular Humanism demands that these fossils are millions of years old, and they control both the fossils to be tested and the testing procedures, ^{14}C testing is never done on fossils. There is only the dogmatic assertion that fossils are now stone and there is no carbon to test.

There have been carbon tests on mollusks that indicate a much younger date on certain samples. Without ^{14}C testing, however, there is no scientific dating of fossils, only religious pronouncements.[30]

Warm Antarctica

There is abundant evidence that Antarctica was once warm. Warm climate animal and plant fossils abound. Antarctica also has a coal bed. Formation of a coal bed requires a massive number of warm climate plants. The ice core samples have discovered that many of these fossils are below sea level.[31] The question is, why? Possible explanations include that Antarctica was once in a warmer latitude and moved, or that the magnetic poles have shifted (as mentioned earlier), or that the oceans have changed dramatically. The facts are clear. A once warm-climate land mass now lies beneath ice three miles thick in spots. The common thread through all of these explanations is the scientific fact of a catastrophic change. Sadly, instead of completely scientific explanations, supposed scientific and academic articles lead off with dogmatic mythological assertions: "around 40 million years ago," "millions of years ago," "40,000 year cycles."

A catastrophe could turn Antarctica from a warm climate into a frozen wasteland very quickly. The articles describing Antarctica's past might have much correct scientific data, but these dogmatic mythological foundational assertions make the entire article read like something from a tabloid.

There is abundant evidence that Antarctica was once warm. Warm climate animal and plant fossils abound.

Ice core samples have revealed that many of these fossils are below sea level.

Ice Core Samples and *Glacier Girl*

Researchers annually take core samples of glaciers and massive ice caps such as those covering Antarctica. They count each layer as a single year and publish a date. As with radiometric dating, it is not possible to know the original condition of the ice cap or glacier. However, unlike radiometric dating, starting with a zero condition (no ice, bare ground) is reasonable. Assuming that the earth is older than the glacier or ice cap is also reasonable. So the speed with which a glacier or ice cap forms is critical to an accurate date.

The layers (of annual ice core samples) are counted as if each layer was a single year and a date is published. The speed with which a glacier forms is critical to an accurate date.

A squadron of P-38s made an emergency landing on a glacier in Greenland on July 15, 1942. For 50 years the squadron of planes had flowed with the glacier, being covered with more ice. One plane was buried in 268 feet of ice. The recovered plane was restored and renamed Glacier Girl.

A squadron of P-38s made an emergency landing on a glacier in Greenland on July 15, 1942. The pilots were rescued and the planes abandoned. On July 15, 1992, the final piece of one P-38 was dug out of the glacier. For 50 years the squadron of planes had flowed with the glacier while being covered with more ice. One plane was pulled out of the glacier more than two miles from the landing point, buried in 268 feet of ice. The recovered plane was restored and renamed Glacier Girl.32

If the same techniques which boldly pronounce with absolute certainty that core samples are tens of thousands of years old were applied to the ice which covered *Glacier Girl*, then that ice would have to be thousands of years old. Yet the scientific fact is that *Glacier Girl* was covered by 268 feet of ice. It is also a scientific fact that this ice was fifty years old. This particular glacier grew at a rate of almost 5.5 feet per year. At this rate, the thickest ice sheet in the world, Terre Adelie in Antarctica, could be formed in just over 2,500 years. Secular Humanists would insist that different conditions in the past required a much longer formation time. Any change in the conditions could just as easily have resulted in a shorter time for formation.

Besides counting the layers in core samples, methods of dating a glacier include testing the oxygen content of the water, studying the presence of CO_2, finding evidence of radioactive decay, and examining pieces of volcanic material. Fred Hall wrote a brief article, "Ice Cores Not All That Simple,"[33] showing how complicated glaciers really are. None of these methods are entirely reliable. While there have been hundreds, perhaps thousands, of computer and theoretical models developed to explain glacier formation, the only scientific observations are in line with the glacier which covered *Glacier Girl.*

Water Scale

Formations like the Grand Canyon were carved by water action. No one disputes this, but water action is a topic on which scientists can still find points of disagreement.

Anyone who has watched a movie from the 1950s or earlier has seen the common, at that time, technique of filming a scale model ship in a tank of water. Even with rather large ships, such as the ones used in Ben Hur, the water never looks quite real. The explanation is that water does not scale, that is, large amounts of water look and behave differently than smaller amounts of water. For realistic water, producers and directors had to either build full sized models or wait decades for 3-D animation.

Since water does not scale visually, scale models using water were believed to be inaccurate also. For example, water can cut channels through layers of mud. The resulting canyons look something like a scale model of the Grand Canyon. These models have been dismissed as unrealistic simply because water does not scale. This idea that water does not scale, however, is not always true. Bridges built in powerful rivers, especially rivers prone to flooding, are often washed away.

Bridges built in powerful rivers, especially rivers prone to flood, are often washed away. Engineers building a new bridge over the Mississippi River at Alton, IL, between 1990 and 1994, built a scale model to help prevent that from happening. The scale model they built used real water to examine the direction and amount of force the Mississippi River would exert on the new bridge.

Engineers building a new bridge over the Mississippi River at Alton, IL, between 1990 and 1994, built a scale model to help prevent that from happening. The scale model they built used real water to examine the direction and amount of force the Mississippi River would exert on the new bridge.34

Though the water did not "look" to scale, the water flow and pressure information was accurate enough to allow the engineers to see what forces they had to contend with. Because of the model, modifications were made in the bridge's design. These modifications are likely the reason the bridge is still standing today.

Water Salinity

The study of water and its properties gives scientists many ways to learn about the earth. It is also a very much-abused study when it comes to dating the earth. One of the most unusual methods of dating is measuring the salt content of the sea. This method assumes a constant and steady addition of salt to the sea by freshwater rivers and a constant and steady evaporation rate.[35]

While this method is often cited in textbooks as one of many dating methods "proving" an ancient earth, it is fraught with so many difficulties that it has few educated defenders. It is usually referred to as an "additional" or "support" method of dating.

The first major scientific problem with using the salt content of the sea as a dating method is the wide disparity in salt content among the world's bodies of water. The Mediterranean Sea has a much higher salt content than the Atlantic, which has a higher salt content than the Antarctic. Is the Mediterranean older than the rest of the oceans of the world? Are the rivers that flow into the Mediterranean saltier than the rest of the rivers of the world? The scientific answer to both of these questions is either "no" or "we do not know".

People have attempted to date the seas using salt content since at least Sir Isaac Newton's time. Simply measuring the contact of salt requires a date no more than 100 million years old. Drs. "Austin and Humphreys calculated that the ocean must be less than 62 million years old. It's important to stress that this is not the actual age, but a maximum age. That is, this evidence is consistent with any age up to 62 million years, including the biblical age of about 6000 years."[36]

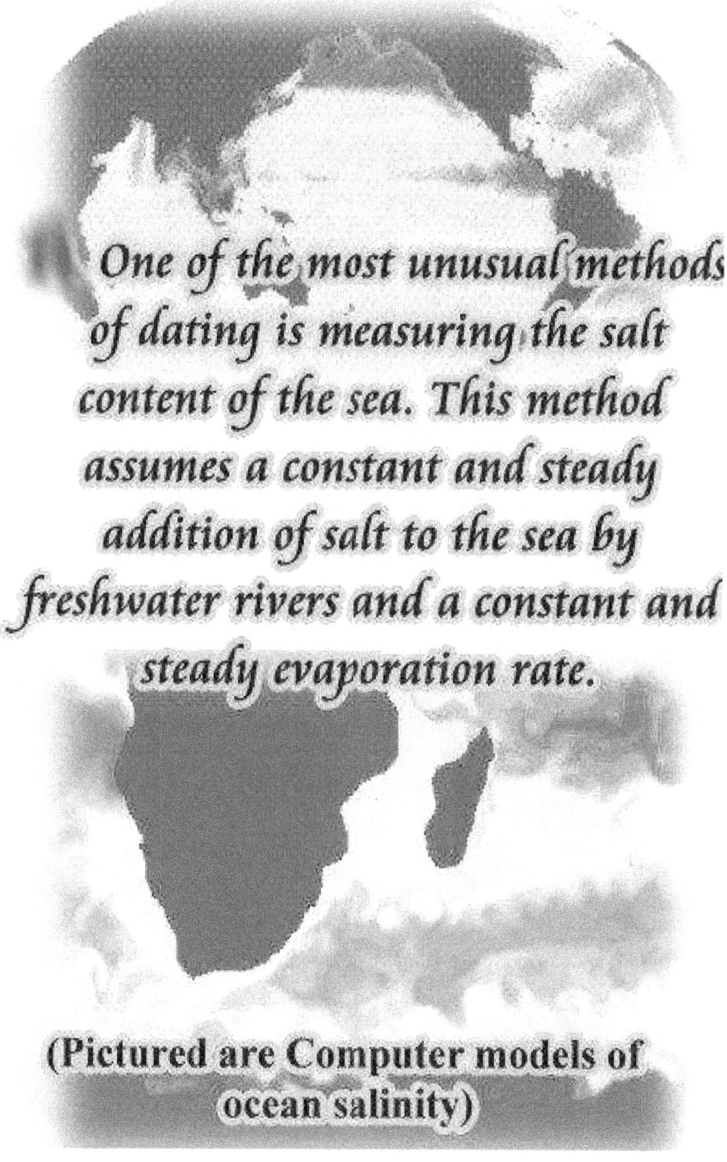

One of the most unusual methods of dating is measuring the salt content of the sea. This method assumes a constant and steady addition of salt to the sea by freshwater rivers and a constant and steady evaporation rate.

(Pictured are Computer models of ocean salinity)

Providence Canyon in southwest Georgia, sometimes called "Georgia's Little Grand Canyon" is 1100 acres of canyons carved out by erosion since the early 1800s.

Providence Canyon

Water's power to shape the landscape provides us with another amazing creation in southwest Georgia. Providence Canyon, sometimes called "Georgia's Little Grand Canyon" is 1100 acres of canyons carved out by erosion since the early 1800s.[37] Though much smaller than the Grand Canyon, it is still one of the largest canyons in America. As the model of the Alton, Illinois bridge helped engineers understand the Mississippi River; Providence Canyon helps us understand the Grand Canyon in Arizona. While neither the Alton Bridge nor the Providence Canyon are perfect models, on a small scale they both accurately model the effects of far greater amounts of water.

Though Providence Canyon is smaller than the Grand Canyon, it has many similar features. The formation of Providence is a scientific fact. Since Providence Canyon is less than two hundred years old, there is no scientific reason to believe the Grand Canyon, or any other canyon, must be millions of years old. All that is needed to make a canyon larger than Providence Canyon is more water, not more time.

Arches National Park

Just a few hundred miles north of the Grand Canyon is Arches National Park in Southeast Utah. When the National Park Service took over management of the park in 1971 there were over 2000 natural sandstone arches. Since then many arches have collapsed, the most famous being the collapse of Wall Arch on August 4-5, 2008. Though the exact number of collapsed arches is not documented, if only one arch were to collapse every three years, in less than 675 years there would not be any arches left. There is no evidence that there were ever hundreds of thousands or millions of arches. The evidence indicates that there were never many more arches than we see now. And there is evidence that many arches have fallen since 1971.

The scientific conclusion, based on the scientifically observed collapse of arches, is that either conditions in the recent past were drastically different to preserve the arches or that the arches are much younger than Secular Humanism proclaims them to be. If conditions were similar to the conditions we know now, the arches could be not older than about 4000 years old. They could easily be younger.[38]

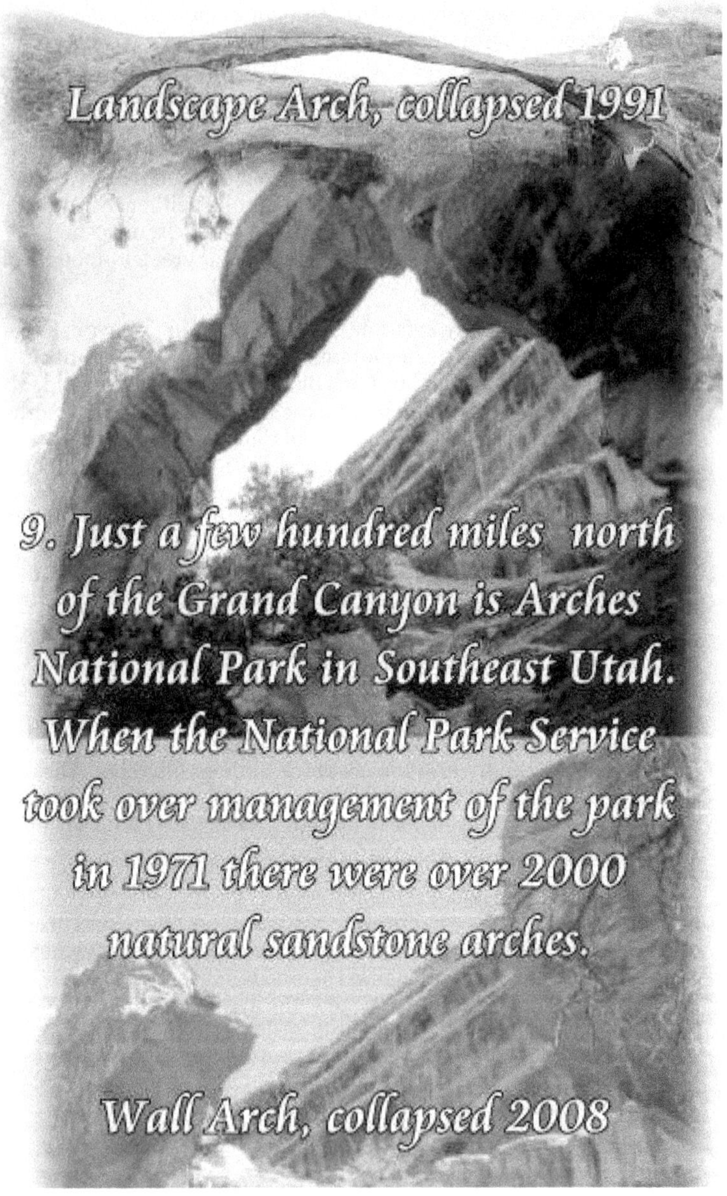
Landscape Arch, collapsed 1991
9. Just a few hundred miles north of the Grand Canyon is Arches National Park in Southeast Utah. When the National Park Service took over management of the park in 1971 there were over 2000 natural sandstone arches.
Wall Arch, collapsed 2008

The picture was taken in late 1987 at level 5 workings in the lead-zinc mine at Mt Isa, in north-western Queensland, Australia.

Photo taken beneath the Lincoln Memorial in the 1960s

Photo Credits[40]

Stalactites and Stalagmites

Stalactites and stalagmites are another geologic feature formed by water. The Lincoln Memorial was built between 1914 and 1922 over land formerly at the bottom of the Potomac River. Stalactites and stalagmites have formed beneath the stairs in the period since the construction was completed (less than 100 years at the time of this writing) as described below.

"... Supports were driven down almost 100 feet to bedrock. This cavernous foundation provides an ideal location for cave-like formations to actively grow. Water on the surface slowly makes its way down through cement stairs into the empty space below. Cement is 'glued' together by calcium carbonate. As the water passes through the cement, it dissolves some calcium carbonate and carries it downward. When the water reaches the open space, it leaves behind the calcium carbonate, creating stalactites and stalagmites. This is the same way cave stalactites and stalagmites form, only instead of passing through cement stairs, natural cave features usually form when ground water passes through limestone. Since the cave formations at the Lincoln Memorial aren't in an actual cave, maybe we should call them 'under-the-stair-ites'."[40]

Dave E. Matson attempts to claim that all the stalactites and stalagmites in existence could not have formed in less than 5000 years.

"The Bulletin of the National Speleological Society (37: p.21, 1975) gives a stalactite/stalagmite growth rate of ... 0.1 to 10 centimeters per thousand years. An exceptional spurt of growth might exceed ... 10 centimeters or 2.5 inches per thousand years. ...Thus, a 60 foot giant, as might be found in Carlsbad Caverns, would have a minimum estimated age of about 180,000 years."[41]

Timpanogos Cave National Monument, in American Fork, Utah, is described in park literature as being roughly 65 million years old. Although the claim that the stalactites and stalagmites are millions of years old is no longer being made, secularists still demand thousands of years for the formation of these cave features, usually tens or hundreds of thousands, not the less than a hundred necessary in the Lincoln Memorial.

"Water trickling through the limestone overlying the caves dissolved calcite and other minerals from the rock. ...The water deposited its mineral load as tiny crystals on a cave ceiling, wall, or floor. Over thousands of years, as countless crystals were deposited, a variety of cave formations took shape--stalactites, stalagmites, flowstone, helictites, and others." [42]

Julia E. Cole, University of Tucson professor of Geosciences, studied a limestone cave in southern AZ. The article described the cave formations as "natural climate archives" and said, "The stalagmite yielded an almost continuous century-by-century climate record spanning 55,000 to 11,000 years ago. ... Each climate regime lasted from a few hundred years to more than one thousand years."[43] The article's photo shows Sarah Truebe, a geosciences doctoral student, with a cave formation less than 2 feet tall. The cave itself appears to be less than ten feet in height. The use of these cave features as "natural climate archives" is based on utter conjecture and uniformitarian presupposition.

Each of these claims is nothing more than a gratuitous assertion. The evidence shows the formation of these features, especially of stalactites, take only decades.[44]

Diamonds

Diamonds are reported by Secular Humanists to be at least 45 million years old, formed 75 miles or deeper beneath the earth. Yet laboratory-produced diamonds are made commercially. In 1953 the first industrial grade laboratory-produced diamonds were made. These tiny laboratory-produced diamonds were and still are manufactured for industrial applications such as cutting tools and electrical coatings. More advanced processes coat lenses with laboratory-produced diamond. The laboratory produced diamond industry gradually increased the size and quality of laboratory-produced diamonds. In early 2010 a 2-carat laboratory-produced gemstone-quality diamond was produced in about three days.

The FTC (Federal Trade Commission) requires the label of laboratory-produced, laboratory-manufactured, or for the product to be identified by the name of the manufacturer along with the specific type of gem rather than using the term synthetic when referring to the type of gem. A laboratory-produced diamond is identical to a geologically-produced diamond is every way; chemically, structurally, and appearance, even on the microscopic level.

A synthetic diamond is still a technically correct term when applied to a laboratory-produced diamond, but some vendors use the term "synthetic" diamond to refer to cubic zirconia, cut glass or any other manmade substitute for a diamond. So the FTC wants to distinguish between real diamonds, both geologic and laboratory-produced, and other crystals which are not diamonds. These other crystals which are not diamonds are often marketed as synthetic diamonds, which they are not.

The existence of laboratory-produced diamonds is a scientific fact. They are produced and reproduced under controlled conditions.

Depending on color desired, other chemicals can be added to the crystal-growing process and the resulting gemstone can be pink, green, blue, yellow, and colorless (white). The diamond mining industry is concerned about the number of laboratory-produced diamonds being manufactured. Proclaiming the youngest naturally-occurring diamond to be 45 million years old is a dogmatic religious pronouncement contrary to science.

Russian Diamond Mine

Laboratory-produced diamonds were commercially made in 1953.

The first laboratory-produced diamonds were industrial grade.

H. Tracy Hall

The most reasonable scientific theory is that diamonds were formed suddenly under the correct conditions.[45]

The RATE (Radioisotopes and the Age of The Earth) research project at the Institute for Creation Research found Carbon 14 in both natural diamonds and ten US coal beds. The upper range of the possible dates for the diamonds was 55,000 years.[46]

"R.E. Taylor of the Department of Anthropology at the University of California-Riverside and of the Cotsen Institute of Archaeology at the University of California-Los Angeles teamed with J. Southon at the Keck Accelerator Mass Spectrometry Laboratory of the Department of Earth System Science at the University of California-Irvine to analyze nine natural diamonds from Brazil. All nine diamonds are conventionally regarded as being at least of early Paleozoic age, that is, at least several hundred million years old. So if they really are that old they should not have any intrinsic ^{14}C in them. Eight of the diamonds yielded radiocarbon 'ages' of 64,900 years to 80,000 years."[46]

Coal and Oil

Carbon can be turned into diamonds, coal and oil. Most of the world uses coal and oil to heat homes and run electric generators. Coal and oil are abundant. Coal was made from plant material that was covered with water and neither coal nor oil is being formed geologically today. There is, however, one possible exception.

When Mount St. Helens erupted in 1980, the explosion filled Spirit Lake with logs. The bottom of the lake was filled with plant material covered in mud from the eruption. This was under the lake water. Examination of this material showed the early stages of the formation of coal. This, however, is a very tiny deposit compared to the massive coal deposits worldwide.[47]

Crude petroleum is also produced on a small scale in laboratories from garbage. Like diamonds and petrified wood, the processes that formed coal beds and oil deposits are not going on today. Something is dramatically different about conditions today. Like diamond formation and petrified wood formation, the only possible scientific example of oil and coal formation shows coal and oil being formed rapidly in a catastrophic event.[48]

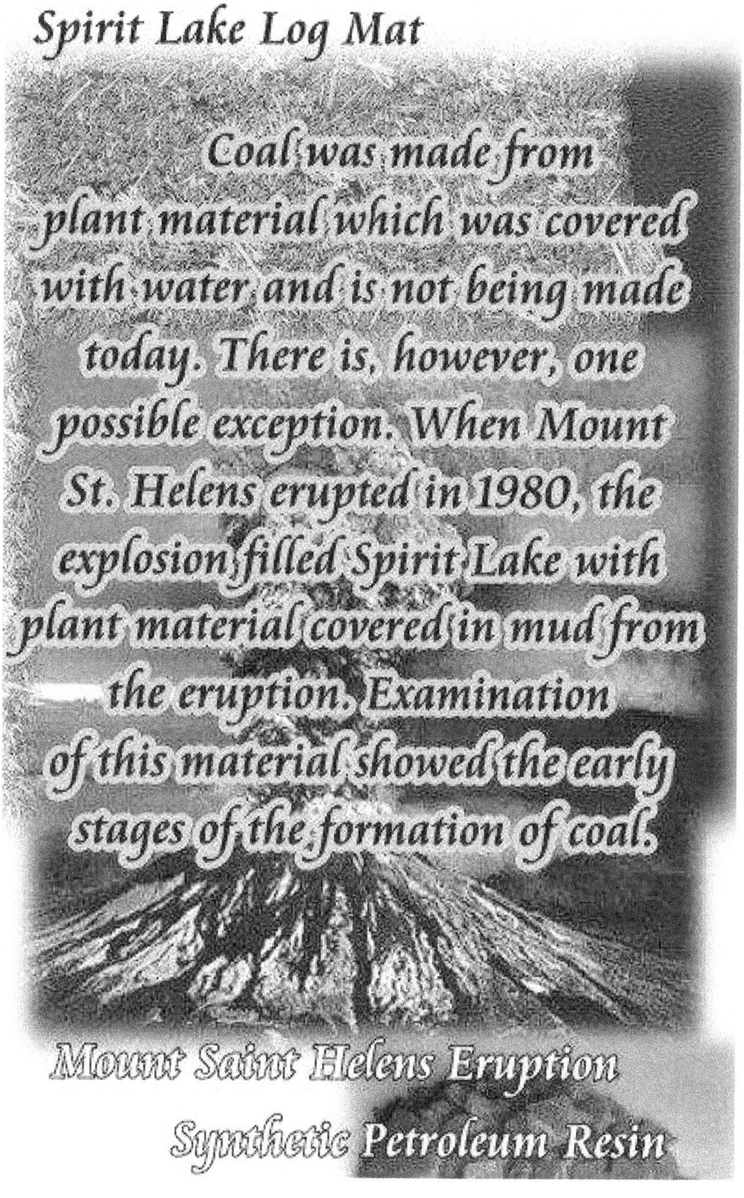

Spirit Lake Log Mat

Coal was made from plant material which was covered with water and is not being made today. There is, however, one possible exception. When Mount St. Helens erupted in 1980, the explosion filled Spirit Lake with plant material covered in mud from the eruption. Examination of this material showed the early stages of the formation of coal.

Mount Saint Helens Eruption

Synthetic Petroleum Resin

Petrified Wood

Just off of Interstate 40 in the Navajo Indian reservation in northeast Arizona is the Petrified Forest. While the Petrified Forest in Arizona is the most well-known of the Petrified Forests, petrified wood can be found all over the world, though it is abundant in dry regions of the western United States. Petrified wood is wood that has turned to stone. The authors have seen petrified tree stumps in South Dakota more than twenty feet in diameter. Perhaps there is a rare exception somewhere, but wood today is not becoming petrified except synthetically. Though modern wood can be synthetically turned into petrified wood, the process only works under highly-controlled conditions.

The existence of synthetic diamonds and manmade petrified wood both scientifically prove that these substances require not immense periods of time but proper conditions to form them. They can be made in days, weeks or months. The religious belief that wood petrified over a great period of time and that the process took place thousands or millions of years ago is without scientific evidence. Even people who insist that wood petrified thousands or millions of years ago must admit wood is not naturally petrifying today. Therefore, something has dramatically changed. Though the most reasonable scientific explanation is a catastrophe, religious dogmas refuse to allow for these scientific explanations.[49]

Japanese scientists fastened pieces of wood in a hot acid lake. They observed that "after only 7 years the wood had turned into stone, petrified with silica."[50]

Wood today is not becoming petrified except synthetically. Though modern wood can be synthetically turned into petrified wood, the process only works under highly controlled conditions.

Electron Microscopic image of laboratory-petrified wood.

Preservation in Ice, Tar, and Peat

There is an entire class of creatures entombed in tar, peat bogs, muck and sand; organic remains clearly younger than fossils. Some of the more well-known of these creatures are woolly mammoths, mastodons, saber-toothed tigers, woolly rhinos, and giant ground sloths. These creatures are not fossilized, that is, turned to stone, but frozen. Though some were preserved in warmer areas by tar, most specimens are frozen and decay quickly when thawed.

Undigested plant remains in their stomachs prove that the animals were frozen quickly. Though pop culture places these animals in the Ice Age, the types of undigested plants found in their stomachs suggest that at the time the animals were frozen they and the plants lived in a warm climate. This indicates that tropical, subtropical or at least temperate conditions existed even in Siberia, Alaska, and northern Canada. Though these creatures obviously died in a catastrophe, this catastrophe was far more recent than the catastrophe which fossilized billions of other creatures worldwide.[51]

Soft Tissue in Dinosaur Bones

Creatures found in tar and ice are said by evolutionists to have come from a later time period than those fossilized, thus minimizing the troublesome issues of their real age. It is harder to dismiss one discovery, soft tissue from the bone of a dinosaur. There is no question that soft tissue deteriorates very rapidly. There is no question as to what such a discovery must mean. Dinosaurs, at least the ones leaving remains with soft tissue, had to have been living at the same time humans lived. The question is, has such a discovery actually been made? Paleontologist Mary Higby Schweitzer of North Carolina University has published her discovery of the remains of blood cells in dinosaur fossils and soft tissue remains in a T. Rex. John Asara of Harvard Medical School and researchers at Palo Alto have verified it.

Blood for transfusions can only be stored for about six weeks. Cryopreservation is only good for about ten years. These facts should help put this discovery into perspective. Not only did Dr. Schweitzer's team find bone cells, blood cells, and proteins, they also found dinosaur DNA.[52]

We should also compare this to the soft tissue discovered in a female wooly mammoth carcass. Even uniformitarians only date this to be 10,000 years old. We know that this is more than twice the actual age of the wooly mammoth. The conditions for preservation of the tissue were much better. It was preserved in permafrost at -10° C. Physiologist Kevin Campbell of the University of Manitoba wrote in an email to Kate Wong in a May 30, 2013 article that, "ancient DNA is highly fragmented and by no means "ready to go" into the next mammoth embryo." He also said "how were these samples preserved in this state for so long?"[53]

So the soft tissue of Ice Age woolly mammoths preserved in very favorable conditions is puzzling. The preservation of dinosaur soft tissue for millions of years is, by comparison, impossible.[54]

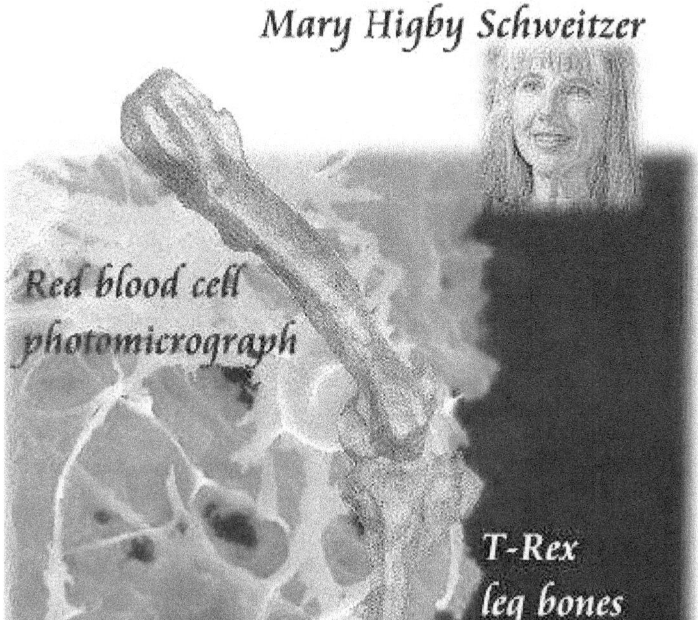

One highly controversial discovery is soft tissue from the bone of a dinosaur. There is no question that soft tissue deteriorates very rapidly and can be at most a few thousand years old.

The evidence is overwhelming. The conclusions, however, are even more astounding. Rather than admit the obvious, that the bones with the remains of soft tissue were young, the published reports maintain that the bones are millions of years old, but some process not now understood preserved the soft tissue. There is no evidence of such an unknown process. This is a classic attempt to make the evidence fit the preconception.[54] It is also a glaring example of professional bigotry. This kind of article can never be published without a claim that the bones are millions of years old.

Mary Schweitzer is firmly committed to ignoring the implications of her work, that these bones are very, very young. That secures her professional position. If she were to acknowledge this implication, that would be the end of her professional career. Eventually well-orchestrated condemnation would cost the author her job, as documented repeatedly in Ben Stein's movie *Expelled*.[55]

No Great Ape Fossils

"No fossils of any of the great apes: gorillas, chimpanzees or orangutans; have ever been found. As far as the fossil record is concerned, they never existed; and yet we know from the evidence of our own eyes that they did, and do."[56]

Though hundreds, perhaps thousands, of news releases, newspaper articles, magazine articles, radio, video, and internet announcements have proclaimed the discovery of a fossil of a great ape, none has ever been verified. Such discoveries have either proven to not be fossilized, and therefore much younger, or not to be a great ape. Some who carefully examine the evidence come to the reasoned conclusion that evolution is not scientifically valid. They do not find reproductive links in the evolutionary chain. Creationists are frequently charged with ignoring the evidence. Richard Dawkins claims to refute the fossil gap arguments in his numerous books, although he doesn't really refute them at all. He just dismisses the arguments with a bald, unsupported statement that large numbers of intermediates exist.

"Creationists are deeply enamored of the fossil record ...[They] repeat, over and over, the mantra that it is full of 'gaps': 'Show me your "intermediates!"' ...We [have]...massive numbers ... to document evolutionary history ... beautiful 'intermediates.' ... The fossil evidence for evolution in many major animal groups is wonderfully strong. Nevertheless there are, of course, gaps, and creationists love them obsessively."[57]

The truth is that there is nothing for mankind to link to. Neanderthals interbred with modern man. A skull found in *Pestera cu Oase*, "The Cave of Bones" in Romania, has characteristics of both so-called "species."

“The skull bearing both older and modern characteristics is discussed in a paper by Erik Trinkaus of Washington University in St. Louis. The report appears in today’s [January 15, 2007] issue of *Proceedings of the National Academy of Sciences*.

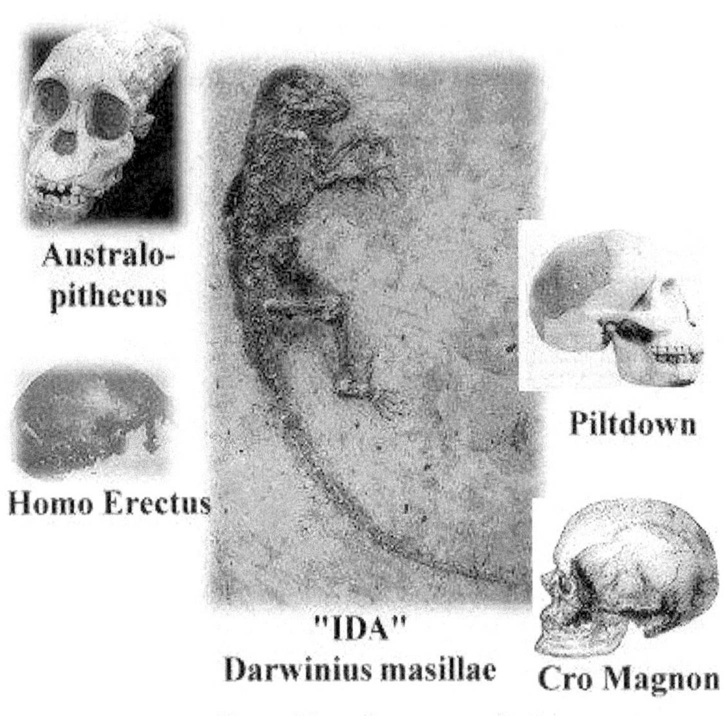

"No fossils of any of the great apes - gorillas, chimpanzees or orangutans - have ever been found. As far as the fossil record is concerned, they never existed; and yet we know from the evidence of our own eyes that they did, and do."

"...The researchers said the skull had the same proportions as a modern human head and lacked the large brow ridge commonly associated with Neanderthals. However, there were also features that are unusual in modern humans, such as frontal flattening, a fairly large bone behind the ear and exceptionally large upper molars, which are seen among Neanderthals and other early hominids.

"Such differences raise important questions about the evolutionary history of modern humans," said co-author João Zilhão of the University of Bristol, England.[58]

Therefore, Neanderthals are men. Without any fossil evidence of creatures for man to evolve from, evolution of humans is a religious leap of faith. There is no evidence of any link and no fossil evidence of anything to link to.

Mitochondrial DNA

Any link would controlled by DNA. The most important aspect of the soft tissue discovery in the dinosaur is the DNA. DNA is in all cells of all living organisms. The tiniest cell in the human body contains the same DNA in the nucleus as the largest cell. This genetic coding determines hair color, shape of our nostrils, and every other detail of our body. As every student of high school biology knows, this DNA inside the nucleus contains genetic material from both our mother and our father. But many people are unaware of another type of DNA known as mitochondrial DNA. Mitochondrial DNA exists within the cell's mitochondria outside of the nucleus and contains only genetic material from our mothers. Since there is no mixing of genetic material, a child's mitochondrial DNA should be an exact duplicate of the mother's mitochondrial DNA.

Mitochondrial DNA controls individual cell functions, not genetically encoded information. Infinite generations with genetically different fathers can have identical mitochondrial DNA but radically different physical characteristics. This should allow for a trace of mitochondrial DNA back to the beginning the human race. We could perform this trace, except for the problem of genetic mutations. Since a child's normal mitochondrial DNA is identical to his mother's, any mutation starts a new line. Minor mutations are difficult to detect and major mutations, such as those caused by massive radiation exposure, produce children who are unable to survive. But a few extremely rare mutations have produced traceable lines.

In 1997, *Nature Genetics* published an article with the innocuous title "A high observed substitution rate in the human mitochondrial DNA control rate." An abstract is available online for free. Though the technical language is absolutely necessary for accuracy, it distracts the average reader. Even with nothing but the abstract, the force of this study is overwhelming.

The most important aspect of the soft tissue discovery in this dinosaur is the DNA. Many people are unaware of another type of DNA known as mitochondrial DNA. Mitochondrial DNA exists within the cell's mitochondria outside of the nucleus and contains only genetic material from our mothers.

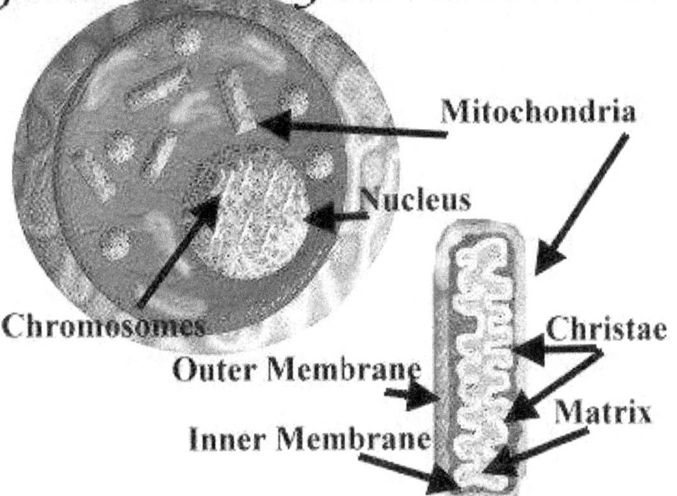

Mitochondrial DNA is not contained in the Nucleus but is in the cytoplasm of the Cell.

"...We report a direct measurement of the intergenerational substitution rate in the human CR

[Control Region – a section of the DNA that controls other sections of DNA]. We compared DNA sequences of two CR hypervariable segments from close maternal relatives, from 134 independent mtDNA lineages spanning 327 generational events. Ten substitutions were observed, resulting in an empirical rate of 1/33 generations, or 2.5/site/Myr. This is roughly twenty-fold higher than estimates derived from phylogenetic analyses. This disparity cannot be accounted for simply by substitutions at mutational hot spots, suggesting additional factors that produce the discrepancy between very near-term and long-term apparent rates of sequence divergence. The data also indicate that extremely rapid segregation of CR sequence variants between generations is common in humans, with a very small mtDNA bottleneck."[59]

What this study did was take mitochondrial DNA samples from living volunteers and compared it to mitochondrial DNA from their ancestors. The test subjects had to have accurate records of their ancestors for hundreds of years, so all test subjects had to be European. Corpses had to be available with accurate records and preserved well enough that mitochondrial DNA could be obtained. The study went back approximately 550 years.

The test results proved that mutations happen at a significantly higher rate than geneticists thought possible. The resulting statistical analysis came to two stunning conclusions.

First, applying this data to other studies gives an approximate date of 6000-6,500 BP (Before Present) for Mitochondrial Eve.[60]

Catastrophes powerful enough to move marine ammonites to the top of Mount Everest, and tilt Lake Titicaca, could easily, temporarily and dramatically, increase the mutation rate, making even the 6000-year-old date too old.

Second is the "very small mtDNA bottleneck." This means that at some point in the history of the human race there were very few women. Bryan Sykes, author of *The Seven Daughters of Eve* believes that all Europeans currently alive can be traced back to one of seven women. Though Sykes is a well-respected English geneticist, as a committed Secular Humanist he makes two common though critical errors. These two errors have become the "standard" which any geneticist who expects to be published must adhere to. These errors are required by the religious dogma of Secular Humanism. Because his religious dogma demands that the human race is much older than the scientific evidence shows, he makes the leap of faith that the

2.5/site/Myr was lower in the past. His second error is assuming by a leap of faith, without any scientific evidence, that these seven women represent the smallest point of the bottleneck.

The Bible says that the sons of Noah brought their wives on the ark. These three women are the smallest point of the bottleneck. Their daughters or granddaughters might be the seven women of Bryan Sykes. Since conditions at that time could easily cause increased genetic mutations, their daughters, granddaughters or great granddaughters could easily be the seven women isolated by Bryan Sykes. When you read *The Seven Daughters of Eve,* understand that the last part of the book is devoted to fictional indoctrination. He novelizes each of these women and places each of them in a "cavewoman" setting. This is as antiscientific an approach as possible. Nevertheless the book was published. The scientific evidence of Mitochondrial DNA concludes that the human race is much younger than the published dates, less than 10,000 years, and that at one time in the very recent past the entire human race had no more than seven women. Bryan Sykes added the cavewoman fictions to assure publication. Such fabrications are the essence of the academic requirements for upholding the secularist dogma.[56]

He also claims that this genetic bottleneck of seven women is only for women of European descent, not the entire human race.

A much better study, without the approval of the academic community, therefore without the publicity, is Dr. Robert W. Carter's *Adam, Eve and Noah vs Modern Genetics.* This article also explores why the Y chromosome supports a recent genetic bottleneck. Dr. Carter states, "There are three main mitochondrial DNA lineages found across the world. The evolutionists have labeled these lines "M", "N", and "R"..."[61]

Thermodynamics

Engineers can earn a PhD in many subcategories of the massive field of thermodynamics. The dynamics of heat affects all other aspects of engineering. The first two laws of thermodynamics are well-tested and well-proved. While the implications are massive, the first two laws are simple. The first law of thermodynamics: The conservation of energy. Energy can be changed from one form to another, but it cannot be created or destroyed. The total amount of energy and matter in the universe remains constant, merely changing from one form to another.

Albert Einstein popularized the first law of thermodynamics with his famous proposition "If a body at rest emits a total energy of E while remaining at rest, then the mass of that body decreases by E/c^2."

This is oversimplified into $E=mc^2$. Though technically this only applies to a body at rest, it is a workable understanding of the concept that matter and energy are interchangeable. In this formula, "c" represents the speed of light, in a vacuum, 299, 792, 458 meters per second or 186,300 miles per second.

Here is a link to a blog which works through the Lorentz transformation to explain how Albert Einstein arrived at his final formula. [62]

Thermodynamics

First Law: Energy changes form, cannot be created or destroyed. Amount of energy and matter constant, only changes form. The universe is either 1) eternal, 2) created out of nothing, or 3) came into existence through some unknown process.

Second Law:
Potential energy always less than initial state.
Entropy = "heat death" for the entire universe. Motionless, at a uniform temperature near absolute zero, broken down into subatomic particles.

According to the first law of thermodynamics the universe is either 1) eternal, 2) created out of nothing, or 3) came into existence through some process that we know nothing about.

The Second Law of Thermodynamics states "in all energy exchanges, if no energy enters or leaves the system, the potential energy of the state will always be less than that of the initial state." This is also commonly referred to as entropy. Another way of stating entropy is that all energy changes are in a downward direction.[63] Without a belief in the religious dogma that the universe is infinite and can therefore obtain energy from "outside" the system (which is scientifically unprovable), entropy will eventually lead to a "heat death" for the entire universe. Everything in the universe will be motionless, at a uniform temperature near absolute zero, broken down into subatomic particles.

Each one of these examples of physical evidence has the same message. To repeat a quote from Dr. Danny R. Faulkner at the beginning of this chapter:

"While the early faint Sun paradox does not tell us that the Solar System is only thousands of years old, it does seem to rule out the age being billions of years."[64]

We can rephrase this statement to make it more inclusive. While none of these points in this chapter tell us that the earth is only thousands of years old, each one individually and all of them collectively seem to rule out the age being billions of years.

We close with the words of the committed Secular Humanist, Isaac Asimov, as he condemns not only his own belief system, but also the belief systems of everyone who reject the evidence for the Word of God.

"I believe in evidence. I believe in observation, measurement, and reasoning, confirmed by independent observers. I'll believe anything, no matter how wild and ridiculous, if there is evidence for it. The wilder and more ridiculous something is, however, the firmer and more solid the evidence will have to be."[65]

Isaac Asimov

"I believe in evidence. I believe in observation, measurement, and reasoning, confirmed by independent observers. I'll believe anything, no matter how wild and ridiculous, if there is evidence for it. The wilder and more ridiculous something is, however, the firmer and more solid the evidence will have to be."

Isaac Asimov

"We can make inspired guesses, but we don't know for certain what physical and chemical properties of the planet's crust, its ocean, and its atmosphere made it so conducive to such a sudden appearance of life..."

---

1 Charles Darwin, "Letter to Asa Gray," (Harvard Professor of Biology), 18 June, 1857.

2 John Adams, "Argument in defence of the [English] soldiers in the Boston Massacre trial," December 1770.

3 Mark Twain, *Life on the Mississippi,* first edition published by Osgood and Company, 1883.

4 Samuel Johnson, *The History of Rasselas, Prince of Abissinia,* 1759.

5 Dennis Prager, "Breastfeeding as a Religion," World Net Daily, http://wnd.com/, posted November 11, 2003 1:00 am Eastern.

6 Richard W. Pogge, Astronomy 162: Introduction to Stars, Galaxies, & the Universe, 2006, http://www.astronomy.ohio-state.edu/-pogge/Ast162/Unit2/sunshine.html

7 "Fusion", *Nobelprize.org* updated 9 Mar 2013 http://nobelprize.org/nobel_prizes/physics/articles/fusion/sun_4.html

8 Ian T Durham, "Hans Bethe" (Biographic article about Hans Bethe), Saint Anselm College, Goffstown, NH, http://www-history.mcs.st-and.ac.uk/Biographies/Bethe.html

9 Akridge, R. 1980. "The Sun Is Shrinking." *Acts & Facts.* 9 (4) and Faulkner, D. 1998. "The Young Faint Sun Paradox and the Age of the Solar System." *Acts & Facts.* 27 (6). [these two articles are quoted and paraphrased from throughout this section]

10 Roger Freedman, Robert Geller, William J. Kaufmann, *Universe: The Solar System,* Macmillan, New York, NY, 2010.

11 Two links to articles which examine the early faint sun paradox problem in more detail:

http://creation.com/our-steady-sun-a-problem-for-billions-of-years

http://creation.com/the-young-faint-sun-paradox-and-the-age-of-the-solar-system

12 Daily Mail online, October 3, 2011 http://www.dailymail.co.uk/sciencetech/article-2044480/NASAs-SDO-satellite-shows-boiling-sun-stunning-detail.html#ixzz2MnMZZ5lS

13 Ethan Siegal PhD in theoretical astrophysics at the University of Florida *Starts with a Bang.* "How the Sun works, from the inside out", originally posted August 12, 2011.

14 D. Russell Humphreys, Steven A. Austin, John R. Baumgardner, and Andrew A. Snelling, "Helium Diffusion Age of 6000 Years Supports Accelerated Nuclear Decay," *Creation Research Society Quarterly Journal. (CRSQ)* Vol 41 No 1 June 2004, *Creation Research.org,* Copyright © 2004 by Creation Research Society. Also Dr. Don DeYoung, *Thousands, Not Billions: Challenging an Icon of Evolution Questioning the Age of the Earth,* Green Forest, AR: Master Books, Inc., 2005.

15 Utah Geological Survey, *Utah.gov.*

16 Radiometric Dating background from the position of those who believe it to be valid can be studied on *TalkOrigins.org.,* especially the article *Radiometric Dating and the Geological Time Scale: Circular Reasoning or Reliable Tools?* Andrew MacRae Copyright 1997-2004 [Text last updated: October 2, 1998] and also these two books: G. Brent Dalrymple, *The Age of the Earth.* Stanford University Press: Stanford, CA, 1991. G. Faure, *Principles of Isotope Geology,* 2nd. edition. John Wiley and Sons: New York, NY, 1986.

17 John Michael Fischer, *Dinosaur bones have been Carbon-14 dated to less than 40,000 years,* http://newgeology.us/presentation48.html, 2012-2014.

18 Press release, Public Information Office, Jet Propulsion Laboratory, California Institute of Technology, *NASA,* July 21, 1994.

19 Andrew A. Snelling, "The Earth's magnetic field and the age of the Earth," first published: *Creation (Creation Ministries International),* 13(4):44-48 September 1991.

20 D. Russell Humphreys, *Earth's Magnetic Field is Decaying Steadily –with a Little Rhythm,* CRSQ (Creation Research Society Quarterly) July 1, 2010. http://www.creationresearch.org/crsq/articles/47/47_3/CRSQ%20 Winter%202011%20Humphreys.pdf

21 Jonathan Sarfati, *The Earth's Magnetic Field: Evidence That the Earth Is Young* http://creation.com/the-earths-magnetic-field-evidence-that-the-earth-is-young

22 Alexandra Witze, "Geomagnetic Flip-Flops in a Flash," *Science News,* September 25, 210 Vol. 178, Number 7, and R.S. Coe, and M. Prevot, 1989. "Evidence suggesting extremely rapid field variation during a geomagnetic reversal," *Earth and Planetary Science Letters, Elsevier,* Amsterdam, Netherlands, vol. 92, pp. 296-297.

23 http://www.answersingenesis.org/home/area/cfol/ch3-grand-canyon.asp

24 Type/Process: Pyroclastic Flow
Volcanic Status: Historical
Image Number: 029-008
Photographer: Norm Banks, 1980 (U.S. Geological Survey)
Summit Elevation: 2549 meters
Latitude/Longitude: 46.20 N / 122.18 W
Timeframe: Last known eruption 1964 or later
Region: Canada and Western USA

25 G.R. Morton, (An old-earth supporter who calls himself a creationist apologist) "Young-Earth Arguments: A Second Look," 1998, *home.entouch.net.*

26 J.B. Delair and E.F. Oppe, "The Lost Sea of Andes," in Charles Hapgood's *The Path of the Pole,* Chilton Book Company, Philadelphia, PA, 1970.

27 Donald W. Patten and Samuel R. Windsor, "Catastrophic Theory of Mountain Uplifts (A Crustal Deformation Theory)," *Catastrophism and Ancient History* Vol. XIII Part 1 January 1991.

28 "Ancient temple found under Lake Titicaca," *BBC News, UK,* Wednesday, 23 August, 2000, 11:04 GMT 12:04.

29 J. P. Davidson, W. E. Reed, and P. M. Davis, "The Rise and Fall of Mountain Ranges," in *Exploring Earth: An Introduction to Physical Geology,* Upper Saddle River, New Jersey, Prentice Hall, 1997.

30 Erich A. Von Fange, "Time Upside Down," *Creation Research Quarterly,* June 1974.

31 *National Geographic,* July 26, 2008, "Tiny Fossils reveal Warm Antarctic Past," and *AntarcticConnection.com* reports on the Antarctic research stations.

32 Sean Pitman, M.D., in a PowerPoint presentation titled "Ancient Ice," created in Jan 2006, including testimony from a phone interview with Bob Cardin, project manager to recover one of the P38s lost on the glacier.

33 Fred Hall, "Ice Cores Not All That Simple," *AEON II:* 1, 1989:199.

34 "Superbridge," *NOVA,* PBS, November 12, 1997.

35 Dr. Nathan Green, online course overview for GEO.101, "Introduction to Geology," Spring 2006, University of Alabama.

36 Jonathan Sarfati, *Salty Seas: Evidence for a Young Earth, Creation* 21(1):16-17, December 1998, http://creation.com/salty-seas-evidence-for-a-young-earth

37 *GeorgiaEncyclopedia.org* gives background on the canyon but attributes its underlying geology to the "millions of years" formation theory. See also "Canyon Creation," by Rebecca Gibson, *Answers in Genesis,* September 2000.

38 National Park Service report on Wall Arch collapse with before and after photos, August 4-5, 2008.

39 Photo of recently-formed stalactites courtesy of Creation Ministries International (see footnote 44 for commentary on the Australian Mine photo). Lincoln Memorial Photo from National Parks services website.

40. National Park Services Website.

41 Dave E. Matson, "How Good Are Those Young-Earth Arguments?" on *Infidels.org*. copyright 1995.

42 *GORP.com* (Great Outdoor Recreation Page.)

43 "Cave Reveals Southwest's Abrupt Climate Swings During Ice Age," *Science Daily.com,* January 25, 2010.

44 http://creation.com/stalactites-do-not-take-millions-of-years

45 American Museum of Natural History website, "How Old are Kimberlites and Diamonds?" see also *Novori.com* for history and manufacture of laboratory produced diamonds.

46 Andrew Snelling (Dr.), "Radiocarbon in Diamonds Confirmed," *Answers in Genesis,* November 7, 2007. (This study was conducted during the *RATE (Radioisotopes and the Age of The Earth)* research project at the Institute for Creation Research.)

47 "Coal, Volcanism and Noah's Flood," *TJ (Technical Journal)* 1(1): *Creation Ministries International,* 11-29 April 1984.

48 A.A. Snelling, "The Recent Origin of Bass Strait Oil and Gas," Creation, 5 (2):43-46 March 1982.5

49 Phil McCafferty, "Instant petrified wood?" *Popular Science,* October 1992, pp. 56-57. also Hamilton Hicks, 'Mineralized sodium silicate solutions for artificial petrification of wood,' United States Patent Number 4,612,050, September 16,1986, pp. 1-3. As cited by: Steven Austin, *CatastroRef*—"Catastrophe Reference Database: Catastrophes in Earth History, Geologic Evidence, Speculation and Theory,*" Institute for Creation Research,* San Diego. Entry no. 267.

50 *Petrified Wood: Fast or Slow?* http://creation.com/petrified-wood-fast-or-slow

51 Michael Oard, *Frozen in Time: The Wooly Mammoth, The Ice Age and the Bible,* Green Forest, AR: Master Books, Inc., 2004.

52 http://creation.com/dino-dna-bone-cells#endRef5

53 http://www.nature.com/news/can-a-mammoth-carcass-really-preserve-flowing-blood-and-possibly-live-cells-1.13103

54 Schweitzer, Mary H. and Jennifer L. Wittmeyer, North Carolina State University; John R. Horner, Montana State University; Jan B. Toporski, Carnegie Institution of Washington Geophysical Laboratory. "Soft-Tissue Vessels and Cellular Preservation in Tyrannosaurus Rex." *Science,* March 25, 2005. (NC State, the N.C. Museum of Natural Sciences and the National Science Foundation funded the research.)

55 Kevin Miller, Ben Stein, writers, Producers Logan Craft, Walt Ruloff and John Sullivan, Director Nathan Frankowski. Assoc. Prod. Mark Mathis. Ed. Simon Tondeur. *Expelled: No Intelligence Allowed.* © 2008 Premise Media Corporation, Rampart Films Production.

56 Bryan Sykes, *The Seven Daughters of Eve: The Science That Reveals Our Genetic Ancestry.* W.W. Norton, New York, N.Y., 2001.

57 Richard Dawkins, *The Greatest Show on Earth,* Free Press, Simon and Schuster, New York, NY, also by Bantam Press Transworld Publishers in Great Britain, 2009.

58 Randolph E. Schmid (Associated Press), "Skull Suggests Interbreeding of Neanderthal and Modern Man," *The Denver Post,* January 15, 2007.

59 Parsons, Thomas J., et. al. "A high observed substitution rate in the human mitochondrial DNA control region." Nature Genetics 15, 363 - 368 (1997).

60 http://creation.com/refuting-evolution-chapter-6-humans-images-of-god-or-advanced-apes#r25

61 http://creation.com/noah-and-genetics

62 http://terrytao.wordpress.com/2007/12/28/einsteins-derivation-of-emc2/

63 M.J. Farabee, *The Online Biology Book* (Farabee is a member of the Biology faculty at Estrella Mountain Community College, Avondale, Arizona. *emc.maricopa.edu*

64 Faulkner, D. 1998. "The Young Faint Sun Paradox and the Age of the Solar System. " Acts & Facts. 27 (6).

65 Isaac Asimov, *The Roving Mind.* Prometheus Books, 1997.

The best gift you can give an author

is an honest, thoughtful review. Please consider leaving one online. Help us understand what you liked and didn't like about the book and why. Help authors reach more readers and spread your influence and ours. If you liked the book, please recommend it to your spouse, friends, pastors, teachers, cashiers, employers, – anybody and everybody you see each day. If you don't know what to say, remember Proverb 16:3 – Commit thy works unto the Lord and thy thoughts shall be established. Thank you!

OTHER BOOKS AND PRODUCTS FROM FINDLEY FAMILY VIDEO PUBLICATIONS

All our books (including Historical Fiction, SciFi, contemporary relationships short stories, and an Archaeological Mystery serial) are linked on our blog.

Elk Jerky for the Soul includes posts on current issues, excerpts from our fiction and nonfiction works, Bible teaching, travel and everyday observations, and more.

https://findleyfamilyvideopublications.com/

Visit our YouTube Channel

https://www.youtube.com/channel/UCGhwNpU115ARMwgYwTIJBrA/featured. Book trailers, video excerpts, project teasers, and more. Science, History, Literature, and biblical worldview studies are the focus of our book and video projects.

Historical Fiction

by Michael J. Findley

The Ephron the Hittite Series (Including boxed set of all titles)

Ephron Son of Zohar

Tawananna Daughter of Zohar

Heth Son of Canaan Son of Ham, Noah

Shelometh Daughter of Yovov Wife of Ephron

Zita Son of Ephron and Shelometh

Adult Romantic Suspense

by Mary C. Findley

The Men of the Realmlands series

Book One: The Baron's Ring

Book Two: The Captain's Blade

Send a White Rose

Chasing the Texas Wind

Carrie's Hired Hand (novella)

Young Adult Historical Adventure

by Mary C. Findley

Hope and the Knight of the Black Lion (plus illustrated version)

The Benny and the Bank Robber Series

Benny and the Bank Robber (Plus homeschool editions for student and teacher with review and vocabulary)

Doctor Dad

The Oregon Sentinel

Lines in Pleasant Places

Science Fiction and Fantasy

by Michael J. Findley

The Empire Saga (all six of the following books in one volume)

City on a Hill and Sojourner (Combined Novella and Short Story)

Nehemiah LLC (Full-length novel available as a standalone ebook, paperback, and hardcover versions)

Empire One: Humiliation

Empire Two: Repentance

Empire Three: Sanctification

Steampunk

by Sophronia Belle Lyon (pen name for Mary C. Findley)

The Alexander Legacy Steampunk Literary Tribute Series

Book One: A Dodge, a Twist, and a Tobacconist (including illustrated version)

Book Two: The Pinocchio Factor

Book Three: The Most Dangerous Game

Book Four: Beware the Bustle

Fantasy/Allegory

by Mary C. Findley

Allegorical clockwork novella inspired by Little Red Riding Hood

The Acolyte's Education

A Paranormal Urban Fantasy serial

His Sign: The Wait Is Over

His Sign 2: The Ezra Solution

Contemporary Fiction

by Mary C. Findley

Romantic Suspense Novella

Fall On Your Knees

Relationships Short Stories

Fifty Shades of Faithful

Fifty Shades of Faithful 2: In Living Color

The Great Thirst Serial Archaeological Mystery (including boxed set of all titles)

Part One: Prepared

Part Two: Purified

Part Three: Pursued

Part Four: Persecuted

Part Five: Persevering

Part Six: Protected

Part Seven: Prevailing

Murder Mystery

Mapped Out Murders

Nonfiction

by Mary C. Findley

Write for the King of Glory, 2nd Edition (updated, with tips on indie writing and publishing)

by Michael J. and Mary C. Findley

The Good, the Bad, and the Ugly: A Readers' and Writers' Guide for Believers

Biblical Studies (Teacher and student editions plus excerpts in OT and NT Manuscript History)

Antidisestablishmentarianism (illustrated and plain versions)

Serial versions, illustrated and plain

What Is an Establishment of Religion?

What Is Secular Humanism?

What Is Science?

What Are the Results of the Establishment of Secular Humanism?

The Conflict of the Ages series (All have teacher and student editions)

I. The Scientific History of Origins

II. The Origin of Evil in the World that Was

III. They Deliberately Forgot: The Flood and the Ice Age

IV. Ice Age Civilizations

V. The Ancient World

by Michael J. Findley

Short Recaps of longer nonfiction works *(Antidisestablishmentarianism* and *Conflict of the Ages)*

Disestablish: An Overview from Creation to the Ice Age

Under the Sun: The Truth about History from the Beginning

*****

Christian Books in Multiple Genres. Join Christian Indie Author ~ Readers Group on Facebook. https://www.facebook.com/groups/291215317668431/

www.ingramcontent.com/pod-product-compliance
Lightning Source LLC
LaVergne TN
LVHW050526160826
845677LV00011B/1965